Sexuality and Gender at Home

Home
Series Editors: Victor Buchli and Rosie Cox

ISSN: 2398-3191

This exciting new series responds to the growing interest in the home as an area of research and teaching. Highly interdisciplinary, titles feature contributions from across the social sciences, including anthropology, material culture studies, architecture and design, sociology, gender studies, migration studies and environmental studies. Relevant to undergraduate and postgraduate students as well as researchers, the series will consolidate the home as a field of study.

Making Homes by Sarah Pink, Kerstin Leder Mackley, Roxana Morosanu, Val Mitchell and Tracy Bhamra

Food, Masculinities, and Home: Interdisciplinary Perspectives edited by Michelle Szabo and Shelley Koch

FURTHER TITLES FORTHCOMING

Sexuality and Gender at Home

Experience, Politics, Transgression

EDITED BY BRENT PILKEY, RACHAEL M. SCICLUNA, BEN CAMPKIN AND BARBARA PENNER

Bloomsbury Academic
An imprint of Bloomsbury Publishing Plc

BLOOMSBURY

LONDON · OXFORD · NEW YORK · NEW DELHI · SYDNEY

Bloomsbury Academic

An imprint of Bloomsbury Publishing Plc

50 Bedford Square
London
WC1B 3DP
UK

1385 Broadway
New York
NY 10018
USA

www.bloomsbury.com

**BLOOMSBURY and the Diana logo are trademarks of
Bloomsbury Publishing Plc**

First published 2017

British Library Cataloguing-in-Publication Data
A catalogue record for this book is available from the British Library.

ISBN: HB: 978-1-4742-3962-2
ePDF: 978-1-4742-3963-9
ePub: 978-1-4742-3964-6

Library of Congress Cataloging-in-Publication Data
A catalog record for this book is available from the Library of Congress.

Cover design: Clare Turner
Cover image: Louise Bourgeois, CELL (HANDS AND MIRROR), 1995. Photo: Peter Bellamy,
© The Easton Foundation / VAGA, New York / DACS, London 2016

Series: Home

Typeset by Deanta Global Publishing Services, Chennai, India

To find out more about our authors and books visit www.bloomsbury.com. Here you
will find extracts, author interviews, details of forthcoming events and the option
to sign up for our newsletters.

Contents

List of figures

List of contributors

Tom Boellstorff is Professor in the Department of Anthropology at the University of California, Irvine, former Editor-in-Chief of *American Anthropologist*, the flagship journal of the American Anthropological Association, and Fellow of the American Association for the Advancement of Science. He is the author of many articles and the books *The Gay Archipelago: Sexuality and Nation in Indonesia* (2005), *A Coincidence of Desires: Anthropology, Queer Studies, Indonesia* (2007), *Coming of Age in Second Life: An Anthropologist Explores the Virtually Human* (2015), as co-author, *Ethnography and Virtual Worlds: A Handbook of Method* (2012); and as co-editor, *Data, Now Bigger and Better!* (2015).

Ben Campkin is the author of *Remaking London: Decline and Regeneration in Urban Culture* (2013), which was commended in the Royal Institute of British Architects President's Awards for Research (2014) and won the Urban Communication Foundation's Jane Jacobs Award (2015). He is co-editor of *Engaged Urbanism: Cities and Methodologies* (2016), *Dirt: New Geographies of Cleanliness and Contamination* (2007/2012) and the series *Urban Pamphleteer* (2013–). He is Senior Lecturer in Architectural History and Theory at The Bartlett School of Architecture, University College London, UK, and Director of UCL's Urban Laboratory.

Lilian Chee is Assistant Professor at the Department of Architecture, National University of Singapore. Her forthcoming book is *Architecture, After Affect* (2017), and she is lead editor of *Asian Cinema and the Use of Space: Interdisciplinary Perspectives* (2015). She conceptualized the architectural essay film *03-Flats* (2014), which won the Best ASEAN documentary at the Salaya International Documentary Film Festival (2015), was critically acclaimed at the Busan Wide Angle Documentary Film competition (2014) and screened at the Venice Architecture Biennale (2016).

Matt Cook is Professor of Modern History at Birkbeck, University of London, UK, and Director of the Raphael Samuel History Centre. He works on histories of sexuality, urban life and domesticity. His most recent book is *Queer Domesticities* (2014). He is currently co-editing a collection on *Queer Interiors* and working on projects about queer life beyond London and about the AIDS crisis in the United Kingdom.

Elizabeth Darling is Reader in Architectural History at Oxford Brookes University, UK. Her research focuses on interwar English modernism, gender and cultural modernity, and often the intersections among them. Her publications include *Re-forming Britain: Narratives of Modernity Before Reconstruction* (2007) and *Wells Coates* (2012), and she is currently working on the book and exhibition that accompany the project to commemorate the centenary of women's entry to the Architectural Association, AA XX 100, and a study of the material and spatial cultures of broadcasting in interwar England.

Alice T. Friedman is the Grace Slack McNeil Professor of the History of American Art at Wellesley College, USA, where she has taught since 1979, and a visiting professor at the Modern Interiors Research Centre at Kingston University, UK. She is the author of many books and articles, including *Women and the Making of the Modern House: A Social and Architectural History* (1998/2010) and *American Glamour and the Evolution of Modern Architecture* (2010).

Andrew Gorman-Murray is a Senior Lecturer in Social Sciences (Geography and Urban Studies) at Western Sydney University, Australia. His primary research interests encompass gender, sexuality and space, and geographies of housing and home. He has conducted a number of projects on LGBT belonging and exclusion across different sites, spaces and scales in Australia, including homes, neighbourhoods, suburbia, rural towns, disaster settings and legal frameworks.

Narmala Halstead is a Reader in Anthropology at the University of East London, UK. She previously held a university lectureship at Cardiff University and also taught at Brunel University. She holds a PhD in Anthropology from Brunel University. She has conducted long-term fieldwork in Guyana and New York. Her research interests include migration, diaspora, violence, state, human rights, power, non-ethnicity, digital anthropology and media. She has published and presented extensively on her research. She leads the Anthropology and Contemporary Worlds Research Group at the University of East London and offers training for an urban anthropology fieldwork programme in London.

Sue Heath is a Professor of Sociology and Co-Director of the Morgan Centre for Research into Everyday Lives at the University of Manchester, UK. She has long-standing research interests in housing and household formation, including shared living arrangements, and most recently has led the Economic and Social Research Council-funded project *Under the Same Roof: The Everyday Relational Practices of Contemporary Communal Living.*

R. Justin Hunt is a producer, lecturer and performer. He is currently co-producer of I'm With You, a London-based performance collective, and Naked Boys Reading, an international literary salon. He is also Executive Producer of Chisenhale Dance Space. He has taught sexuality studies for nearly six years at Syracuse University, London, UK. He is often seen out as his alter ego, Dr Sharon Husbands. He received his PhD in performance from Roehampton University, UK.

Dana Kaplan is a cultural sociologist, specializing in critical heterosexualities, middle-class culture and neoliberal subjectification. She earned her PhD from the Department of Sociology and Anthropology at the Hebrew University, Israel. Her current research projects include the intersection of beauty and class in Israel as well as urban branding and sexual outlooks.

Ellen Lewin is Professor in the Departments of Gender, Women's and Sexuality Studies and Anthropology at the University of Iowa, USA. She is the author of three ethnographies on gay and lesbian families: *Lesbian Mothers (1993)*, *Recognizing Ourselves (1998)* and *Gay Fatherhood (2009)*, and the co-editor (with William Leap) of three collections on lesbian and gay anthropology: *Out in the Field (1996)*, *Out in Theory (2002)* and *Out in Public (2009)*. Her work in feminist anthropology includes *Feminist Anthropology: A Reader (2005)* and a new volume, co-edited with Leni M. Silverstein, *Mapping Feminist Anthropology in the Twenty-First Century (2016)*.

Laura Marshall is a postgraduate researcher in the Department of Geography at University College London (UCL), UK. Influenced by a background in urban studies and international studies, Laura's interdisciplinary research interests coalesce around questions of gender diversity, sexuality and space, as well as using visual and participatory methodologies to produce scholar/activist research. She has worked with the UCL Urban Laboratory on the project 'LGBTQI nightlife spaces in London: 1986 to the present' and co-founded the UCL Gender Diversity Forum.

Barbara Penner is Senior Lecturer in Architectural History at The Bartlett School of Architecture, University College London, UK. She is the author of *Bathroom (2013)*, awarded the 2014 RIBA President's Award for Outstanding University-Located Research, and *Newlyweds on Tour: Honeymooning in Nineteenth-Century America (2009)*. She is co-editor of *Forty Ways to Think about Architecture (2014)*, *Ladies and Gents: Public Toilets and Gender (2009)*, and *Gender Space Architecture (2000)*. She has recently contributed chapters to *Archi.Pop (2015)*, *Globalization in Practice (2014)*, and *Use Matters (2013)*.

She is a regular contributor to the architectural journals *Places* and *Architectural Review*.

Brent Pilkey is a Senior Teaching Fellow at both The Bartlett School of Architecture and The Centre for Advancing Learning and Teaching, University College London, UK. His doctoral research and subsequent dissemination bring together queer theory with the disciplines of architectural history and human geography, with a particular focus on non-celebrated LGBTQ domesticity in London, UK. The work is featured in publications in *Geographical Research*, *Gender, Place and Culture*, *Harvard Design Magazine* and *Home Cultures*.

Rachael M Scicluna is a Lecturer at the School of Anthropology and Conservation at The University of Kent, UK, and an Honorary Research Fellow in Social Anthropology at the Morgan Centre for Research into Everyday Lives, University of Manchester. She is the author of an ethnography on the domestic lives of older lesbians, *Home and Sexuality: The 'Other' Side of the Kitchen* (2017). Rachael is also Co-Director of the Home and Research Network based at the University of Kent. Her research and practice explore the relationship between the anthropology of alternative kinship and family formations, sexuality, politics and home in England and South Europe.

Matt Smith is a lecturer, artist and curator. He undertook an Arts and Humanities Research Council-funded, practice-based PhD in queer craft at the University of Brighton, UK, where he lectures on design. He gives regular talks about his practice (Konstfack Stockholm, Tate Modern, Valand Academy Gothenberg, KHIB Bergen). Solo exhibitions include *Milk* (Aspex, 2010), *Queering the Museum* (Birmingham Museum and Art Gallery, 2010–11) and *Other Stories* (University of Leeds, 2012). He was Artist in Residence in the Victoria and Albert Ceramics Galleries in 2015/16.

Series preface:
Why home?

Rosie Cox and Victor Buchli

The home is where people are made and undone. As life is increasingly seen as precarious, fluid, mobile and globalised, there is a growing interest in the home: what it is, what it means to various groups of people, how it constitutes them, and how it relates to other spheres of life both in the present and in the past. Home is both physical and metaphorical, local and national, a place of belonging and of exclusion. It is at the heart of the most seemingly mundane spaces and experiences – the site of quotidian activities such as eating, washing, raising children, and loving. Yet it is precisely the purportedly banal nature of the home that masks its deep importance for the underlying assumptions that structure social and political life. Home reveals the importance of routine activities, such as consumption to highly significant and urgent wide ranging issues and processes such as the maintenance of and challenges to global capitalism and our relationship to the natural environment.

Amongst academic writers home is increasingly problematised, interrogated and reconsidered. Long understood as an axis of gender inequality, home is also seen as a site for the making of class, racial and ethnic identities; a space of negotiation and resistance as well as oppression and a place where such relationships are undone as well as made. As a topic of study it is the natural analytical unit for a number of disciplines and with relevance to a wide range of cultural and historical settings. The home is probably one of the few truly universal categories upon which an interdisciplinary programme of research can be conducted and which over recent years has resulted in a distinctive analytical category with relevance across disciplines, times and cultures.

This book series offers a space to foster these debates and to move forward our thinking about the home. The books in this series range across the social and historical sciences, drawing out the cross-cutting themes and interrelationships within writings on home and providing us with new perspectives on this intimate space. While our understanding of 'home' is expansive, and open to interrogation, it is not unbounded. In honing our understandings of what 'home' is, this series aims to disturb and it goes beyond the domestic including to sites and states of dispossession and homelessness and experiences of the 'unhomely'.

Preface

Tom Boellstorff

Each chapter of this book represents a fascinating analysis regarding linkages between sexuality, gender and the home. The general introduction and three section introductions do their work well; my goal in this brief preface is not to resituate what has been so well situated. Rather, I set out four provocations that build on these chapters' arguments. I hope these thoughts will contribute to a conceptual toolkit with which to relate *Sexuality and Gender at Home* to wider debates.

Let us begin with Geertz's observation:

> The history of anthropology has in large part consisted in taking concepts put together in the West ('religion', 'family', 'class', 'state'), trying to apply them in non-Western contexts, finding that they fit there rather badly at best, laboring to rework them so that they fit rather better, and then discovering in the end that, however reworked, many of the problems they pose – the nature of belief, the foundations of obligation, the inequality of life chances, the legitimacy of domination – remain clearly recognizable, quite alive (1990: 77).

This issue of navigating between the spectre of overgeneralization and the spectre of over-specification is, of course, not unique to anthropology. It is a productive tension animating social inquiry in the broadest sense. Furthermore, Geertz could have well added 'home' to his list of key concepts. While there seems to be no known culture without a notion of the home, what 'home' might mean and how that might be instantiated in political economy and everyday practice is fundamentally contextual. But one feature commonly found associated with the home is a notion of kinship, and gender and sexuality thus represent key points of departure. A second feature is space, both in the concrete sense of a domicile and in the discursive sense of a domestic sphere. A third feature intersecting with 'the home' in a widespread and consequential manner is a notion of labour: this was somewhat elided by modernist notions of the public/private binarism, but the contributors to this book show repeatedly how the delinking of labour from the home was largely a rhetorical move predicated on treating many forms of labour as not 'labour' at all.

With all this in mind, the first of my four provocations involves a notion of home as an embodiment. The consideration of space in the context of the home is not limited to buildings and furnishings. Might bodies be the alchemy by which a house becomes a home? What forms can domestic embodiments take, through and beyond the prisms of sexuality and gender? What are the relationships between hegemonies of heterosexuality and cisgenderism as cultural logics of embodiment, on the one hand, and as cultural logics of the home, on the other?

These questions of home as embodiment build on the spatial, geographical and even architectural foci many authors bring to their insightful interventions. We can complement this with attention to time, an issue explored in several chapters. How might we consider the home as temporality? Might some places be homes only at certain distinct times of day? How might homes be constituted, not just through materiality, but through distinct tempos with their own rhythms of sociality?

A third trajectory along which to extend our analyses is the question of home as governmentality. Throughout human history, we find great variation in the relationship between forms of state power and the home. In cases where authority is directly derived from kinship, the home may be a locus of social power in a most immediate sense. However, across a wide range of pre-capitalist societies (and not just in the West), many forms of state power paid little attention to the home. In such cases, the home might be a site of production and thus a source of tribute, but rulers often had neither the resources nor the conceptual horizon to concern themselves with the domestic lives of their subjects, leaving such considerations to their allies in the religious sphere. In the modern era, a binarism of public/private has been central to both capitalism and nation states. This centrality is anchored – not undermined – by the ways in which this binarism is rhetorical versus material, as well as the astonishing range of forms it takes.

A fascinating issue addressed throughout this book and deserving of further study is the deployment of 'the home' as a technology of governmentality. In his essay introducing the concept of governmentality, Foucault explored the historical rise of new modalities for the extension of state power into the public sphere, for instance via the rise of the notion of the 'population', the invention of statistics and the development of the discipline of public health (Foucault 1991). Foucault observed that central to these modalities of modern power was a sense of continuity between the government of a society, a family and one's self. He then noted that 'the central term of this continuity is the government of the family, termed *economy*. ... This, I believe, is the essential issue in the establishment of the art of government: introduction of economy into political practice' (ibid: 92). 'Economy' here harks back to the original Greek meaning of the management of the home, traces of which remain in the phrase 'home economics'. However, Foucault contended that 'the perspective of population, the reality accorded to specific phenomena of population, render possible the final elimination of the model of the family and the recentring of the notion of economy ... [the family] now disappears as the model of government, except for a certain number of residual themes of a religious or moral nature' (ibid: 99). But Foucault emphasizes that it is precisely with the eclipse of the family (really, the household) as a model or end of government that the home could gain a pivotal role as 'the privileged instrument for the government of the population' (ibid: 100). The contributions to this book show how, in a range of contemporary contexts, the queering of the home can variously destabilize or retrench its role as an instrument for governmentality. The outcome is not pre-set or inevitable: it depends on sociopolitical context.

This question of emergence leads me to my fourth provocation, what I see as the most fundamental dilemma in the study of sexuality and gender: the question of normativity. As Robyn Wiegman has noted, 'In the consolidation of queer "studies" as an institutionalized project of anti-normativity, queer critique has undergone its most sustained and confounding normalization, one that operates to define the contours of the field and the core critical grammar that drives its political intentions' (Wiegman 2012: 305). Far too often, we think we know 'normativity' when we see it, and we think we know it is bad. It is surely comforting to have such pre-theoretical certainty, but it is empirically inaccurate and politically limiting. The home provides a powerful context from which to challenge what I have elsewhere termed *queernormativity* (Boellstorff 2007). To assume that the domestic is always already complicit with structures of power is too facile, however reassuring, for an analysis of the home as it intersects with gender and sexuality. Sometimes the home may be normative, sometimes not. But the complexities of that normativity are not isomorphic with a binarism of public/private, nor is the 'normative' necessarily less politically potent than the 'transgressive'. Consider the original model of the norm, the Gaussian bell curve. To be an outlier has its own political possibilities. But to shift the centre has possibilities as well. Assimilation can be a powerful force for change (as those of us who remember the Borg from *Star Trek: The Next Generation* recall all too well!).

I invite you to bring analytics of embodiment, temporality, governmentality and normativity to your reading of the chapters that follow. You will find these topics in the text itself, and building on that foundation, find tools for extending our conversations regarding these most important questions of sexuality and gender at home.

References

Boellstorff, T. (2007). 'When marriage falls: Queer coincidences in straight time'. *GLQ: A Journal of Gay and Lesbian Studies* 13, nos. 2/3: 227–48.

Foucault, M. (1991). "Governmentality." In *The Foucault Effect: Studies in Governmentality*, edited by G. Burchell, C. Gordon and P. Miller, 87–104. Chicago: University of Chicago Press.

Geertz, C. (1990). '"Popular art" and the Javanese tradition'. *Indonesia* 50: 77–94.

Wiegman, R. (2012). *Object Lessons*. Durham: Duke University Press.

Introduction

Brent Pilkey, Rachael M. Scicluna,
Ben Campkin and Barbara Penner

In December 2012, fifty artists, scholars, activists and built environment practitioners from all over the world gathered for a workshop in London to present and discuss their work on the intertwining of sexuality and the home.[1] This event offered the opportunity to think through, as a trans-disciplinary concern, the ways in which sexualities and homes, as conceptual categories and as lived experiences, are mutually constituted. Participants were concerned, in other words, with the question of how sexualities are informed by the domestic sphere and how the home has, in different cultural and historical situations, shaped sexuality.

The chapters in this book present the workshop contributions and expand on them, also focusing on gender as an explicit focus. The event included a rich variety of discussions of embodied subjectivities, lived practices, social identities and institutional categories of sexuality and gender, and dealt with the home, domesticity and the spaces and structures through which they are produced in nuanced ways – as conceptual categories, designed spaces and materially experienced realities. Hence, the authors of the following chapters also focus on homes, sexuality and gender in a range of configurations, where each is instituted in relation to the others in dynamic ways. They work at scales ranging from the individual embodied subject to the home environment itself, to that of the social contexts, economies, local and national identities through which they are construed. The collection is one of the first to explicitly focus on how home, sexuality and gender are formed, performed and overlap, and on how they structure lives as well as the possibilities and limits of transgression.

Reading the collection cover to cover, or in any another sequence, readers will come to further appreciate the varied and significant role sexuality and gender play in domestic and daily life, and vice versa. They will encounter examples that demonstrate how these dimensions of life are intertwined and how they reflect and enact belief systems and ideologies. Retaining the ethos of the original workshop on 'Sexuality at Home', the anthology does not attempt to be definitive or exhaustive. Nor does it attempt a linear chronological journey, as that would falsely convey a simple evolution of relations. Instead, it seeks to open doors, windows and other apertures into topics common to many disciplines and practices. In short, it provides a space for the reader to make themselves at home, but one where they may be unsettled through encounters with unfamiliar ideas and new connections.

Although this is one of the first collections to explicitly bring sexuality, gender and the home together under one roof, with the rise of theorized feminism in the 1970s, and gay and lesbian studies in the 1980s, gender and sexuality emerged as significant in understanding larger social issues including, for example, material inequality as manifest in domestic spaces and practices (Hayden 1981; Matrix 1984). Scholars from many disciplines, including our own – architecture and architectural history and social anthropology – have increasingly paid attention to these individual and intersecting categories of analysis, again very often using home as a lens through which to view them (see, for example, Agrest, Conway and Weisman 1996; Ardener 1997[1993]; Attwood 2005; Birdwell-Pheasant and Lawrence-Zúñiga 1999; Blunt 2005; Blunt and Dowling 2006; Briganti and Mezei 2012; Buchli 2013; Carsten and Hugh-Jones 1995; Cieraad 1999; Coleman, Danze and Henderson 1996; Colomina 1992; Douglas 1991; Groman-Murray 2006; Hurdley 2013; Lewin 2006; Mauss (1979[1950]; Miller 2001; Morrison 2013; Oakley 1974; Potvin 2013; and Tolia-Kelly 2004). Indeed, Hilde Heynen and Gülsüm Baydar provided an important precedent for our work in their 2005 edited collection, *Negotiating Domesticity*, which considered gender in relation to home and also devoted a section to considering issues of sexuality (Heynen and Baydar 2005, see especially Bonnevier's chapter; see also Bonnevier 2007). Yet, outside of this body of work, academic debates until the latter part of the twentieth century were dominated by straight, white, European male voices (Okely and Callaway 1992; Smith and Smith 1981). This is still the case, but the opening up of new disciplinary approaches in the 1990s and 2000s created room for alternative and often marginalized voices.

In our approach to the intertwining lines between sexuality, gender and home, we take inspiration from the social anthropologist Tim Ingold's understanding of how human relations 'unfold within the weave of the world' (Ingold 2011a: 9). The intimate understanding of life as being woven evokes a sensorial aspect of dwelling, similar to the effect triggered by some of the works of the French-American artist Louise Bourgeois, as illustrated on the front cover. *Cell (Hands and Mirror)*, 1995, is a large-scale sculptural work, in which audiences are encouraged to look into each interior cell to see different arrangements of symbolically loaded objects and sculpted fragments of bodies. The experience of this uncanny dwelling is disorienting and evoked through multiple senses, memory and imagination. Through such a sensory and incomplete evocation of dwelling, the home – its meaning, image, built form, myth and status – appears as not only a built environment, or the outcome of such, but a web of relations, the fabric of life, in and with which lives unfold in time and space.

The built environments that we design and inhabit provide a sometimes malleable frame for our sexual lives, our sexualities, our genders, gendered identities and experiences – that is, they shape us and we them (Williams 2013; Baydar 2012). Sexuality is often viewed through a spatial metaphor, specifically through the concept of sexual orientation (Ahmed 2006; Castiglia and Reed 2012: 75; Probyn 2003). As feminist architectural and anthropological studies from the 1970s and 1980s pointed out, gender can also be thought about through the contestation of space, and the production and experience of architecture and cities can contribute to gender-based discrimination (Ardener 1997[1993]); Rendell 2000). Such work has drawn attention to the gendered politics of space through notions of control, restriction and liberation, visibility and invisibility, in both public and private places. A substantial body of literature looks at the production of gender in the domestic sphere in terms of masculinities and femininities (Anderson 2000; Blunt and Rose 1994; Cox 2006; Cox 2013; Gregson and Lowe 1994; Treas and Drobnic 2010; Oakley 1974). More recently, there have been calls for attention to the cisnormative – as well as hetero-patriarchal – social production of space, including from trans and non-binary positions (Browne et al. 2010 and Marshall, this book). The chapters in this collection build on such theoretical and empirical advances, paying specific attention to the configuration of the home in relation to diverse sexualities and genders.

Experience, politics, transgression

Focusing on the home, sexuality and gender through experience, politics and transgression, many chapters in this collection work to deconstruct the heteronormative bias in domestic arrangements and shed light on why alternative identities and practices have been oppressed by and/or overlooked in the design of the spaces and institutions of domesticity. Contemporary academic work is often steeped in the assumptions of patriarchal and heteronormative positions in terms of its privileging of certain forms of social relations, such as the heterosexual couple (Blackwood 2005), and in the way that others are 'muted' or misrecognized (Ardener 1997). Such biases and misconceptions ought to be taken into consideration when scrutinizing the frequently heteronormative foundations of the concept of home, homes themselves, and the idealized family structures they reinforce. This book therefore intentionally features a wide variety of intimate relationships, opening up opportunities to consider how they have been experienced in different settings at home and beyond. Seen overall, these domestic scenes move away from binary understandings of sexuality or gender.

In 1992, architectural historian Beatriz Colomina published *Sexuality and Space* (Colomina 1992), which developed out of a conference of the same name held at Princeton School of Architecture in 1990. This was to become a landmark text, highlighting the ways in which space, and representations of space, produce and reproduce gender (Penner 2005: 89). Widely influential, *Sexuality and Space* bolstered the feminist and interdisciplinary spatial critique of patriarchal societies. It has been an important impetus for our own project – in its effort to think through sexuality and gender at home – as well as being a pioneering work that paved the way for other texts that look at the built environment, domesticity, gender, and sexuality from feminist and queer perspectives (see, for example, Blunt and Dowling 2006; Rendell, Penner and Borden 2000; Betsky 1995; Agrest, Conway and Weisman 1996; Carrington 1999; Coleman, Danze and Henderson 1996; Dines 2010; Durning and Wrigley 2000; Friedman 1990; Ruedi, Wigglesworth and McCorquodale 1996; and Williams 2013).

Alongside feminist critiques of the gendering of space, including feminist architectural histories and practices, queer theory has attended to the organizing structure of discourses on sexuality. Queer scholars and activists have, in similarity with feminists, taken up the work of Michel Foucault on the emergence of the modern sexual subject and the discourses and institutions of sexuality (Foucault 1979, 1990, 1992). Following the earlier feminist tradition of challenging structural binaries, and building on the arguments that 'space is gendered and that space is sexed' and that 'gender, sex and sexuality are all spaced', queer theorists have focused on the deconstruction of dominant, heteronormative – and homonormative – sexual identities, and have privileged other nonconforming transgressive or dissident sexualities which trouble them (Bell et al. 1994: 32).

These scholars have built on the powerful work of gender and queer theorist Judith Butler, specifically the thesis on performativity she developed in *Gender Trouble: Feminism and the Subversion of Identity* (Butler 1999 [1990]), and which she and others have subsequently developed. Butler dismantles the social construction of gender and sexuality and complicates any simplistic hierarchy of one over the other. According to Butler, sexual practices do not produce gender, as such. Rather, the policing of gender and maintenance of gender hierarchy work violently to establish the pre-eminence of heterosexuality (Butler 1999 [1990]: xii). Furthermore, the currents of heteronormative power are so successful that gender is often performed – through repetition and ritual acts – unknowingly by subjects in ways that meet institutionally naturalized expectations. In her groundbreaking work, drawing on John Langshaw Austin's performative linguistic theory (1975), Butler rejected essentialist categories of gender and sexual identity, arguing rather that they are mutually constructed through embodied and culturally conditioned acts, situated in specific times and spaces.

Queer scholars of domesticity have also been informed by Eve Kosofsky Sedgwick's understanding of, on the one hand, how sexualities are spatialized, and, on the other, how conventions and institutions can be queered (Kosofsky Sedgwick 1990). Such insights from queer theory have travelled into the spheres of human and social geography, anthropology and architectural history, among other spatial disciplines, and a growing body of literature continues earlier attempts to destabilize the heteronormative ideology of space (Andersson 2011; Brown 2008; Castiglia and Reed 2012; Collins 2004); Rushbrook 2003, and home and domesticity, specifically (Reed 1996; Scicluna 2013, 2015, 2017; Cook 2014; Gorman-Murray 2015).

Studies at the nexus of sexuality, gender and the home aim to open up this space – and its constituent practices – for a plurality of identity formations and subjective experiences: they may highlight a multiplicity of lived realities and 'alternative domesticities' (Pilkey, Scicluna and Gorman-Murray 2015; Das, Ellen and Leonard 2008; Procupez 2008) or contribute to the collapse of dualistic thinking (Csordas 2002; Ingold 2011b; Scicluna 2015). They also introduce new complexity in understanding how identities – unfolding in space and time – are made up of intersecting constructions that include not only gender and sexuality but also ethnicity, class, ability and other status markers. Examining how homes and domestic practices are ideologically produced and often work against heterogeneity, we can also pay attention to ingrained inequalities in the division of domestic privileges and labour, and practices of comportment in home environs. Such themes are at the core of this collection.

As Butler and other writers discussed above established, there is a close link between social and cultural definitions of gender and those of sexual orientation, identity and desire. Scholarly literature that seeks to focus on gender invariably engages sexuality. For people who experience marginalization and/or violence because of their gender identity or sexuality, collective and individual responses through identity and visibility politics have been vital (Sullivan 2003: 50). In this book, we seek to work against the generalization of specific groups and to emphasize differentiated, embodied experiences. We therefore use umbrella terms such as 'LGBTQ' (lesbian, gay, bisexual, transgender and queer), 'normative', 'heterosexual', 'homosexual' and 'straight' cautiously and reflexively. We note that there is a relative dearth of literature on transgender, non-binary and bisexual experiences of home, and we hope that the links to emerging scholarship on trans experiences here suggest the need and potential for future work. Embodied subjectivities and lived experiences defy separation into reductively simple analytical categories, as the work focusing on transgender identities clearly shows (Felsenthal 2009; Halberstam 2005).

This collection builds on gendered studies of home, which have predominantly focused on female experiences of domesticity, by also taking human sexuality at home as a central and cross-cutting theme. Sexuality here not only refers to sex itself, taking place at home or in home-like settings, but also psychic and embodied dimensions shaped by multiple cultural and ideological factors. The contributing authors read the intersection of sexuality and gender at home in nuanced ways. Some offer historical studies of same-sex occupied homes; others look at more contemporary lived realities; others still are concerned with the politics of sexual practices and expressions of sexuality at home and in public, or with the possibilities of challenging restrictive normative ideologies through the sexualized body. Although, as editors, we did not prescribe rigid thematic instructions – indeed authors were encouraged to approach the book's theme from their own perspectives and expertise – collectively, contributors are explicitly concerned with issues of social justice and seek to challenge narrow views of the home as a site constituted, occupied and performed by 'appropriately' gendered and sexed bodies. They critique the idealized heteronormative arrangements that oppress other practices, tenure types, relationship configurations and identities. As cultural historian Matt Cook (2014) has written, heteronormativity has bearing on *everyone's* experiences of home.

Structure of the book

The collection is divided into three sections – Making Home, Queering Home and Beyond Home – with chapters grouped according to their approach to sexuality and gender at home. The first section comprises four researchers who look at sexuality and gender at home by showing how home is a place constructed and framed within the limits of hegemonic order. The lives that are discussed in these chapters are very much formed in response to the restrictions imposed by institutions that uphold normative gender hierarchies, sexualities and domestic spaces. The second section gathers together five chapters that uncover representations and spatial analyses of queerness and sexuality at home in recent and past histories (of both privileged and everyday lives). The experiences highlighted foreground the politics of making a home for queer sexualities as well as the ways in which these lives are able to begin to transgress social and spatial norms. The final section sees five authors examine accounts of the performativity of sexualities and genders at home, by moving beyond the threshold. Through imagining homeliness beyond home, these authors begin to transgress narrow and restrictive thinking on domestic environments, and open up broader questions of context and relationality. Each of the three sections is prefaced with a short editorial introduction, which sets up the main themes and arguments the chapters present.

Collectively, the fourteen chapters provide insights into how people negotiate with institutions, and through a focus on lived experience reveal the messiness of the everyday in all its diversity and complexity. In such a short anthology, there will inevitably be gaps and themes that are not taken up. An attempt has been made to include work that engages with a diversity of embodied experiences globally. The book presents work on and from subjects and spaces in Guyana, Singapore, the United States, the United Kingdom, Australia and Israel. It by no means entirely captures the actual diversity of work going on in the field. We conclude here by pointing to a need to collate and connect other work internationally, and to highlight and foster new comparative approaches informed, for example, by postcolonial analyses. It is the editors' hope that this collection will inspire future work critically tracking the multiple ways sexuality and gender are embedded in and are mutually constitutive of homes around the world.

Note

1 'Sexuality at Home', Bartlett School of Architecture, University College London, 11 December 2012, https://www.bartlett.ucl.ac.uk/architecture/events/sexuality-at-home (accessed 6 August 2016).

References

Agrest, D., P. Conway and L. Weisman, (eds) (1996). *The Sex of Architecture*. New York: Harry N. Abrams.

Ahmed, S. (2006). *Queer Phenomenology: Orientations, Objects, others*. Durham, NC: Duke University Press.

Anderson, B. (2000). *Doing the Dirty Work? The Global Politics of Domestic Labour*. London: Zed Books.

Andersson, J. (2011). 'Vauxhall's post-industrial pleasure gardens: "Death wish" and hedonism in 21st century London'. *Urban Studies* 48, no. 1: 85–100.

Ardener, S. (ed.) (1997[1993]). *Women and Space: Ground Rules and Social Maps*. Oxford: Berg.

Attwood, F. (2005). 'Inside out: Men on the home front'. *Journal of Consumer Culture* 5, no. 1: 87–107.

Austin, J.L. (1975[1955]). *How to do Things with Words*. Oxford: Clarendon Press.

Baydar, G. (2012). 'Sexualised productions of space'. *Gender, Place and Culture: A Journal of Feminist Geography* 19, no. 6 (December): 699–706.

Bell, D., J. Binnie, J. Cream and G. Valentine (1994). 'All hyped up and no place to go'. *Gender, Place and Culture: A Journal of Feminist Geography* 1, no. 1: 31–47.

Betsky, A. (1995). *Building Sex: Men Women and the Construction of Sexuality*. New York: William Morrow.

Birdwell-Pheasant, D. and D. Lawrence-Zúñiga (1999). *House Life: Space, Place and Family in Europe*. Oxford: Berg.

Blackwood, E. (2005). 'Wedding bell blues: Marriage, missing men, and matrifocal follies'. *American Ethnologist* 32, no. 1: 3–19.

Blunt, A. (2005). *Domicile and Diaspora: Anglo-Indian Women and the Spatial Politics of Home*. Oxford: Blackwell.

Blunt, A. and R. Dowling (2006). *Home (Key Ideas in Geography)*. London: Routledge.

Blunt, A. and G. Rose (1994). *Writing Women and Space*. London: The Guildford Press.

Bonnevier, K. (2005). 'A queer analysis of Eileen Gray's E. 1027'. In *Negotiating Domesticity: Spatial Productions of Gender in Modern Architecture*, edited by H. Heynen and G. Baydar, 162–180. Abingdon: Routledge.

Bonnevier, K. (2007). *Behind Straight Curtains: Towards a Queer Feminist Theory of Architecture*. Stockholm: Axl Books.

Briganti, C. and K. Mezei (2012). *The Domestic Space Reader*. Toronto: University of Toronto Press.

Brown, G. (2008). 'Urban (homo)sexualities: Ordinary cities and ordinary sexualities'. *Geography Compass* 2, no. 4: 1215–31.

Browne, K., C. J. Nash and S. Hines (2010). 'Introduction: Towards trans geographies'. *Gender, Place & Culture: A Journal of Feminist Geography* 17, no. 5: 573–7.

Buchli, V. (2013). *An Anthropology of Architecture*. London: Bloomsbury.

Butler, J. (1999 [1990]). *Gender Trouble: Feminism and the Subversion of Identity*. London: Routledge.

Carrington, C. (1999). *No Place Like Home: Relationships and Family Life Among Lesbians and Gay Men*. Chicago: University of Chicago Press.

Carsten, J. and S. Hugh-Jones (1995). *About the House: Levi-Strauss and Beyond*. Cambridge, UK: Cambridge University Press.

Castiglia, C. and C. Reed (2012). *If Memory Serves: Gay Men, AIDS, and the Promise of the Queer Past*. London: University of Minnesota Press.

Cieraad, I. (ed.) (1999). *At Home: An Anthropology of Domestic Space*. Syracuse, New York: Syracuse University Press.

Coleman, D., E. Danze and C. Henderson, (eds) (1996). *Architecture and Feminism*. New York: Princeton Architectural Press.

Collins, A. (2004). 'Sexual dissidence, enterprise and assimilation: Bedfellows in urban regeneration'. *Urban Studies* 41, no. 9 (August): 1789–1806.

Colomina, B. (ed.) (1992). *Sexuality and Space*. New York: Princeton Architectural Press.

Cook, M. (2014). *Queer Domesticities: Homosexuality and Home Life in Twentieth Century London*. London: Palgrave Macmillan.

Cox, R. (2006). *The Servant Problem: Domestic Employment in a Global Economy*. London: I. B. Tauris.

Cox, R. (2013). 'The complications of "Hiring a Hubby": Gender relations and the commoditisation of home maintenance in New Zealand'. *Social and Cultural Geography* 14, no. 5: 575–90.

Csordas, T. J. (2002). *Body/Meaning/Healing*. London: Palgrave Macmillan.

Das, V., J. M. Ellen and L. Leonard (2008). 'On the modalities of the domestic'. *Home Cultures* 5, no. 3: 349–71.

Dines, M. (2010). *Gay Suburban Narratives in American and British Culture: Homecoming Queens*. Basingstoke: Palgrave Macmillan.

Douglas, M. (1991). 'The idea of a home: A kind of space'. *Social Research* 58, no. 1: 287–307.

Durning, L. and R. Wrigley, eds (2000). *Gender and Architecture: History, Interpretation and Practice*. Chichester, UK: Wiley.

Felsenthal, K. (2009). 'Creating the queendom: A lens on Transy House'. *Home Cultures* 6, no. 3: 243–60.

Foucault, M. (1979) [1976]. *The History of Sexuality Volume 1: An Introduction*. London: Allen Lane.

Foucault, M. (1992) [1984]. *The History of Sexuality Volume 2: The use of Pleasure*. London: Penguin Books.

Foucault, M. (1990) [1984]. *The History of Sexuality Volume 3: The Care of the Self*. London: Penguin Books.

Friedman, A. T. (1990). *Women and the Making of the Modern Home: A Social and Architectural History*. New York: Harry N. Abrams.

Gorman-Murray, A. (2006). 'Queering home or domesticating deviance?: Interrogating gay domesticity through lifestyle television'. *International Journal of Cultural Studies* 9, no. 2: 227–47.

Gorman-Murray, A. (2015). 'Twentysomethings and twentagers: Subjectivities, spaces and young men at home'. *Gender, Place and Culture: A Journal of Feminist Geography* 22, no. 3: 422–39.

Gregson, N. and M. Lowe (1994). *Servicing the Middle Classes: Class, Gender and Waged Domestic Labour in Contemporary Britain*. London: Routledge.

Halberstam, J. (2005). *A Queer Time and Place: Transgender Bodies, Subcultural Lives*. New York: New York University Press.

Hayden, D. (1981). *The Grand Domestic Revolution: A History of Feminist Designs for American Homes, Neighborhoods, and Cities*. Cambridge, MA: MIT Press.

Heynen, H. and G. Baydar, (eds) (2005). *Negotiating Domesticity: Spatial Productions of Gender in Modern Architecture*. Abingdon: Routledge.

Hurdley, R. (2013). *Home, Materiality, Memory and Belonging*. London: Palgrave Macmillan.

Ingold, T. (2011a). 'Against space: Place, movement, knowledge'. *In Boundless Worlds: An Anthropological Approach to Movement*, edited by P. Wynn Kirby, 29–43. New York: Berghahn Books.

Ingold, T. (2011b). *Being Alive: Essays on Movement, Knowledge and Description*. London: Routledge.

Kosofsky Sedgwick, E. (1990). *Epistemology of the Closet*. Berkley and Los Angeles: University of California Press.

Lewin, E. (ed.) (2006). *Feminist Anthropology: A Reader*. Malden, MA: Blackwell.

Matrix (1985). *Making Space: Women and the Man Made Environment*. London: Pluto Press.

Mauss, M. (1979 [1950]). *Seasonal Variations of the Eskimo: A Study in Social Morphology*. London: Routledge.

Miller, D. (2001). *Home Possessions*. Oxford: Berg.

Morrison, C. A. (2013). 'Homemaking in New Zealand: Thinking through the mutually constitutive relationship between domestic material objects, heterosexuality and home'. *Gender, Place and Culture: A Journal of Feminist Geography* 20, no. 4: 413–31.

Oakley, A. (1974). *The Sociology of Housework*. Bath: The Pitman Press.

Okely, J. and H. Callaway (eds) (1992). *Anthropology and Autobiography*. London: Routledge.

Penner, B. (2005). 'Researching female public toilets: Gendered spaces, disciplinary limits'. *Journal of International Women's Studies* 6, no. 2 (June): 81–98.

Pilkey, B., R. M. Scicluna and A. Gorman-Murray (2015). 'Alternative domesticities'. *Home Cultures* 12, no. 2 (special issue 'Queer domesticities: Sexuality, identity and politics at home'): 127–38.

Potvin, J. (2013). 'Guilty by design/guilty by desire: Queering bourgeois domesticity'. In *The Handbook of Interior Architecture and Design*, edited by G. Brooker and L. Weinthal, 291–303. London: Bloomsbury.

Probyn, E. (2003). 'The spatial imperative of subjectivity'. In *Handbook of Cultural Geography*, edited by K. Anderson, M. Domosh, S. Pile and N. Thrift, 290–9. London: Sage.

Procupez, V. (2008). 'Beyond home: Forging the domestic in shared housing'. *Home Cultures* 5, no. 3: 327–48.

Reed, C. (ed.) (1996). *Not at Home: The Suppression of Domesticity in Modern Art and Architecture*. London: Thames & Hudson.

Rendell, J. (2000). 'Introduction: "Gender space architecture"'. In *Gender Space Architecture*, edited by J. Rendell, B. Penner and I. Borden, 225–39. London: Routledge.

Rendell, J., B. Penner and I. Borden (eds) (2000). *Gender Space Architecture*. London: Routledge.

Ruedi, K., S. Wigglesworth and D. McCorquodale (eds) (1996). *Desiring Practices: Architecture, Gender and the Interdisciplinary*. London: Black Dog Publishing.

Rushbrook, D. (2003). 'Cities, queer space, and the cosmopolitan tourist'. *GLQ: A Journal of Lesbian and Gay Studies* 8, no. 1–2: 198.

Scicluna, R. M. (2013). *The 'Other' Side of the Domestic Kitchen: An Anthropological Approach to the Domestic Unit and Older Lesbians*. Ph.D. diss., The Open University.

Scicluna, R. M. (2015). 'Thinking through domestic pluralities: Kitchen stories from the lives of older lesbians in London'. *Home Cultures* 12, no.2: 169–91.

Scicluna, R. M. (2017). *Home and Sexuality: The 'Other' Side of the Kitchen*. London: Palgrave Macmillan.

Smith, B. and B. Smith (1981). 'Across the kitchen table: A sister-to-sister dialogue'. In *The Bridge Called my Back: Writings by Radical Women of Color*, edited by C. Moraga and G. Analdua, 123–40. New York: Kitchen Table, Women of Color Press.

Sullivan, N. (2003). *A Critical Introduction to Queer Theory*. Edinburgh: Edinburgh University Press.

Tolia-Kelly, D. P. (2004). 'Locating processes of identification: Studying the precipitates of re-memory through artefacts in the British Asian home'. *Transactions of the Institute of British Geographers* 29, no. 3: 314–29.

Treas, J. and S. Drobnic (2010). *Dividing the Domestic: Men, Women, and Household Work in Cross-national Perspective*. Palo Alto, CA: Stanford University Press.

Williams, R. J. (2013). *Sex and Buildings: Modern Architecture and the Sexual Revolution*. London: Reaktion Books.

PART ONE

Making home

Introduction: Making home

Barbara Penner and Rachael M. Scicluna

What is a home? In this essay collection, we have deliberately interpreted 'home' in its most capacious way. At its most basic, 'home' may refer to a physical site – a house – but it may equally be a symbol of individual and collective values, aspirations and memories, that act upon and attach people just as surely as an actual dwelling may do. Looking at home in this way – as a space, as a material object, and as a socially constructed symbol – helps to explain why there remains a general investment in the ideal of home as a private, safe, privileged place, even if homes can be experienced as places of labour, disappointment, conflict, abuse and exploitation (Cieraad 1999; Coontz 1992; Das, Ellen and Leonard 2008; Gorman-Murray 2012). As the British anthropologist Mary Douglas (1991: 289) has remarked, 'Happiness in not guaranteed in a home,' but this does not stop people from finding it a powerfully resonant concept and from working hard to make it a reality.

For, as the essays in this collection remind us, making one's physical home live up to an ideal is hard work that requires continual management, affective labour and imagination – many acts, routines and gestures, small and large – in order to be constructed and sustained. Far from standing outside of existing power structures of law, economy, politics, religion, race, history and kinship, home is a nexus of these intermingling flows of power, but, importantly, as the four essays in this section show, these do not completely determine its meaning. As material culture scholar Alison J. Clarke concluded, following her ethnographic study of working-class British women, individual relationships to home environments cannot be characterized simply as normative or coercive, emulative or expressive, but involve 'a more complex process of projection and interiorization that continues to evolve' (Clarke 2001: 43).

Acknowledging this evolving process of homemaking implicitly rejects the idea of home as a fixed and uniform entity with a singular meaning, but focuses – as the four essays in this section do – on the labour, effort and strategies adopted to realize it and the manifold forces which continually inflect it. Specifically, the essays here engage with the homemaking strategies of inhabitants who do not conform to the norm in terms of their gender, sexuality or marital status. Heteronormativity has fostered the heterosexual nuclear family as the ideal social formation, which has become part of the collective domestic imagination. Thus, the practices and social and spatial relations within the heterosexual nuclear family (or extended family) are used as yardsticks of normality, belonging, intimacy and happiness. All four authors provide detailed examples of how nonconforming individuals and families negotiate with these institutional benchmarks and shared cultural scripts in order to create alternative domesticities, often in the face of uncertainty, discrimination, hostility and violence.

As Elizabeth Darling establishes, architecture and its representations are important tools of heteronormative naturalization, modelling particular social relationships by means of domestic arrangements and décor. Darling considers three residential projects in 1930s London that deployed the language of modernism to represent ideal marital-sexual relationships, but to different ends. Darling's first example, 1 Kensington Palace Gardens (1932) by Wells Coates, was a 'love nest' for a newly wed couple that, through media coverage of the conjugal bedroom, normalized a bourgeois model of marriage in which mutually pleasurable sex played a newly significant part. Darling also finds a similar emphasis on the marital bedroom and the conjugal bed in another example, Kensal House (1936), a social housing block by Elizabeth Denby and Maxwell Fry, where the insistence on the working-class married couple's right to sexual privacy was even more radical and progressive. But in Darling's example of 34 Gordon Square (1934), also by Coates, the modernist idiom becomes instead a means of securing respectability for a marriage of convenience, in which one partner was gay. In Darling's case studies, then, modernism is used both to promote new norms of conjugal sexuality and to mask non-normative ones, reminding us that architecture cannot always be treated as a stable or authentic index of lived social-sexual relations.

Lilian Chee's chapter examines Singapore's public housing in relation to sexuality and gender, specifically highlighting how heteronormativity also affects heterosexuals who feel they do not fit into the idealized picture of the happy family (see Wilkinson 2014 on single individuals). Chee first tracks the way in which state-sponsored architecture in Singapore has been able to foster the ideals and aspirations of the heteronormative nuclear family by aggressively linking heterosexual coupledom to the right to housing, a situation that renders the existence of single women in public housing precarious if not unimaginable. Nonetheless, in discussing the film essay on the lives of three single women, *03-FLATS* (dir. Lei Yuan Bin, 2014), Chee explores how they have managed to carve out a place for themselves within a system designed to erase them and how their daily embodied routines and life rhythms inscribe a powerful counternarrative to official heteronormative policies. In a similar vein, Heath and Scicluna's chapter studies the phenomenon of groups of people who are not family relations sharing domestic space in England. The authors consider some of the ways in which sexual intimacy plays out in shared households, including how these interactions may change at different points in a relationship or across the life course. This work shows how many forms of intimacy and domesticity exist that, intentionally or not, destabilize the persistent conflation of home with the nuclear family.

Finally, Ellen Lewin's chapter provides a clear-sighted case study of motivations: Why do groups that are implicitly excluded from heteronormativity strive to reproduce a traditional home, as evoked by the image of a 'picket fence'? What do they feel is at stake? Indeed, it is not obvious why, despite decades of sustained critique from feminists and queer theorists, marriage, children and their concomitant, the single-family home, remain such potent aspirations for many otherwise nonconforming individuals. Through her detailed ethnographic exploration of gay fatherhood in Chicago, USA, Lewin makes the important point that, for her participants, home is fundamentally associated with comfort, safety and affection and demonstrates how it emerges as the moral centre of their lives. Her chapter further suggests that, far from becoming less politically relevant, home may become even more significant for disenfranchised social groups seeking security, stability and legitimacy.

For all its associations with heteronormativity and dominant ideologies, then, the four essays in this section underscore the sense of home as a place where alternative and sometimes resistant identities and subjectivities can be cultivated. In this, they link to the work of the feminist bell hooks, who beautifully reminds us of what homemaking can do socially and politically for minority social groups. In her account of the meaning of home for African Americans, hooks notes that, historically, it was the place where 'we could be affirmed in our minds and hearts despite poverty, hardship and deprivation, where we could restore to ourselves the dignity denied us on the outside in the public world' ([1990] 2015: 42). Yet hooks is also careful to stress the daily, affective labour required on the part of African–American women, who must dig deep to create homes out of adverse conditions – a powerful reminder that home, especially now in our own globalized age of conflict, migration and environmental and economic precarity, is a privilege that can never simply be assumed.

References

Cieraad, I. (1999). 'Introduction: Anthropology at home'. In *At Home: An Anthropology of Domestic Space*, edited by I. Cieraad, 1–12. New York: Syracuse University Press.

Clarke, A. J. (2001). 'The aesthetics of social aspiration'. In *Home Possessions: Material Culture Behind Closed Doors*, edited by D. Miller, 23–46. Oxford: Berg.

Coontz, S. (1992). *The Way We Never Were: American Families and the Nostalgia Trap*. New York: Basic Books.

Das, V., J. Ellen and L. Leonard (2008). 'On the modalities of the domestic'. *Home Cultures* 5, no. 3: 348–72.

Douglas, M. (1991). 'The idea of a home: A kind of space'. *Social Research* 58, no. 1: 287–307.

Gorman-Murray, A. (2012). 'Que(e)rying homonormativity: The everyday politics of lesbian and gay homemaking'. Paper presented at the *Sexuality at Home Workshop*, London, 10–11 December 2012. Audio available online: http://www.ucl.ac.uk/urbanlab/news/SexualityatHome.

hooks, b. ([1990] 2015). 'Homeplace: A site of resistance'. In *Yearning: Race, Gender, and Cultural Politics*, 41–50. Abingdon: Routledge.

Wilkinson, E. (2014). 'Single people's geographies of home: Intimacy and friendship beyond the family'. *Environment and Planning A* 46, no. 10: 2452–68.

1

Class, sexuality and home in interwar London

Elizabeth Darling

In February 1932, the young architect Acheson Best Overend (1909–77) wrote from London to his family in Melbourne, describing the latest project on which his skills as a draughtsman were deployed while he worked in the office of Wells Coates (1895–1958). Australian tongue firmly in his cheek, he reported: 'We are in the throes of designing the interiors of a love nest for one of the Socialist members in Parliament ... just the bare 2500 pounds on three rooms' (Overend 1932). He was referring to the transformation of the ground and first floor of the substantial mansion overlooking Hyde Park owned by the MP, George Russell Strauss (1901–93), to which he would bring his new bride, Patricia O'Flynn (d.1987), following their marriage in March 1932. The substitution of some of the house's elaborate late nineteenth-century interiors with Coates's calm modernist idiom served to symbolize both the advent of its new incumbents and, more generally, the order of things that both client and architect envisaged for the modern world.

The idea of a home as a 'love nest', and the requirement of a particular and novel setting to this end, establish the core themes of this chapter, which explores how ideas about marriage, sex and sexuality were rehearsed in architectural form in the interwar decades. This was a period when the transition from the idea of marriage as a pragmatic union to one founded on romantic love, which had emerged as part of bourgeois ideology during the nineteenth century, was both refined and began to become more widespread. The result was a model of marital relationships that has remained largely

FIGURE 1.1 *Two views of the principal bedroom of 1 Kensington Palace Gardens before its refurbishment by Wells Coates for George Russell Strauss, 1890s (destroyed). Courtesy of the Cohn Family.*

dominant until the recent present (Gillis 1995: 148–50). The social historian Judy Giles summarizes the interwar shift neatly, speaking of 'new forms of conjugal heterosexuality not necessarily linked to procreation' (Giles 1995: 97). This reflected the general impulse in modernity for 'emotional and social betterment' as well as a desire for material enhancement (Giles 2004: 62). The former also inaugurated a concomitant ordering of other forms of sexuality – free, same-sex, commercialized – as 'dangerous' (Giles 1995: 122) at the same time as it signalled a recognition (and de facto legitimation, perhaps) of practices which, especially in the case of homosexual love, were becoming forms of identity as we know them now.

That these concepts were shifting rather than settled, contested rather than consensual and nuanced by class and sexuality is reflected in the choice of examples discussed here. Two were new interiors in existing buildings: the 'love nest', 1 Kensington Palace Gardens, completed in Spring 1932; the other, the upper floors of 34 Gordon Square, completed towards the

FIGURE 1.2 *The principal bedroom at 1 Kensington Palace Gardens, as redesigned by Wells Coates, 1932 (destroyed). Courtesy of the Cohn Family.*

end of 1934 by Wells Coates for the actors Elsa Lanchester (1902–86) and Charles Laughton (1899–1962). The third is Kensal House, Ladbroke Grove, a purpose-built block of social housing designed by a team led by Elizabeth Denby (1894–1965) and Maxwell Fry (1899–1987) for the Capitol Housing Association (a subsidiary of the Gas, Light and Coke Company), which was opened in late 1936. All are in London, and all took the vanguard forms of modernism in their design. Each was featured extensively across a range of media – though 34 Gordon Square less so – with some emphasis placed on images of their bedrooms. Each embodies particular aspects of the shifts outlined above, while the combination of metropolitan location, architectural language and their mediation suggests that they were intended by their clients, architects and journalists (or some admixture thereof) as models to be disseminated from the nation's centre.

1 Kensington Palace Gardens

Following their wedding, Strauss and his new bride, O'Flynn, took up residence at 1 Kensington Palace Gardens (1KPG). This had been Strauss's family home. He had inherited the substantial Italianate mansion, and a considerable fortune, from his metal merchant father who had died in 1920. He was also heir to the house's interiors: elaborate confections of painted walls and decoratively carved furniture, commissioned at the time of his parents' marriage in the 1890s (Fig. 1.1). Strauss spent approximately £150,000 in today's values (Offer and Williamson 2015) on the transformation of the main public spaces on the ground floor of the house (entrance hall, new dining and living room, ballroom), a modernized kitchen in the basement, and upstairs, a new principal bedroom with anteroom, boudoir, dressing room and a refurbished bathroom nearby. The rest of the house was left unchanged (Strauss Family 2009).

The dismantling of the parental home and its marked transformation by a son for his bride make for a very obvious symbolism of the supplanting of one generation by the next. But to contemporaries, a further symbolism might also have registered: the interior as a statement of an eminently modern marriage. The configuration of space in this 'love nest', in Overend's perceptive phrase, and in particular the glamour and nature of the bedroom and its fittings, was a clear statement of (a declaration of faith in) the new paradigm of bourgeois marriage. For the idea of the companionate marriage, in which a woman and man were seen as equal partners and sex a vital expression of their union, was a concept promulgated by and (largely) for the middle classes (Giles 1995: 97).

In what Hilary Hinds so evocatively calls the new 'marital economy', certain themes were foregrounded (Hinds 2010: 294). Fostered by the writings of pre-war sexologists, these themes stressed women's right to sexual pleasure, while after 1918, campaigners such as Marie Stopes argued that the married woman's role was as much sexual as it was maternal and it was understood that 'sexual expression by both sexes (within marriage) was essential to, if not the core of, a sense of self-identity' (Holtzman 1982: 42–3; Giles 1995: 123). Crucial here was the growing access for middle-class women to birth control, which allowed family size (and the fear of endless childbearing) and thus maternal responsibility to diminish. A corollary of this was the concept of woman's 'sexual authority', which enabled her to expect her husband to give her pleasure as well as respect her desire (or otherwise) for sex (Holtzman 1982: 45). Thus, a modern middle-class woman might be expected to cultivate her attractiveness as hostess, mother and sexual partner. As the wife of an MP, the reconfigured ground floor spaces of 1 Kensington Palace Gardens (1KPG) certainly provided a setting in which O'Flynn could perform the first role; the modernity of their design connoting, as noted above, the progressiveness of the couple's selves and their politics (Strauss stood to the far left of the Labour Party, O'Flynn was a committed Labour Party member and much interested in issues of working-class poverty and of birth control). The vital complement to this, however, was the reordered environment of the spaces upstairs.

Coates's redesign created a series of spaces that, at the same time as they enabled the Strausses to assume their public roles of politician and wife, provided the setting in which they could perform their private roles as life partners. Thus, the bedroom was complemented by a dressing room and a boudoir for O'Flynn and an anteroom for Strauss. The boudoir, furnished with writing desk and chair, easy chair and bookshelves, was the space in which O'Flynn curated the couple's social calendar (Fig. 1.3). The dressing room, with power points for an

FIGURE 1.3 *The dressing table in the bedroom at 1 Kensington Palace Gardens, 1932 (destroyed). Courtesy of the Cohn Family.*

electric iron and a sewing machine and with a large mirror, was the site where the appropriate outfit for the day or evening event could be prepared and donned. The anteroom served this function for her husband (Coates 1932b).

Linking the public and private sides of the marriage was the dressing table in the bedroom. A custom-made and substantial piece of furniture, Coates designed it so that all the paraphernalia of make-up was easily to hand: each drawer was pivoted to turn out, presenting products as though in a shop display (Coates 1932b). The main feature was, however, the arrangement of the mirrors. To either side of the main glass stood separate glasses, tinted blue on one side and peach on the other. The former colour, Overend reported, showed up the flaws that needed correction with make-up and powder (Overend 1935).[1] Once done, at the turn of a mechanism, the mirrors reversed so that O'Flynn could see her final appearance in the more flattering pinkish light (a tint also used in the dressing room mirror). At this machine for beautification, then, O'Flynn could complete her toilette before making her descent to the public rooms on the ground floor or prepare herself for bed.

As the most intimate part of the 'love nest', the bedroom was at the core of Coates's design and we might read the sumptuousness of its fittings and fabrics as a celebration of that intimacy (Figure 1.2). This began with the carpet, which, as Overend wrote, 'gives a warm softness and quietness which form the most pleasing features of the modern adult bedroom'. Next came the mirrored wall. This, the Australian noted impishly, at the same time as it gave a greater suggestion of space, 'also affords quite a deal of interest and amusement when fooling about going to bed and getting up on bright and cheerful mornings. The effect might be salutary also for people just letting themselves run to seed' (a reminder that the form of the body became increasingly important in the new sexual regime).

Above all, it was the beds that formed the centrepiece of the room. In that new 'marital economy of sexual intimacy', the choice of twin beds to furnish the middle-class principal bedroom in place of the Victorian double bed was key. They symbolized that the couple were a pair of separable equals and functioned as a powerful negotiating tool for the woman partner (Hinds 2010: 294). Unlike in a double bed, in which intimacy might be said to be forced, the twin beds (thanks to castors) could be pushed together (as they are in Figure 1.2, though note the distinct pillows, compared with the bolster of the 1890s bed, and the counterpane that covers the divide between the two beds) for a wanted intimacy, or kept apart when sexual intimacy was not welcome. Thus, spatially, the beds were far more dominant than in the 1890s interior. They stood proud in the room, framed by fitted wardrobes, and were reflected in the glazed wall and dressing table mirrors. The silky chartreuse green counterpane further delineated them from the muted colours of the carpet (beige) and the fittings (grey-stained sycamore veneer).

In this 'mise-en-scene for the "married couple"', Strauss and O'Flynn conformed to contemporary expectations of what an (upper) middle-class marriage should be (Hinds 2010: 294) and, with their architect, offered a particularly sophisticated and future-oriented image of its form. As such, it and the rest of the 'love nest' were widely mediated. Just a few months after its completion, Coates included a considerable number of the before and after images of the interiors in his major article for the *Architectural Review* 'Furniture Today Furniture Tomorrow – Leaves from a Meta-technical Notebook' (Coates 1932a), listing with glee the contents of the 1890s bedroom ('kidney shaped dressing table with silk brocade drapery, two ornamental jardinières, a paper cylinder and brown parquet linoleum'). The contrasting images became commonplace in 1930s design literature and may be found, for example, in the pamphlet that accompanied a series on design produced by the BBC in April 1933 (Carrington 1933). Later, and indicative of the dissemination of these ideas beyond the highbrow realms of the national programme, they were featured in *Interior Decorating*, number 13 of The Studio Publication's 'How to' series (Miller 1937: 70–4). The spread of such ideals beyond the middle classes is a theme to which this chapter will return. In the meantime, attention turns to an interior that was again designed by Coates but that offered a rather different representation of the forms of marriage in the interwar decades.

34 Gordon Square

Strauss and O'Flynn had met their architect, Coates, through a friendship network that was distinctly bohemian (Darling 2007: 34–6) and included his clients for 34 Gordon Square (34GS), Elsa Lanchester and Charles Laughton. In contrast to the Strausses, however, the actors' relationship was less straightforward: the outcome of a complex negotiation that accommodated an older and more pragmatic view of marriage with the more 'dangerous' forms of sexuality outlined above.

The pair had met in 1927 when both appeared in the play *Mr Prohack*. She was a dancer and actress who had lived independently since her early teens and who had run a bohemian nightclub, the Cave of Harmony (which also served as her home). Her familiarity with the unconventional is reflected in a performance she choreographed using one of the sexologist Krafft-Ebbings's case studies as its theme (Lanchester 1983: 70). Before meeting Laughton, she had enjoyed a series of affairs and undergone at least one abortion (the actress Tallulah Bankhead advising her on whom to consult). The possibility of a new phase of her career, marked by a performance in the West End, and a growing weariness of her own independence is indicated by Lanchester's recollection of what brought the pair together: 'We found in each other a mutual friendship that we both needed badly – Charles because he felt lonely and was called ugly, and I because I was too "bohemian", with too many odd friends who stayed up half the night' (Lanchester 1983: 83). Although outwardly Laughton was far more conventional – the son of Yorkshire hoteliers, his mother a devout Roman Catholic – it was this bond of 'mutual oddity' that enabled them to overcome the obstacles that the evolution of contemporary sexualities put in their way (Callow 1987: 277).

Initially, all seems to have flourished between them and the couple moved in together. By early 1929, however, they felt an increasing tension between their 'free love' union (which echoed that of Lanchester's parents, who had never married) and their reputation, as their careers – Laughton's especially – brought them more into the public eye. She recalled: 'Charles and I were too shy to remain unmarried. To go on living together was just too embarrassing for us to cope with. Certainly, it would have acted as a brake to Charles's growing career and also hurt his northern hotelier family and his Catholic mother' (Lanchester 1983: 90). Regardless of their particular desires, the 'dangerous' had to be put aside in order to secure their long-term future. Their marriage was the first step in the formation of what a biographer has called 'Charles Laughton inc ... a kind of corporation ... with very few shareholders outside the two of them' whose primary function was to promote him and his work by any means necessary (Singer 1954: 53).

The aura of respectability and normality that marriage bestowed (for good measure, it was announced in *The Tatler*) became even more important when, in spring 1930, Laughton revealed to Lanchester that he was gay. This followed an incident in which a rent boy, seeking to extort money from him, was arrested outside their front door for suspicious behaviour; Laughton was subsequently called as a witness at the trial (although his name was kept out of the papers). Notwithstanding Lanchester's many friends in London's gay community (John Banting, Cedric Morris, Arthur Lett-Haines, Robert Medley and Rupert Doone, inter alia), and reflecting her husband's skill at concealing his inclinations (the 'loneliness' to which she responded was perhaps this), the news came as a complete shock. Once she had rallied, however, the promotion of 'Charles Laughton Inc.' returned as her priority.

In a climate in which the codification of homosexuality as dangerous was leading to a growing number of prosecutions (as Laughton's experience demonstrated), she knew that if the news of his dangerous sexuality got out, 'it would have ruined him' (Sigal 1983: 8). It thus became even more important to project their image as the happily married couple of contemporary middle-class convention. The contrast between public and private faces meant that their marriage evolved in effect into a pragmatic relationship in which romantic love was decoupled from the conjugal, one more reminiscent of the forms of marriage which the nineteenth century had begun to displace. This status allowed, as the historian John Gillis notes, the marital state to continue unthreatened by homosexual or other affairs (Gillis 1995: 148). Although according to Lanchester, the couple hardly discussed what had happened, not least because she felt 'he was not capable of that' (being too closeted), there was one significant material outcome, one which demonstrates how symbolic furniture can be (Sigal 1983: 8). When Laughton confessed that he had had the boy on their sofa, Lanchester insisted they got rid of it (Lanchester 1983: 90).

It was in this context that Lanchester commissioned Coates to design a home for the pair. The development of Laughton's career had seen him travel frequently between Hollywood and London since their wedding, and it was not until he committed to performing in the 1933–4 season at the Old Vic that the couple considered themselves able to settle permanently. Lanchester spent much of the autumn of 1933 searching for a suitable home, eventually settling on the upper three floors of a house in Bloomsbury's Gordon Square.

In some respects, the commission had much in common with 1KPG. In both instances, Coates grappled with an over-decorated set of nineteenth-century interiors. Lanchester reported that 'the sitting room was done in

"Victorian Chinese": a sort of egg-yellow ensemble and a wealth of tea-caddies' (Lanchester 1938: 134). Coates deployed the same vocabulary of sliding screens, muted colour palette and built-in furniture to replace such décor. And while both were designed as marital homes, here the similarity ended. Whereas at 1KPG, public and private spaces were complements in the formation of the Strausses' companionate marriage, at 34 Gordon Square (34GS) they were competing narratives. It was to be no 'love nest', but the headquarters of 'Charles Laughton Inc.'

As such, the public spaces, all on the first floor, were designed to create a setting for the pair to enact their coupledom. The principal space was a combined living and dining room that was divided by sliding screen doors to be opened or closed, depending on how the couple were entertaining. This they did a good deal, working hard to convey that they were a loving and intimate couple. A contemporary recalled, 'They never left each other alone in public. They were always mauling each other.' She added, perceptively, that she assumed therefore that they 'were not very sexually involved' (Benita Armstrong in Callow 1987: 277). These were discrete performances, then, as time-limited as a play, and visitors were generally discouraged from staying the night.

The first floor was the business floor. Visitors were to remain at this level, their exposure to the couple carefully controlled. Upstairs was different, the place for the realities and practicalities of their relationship. The out-of-step pragmatism of their marriage was signalled by the fact that they had separate bedrooms, each designed to reflect their personal tastes and needs. Lanchester's simply had a bed – its striped bed linen matching the curtains made from gentleman's shirting material – wardrobe, dressing table and easy chair (Fig. 1.4). Laughton's was a shrine to himself and contained a sunlamp above the bed, some of his art collection on the wall as well as a bedside cabinet for the china he collected from street markets and junk shops (Fig. 1.5). Coates was also reported to have designed him a small gymnasium (Meynell 1971: 217–18), though whether this was within the bedroom is unclear. If there were conjugal relationships to be enjoyed at home (and romantic interludes with others outside the home were surely more the norm for both), it was perhaps Lanchester who allowed Laughton into her room – a rare moment of identification with more up-to-date forms of female sexuality.

Whatever the relationship embodied in the actors' bedrooms, in the public mind Lanchester worked hard to project the more modern image of the couple as heterosexual soulmates and good friends. She thereby contributed to the more general dissemination of the model of modern marriage echoed in contemporary women's magazines as well as contributing to the assimilation of film actors into the aspirational condition of what we would now call 'celebrity culture'. Lanchester exercised a firm control over this process, something reflected in the way she discussed their home. Laughton's filming commitments meant that, almost as soon as the interiors were finished, the couple left for Hollywood, and it was a few years before they worked in London again and took up residence. It was at this point that Lanchester used the interiors to promote their coupledom (presumably as publicity for current projects). In 1938, her book *Charles Laughton and I* was published. A wife's account of her more famous husband, the creation of their home took up several pages (Lanchester 1938: 134–5 and 189–201). She presents the flat as a setting for their marital life and an exercise in Laughton's taste as both client and collector of art and ceramics, writing how she derived 'pleasure out

FIGURE 1.4 *Elsa Lanchester's bedroom at 34 Gordon Square, by Wells Coates, 1934 (destroyed).* © *The British Library Board, LOU.LON 571 [1938].*

FIGURE 1.5 *Charles Laughton's bedroom at 34 Gordon Square, by Wells Coates, 1934 (destroyed).* © *The British Library Board, LOU.LON 571 [1938].*

of being married to a successful magpie' (Lanchester 1938: 196). In this book, the bedrooms were not featured, the images focusing on the public spaces and including several of Lanchester looking adoringly at Laughton.

That same year, presumably as promotion for the book (as well as their public image), the interiors were featured in an article for the magazine *Woman's Journal* entitled 'Background for Talent' (Woollcombe 1938: 52–5). That their talent was to persuade the public about the happiness and authenticity of their marriage bypassed the journalist. She was content to offer a rather bland description of the interiors with no comments on the particular nature of the furnishings (including the bedrooms; their only published depiction). Her focus instead was on the materials used and the décor as a whole, along similar lines to the 'How to' book in which the 1KPG interiors had appeared. Likely under Lanchester's direction, the text also emphasized Laughton's career and presents her (despite the fact she continued to act) very much as wife and helpmate, an image reinforced by a photograph of the couple sitting together reading a book.

While both 1KPG and 34GS were interiors for elite couples within the middle class, each, in its own way, conformed to the increasingly dominant notion of what more widely constituted a modern marriage within that class. We have also seen how their mediation both reinforced and disseminated this model beyond that class. How an environment might be physically configured to spread the new paradigm is the subject of the final section of this chapter.

Kensal House

If, as Judy Giles noted, the majority of the middle classes benefitted from the possibilities for material, social and emotional betterment that modernity offered in the interwar decades, the same could not be said for the men and women of the nation's working classes. For some, material conditions did improve under the post-war housing acts and, from the mid-1930s, the inauguration of a more thoroughgoing slum clearance programme. At the same time, maternal and child welfare provision increased and the upper echelons of the working classes (especially those in areas where new industries predominated, such as the South East and Midlands) could contemplate home ownership and through it access to the emerging consumer society, although most workers could be said to have been prevented from experiencing progress fully. Certainly, this was the perception of many social reformers and enlightened local councils throughout the period, but their attempts to bring workers into modernity were often circumscribed by a focus solely on material betterment and concomitantly, as Giles notes, by particular ideas of the role of women within working-class marriage (Giles 1995: 124). So while feminist campaigners like Stopes 'ostensibly believed' that all women should enjoy the emotional betterment represented by 'meaningful sexual relationships', Giles argues that a class bias that conceived of working-class women first and foremost as housewives and mothers caused them to focus on the provision of advice and reform measures in these areas (Giles 1995: 124). There were, however, some reformers who moved beyond this bias and for whom emotional emancipation was understood as an absolutely integral part of working women's progress. Kensal House was perhaps the most emphatic statement of such ideas, evidenced in the form and planning of the scheme and the social programme that accompanied it (Fig. 1.6).

Kensal House had always been intended as a model environment. It originated in a 1933 proposal by the Gas, Light and Coke Company's directors to build a block of workers' flats that would demonstrate the cheapness and efficiency of its fuels and equipment at a time when the central government was legislating for slum clearance. For its design, the Company drew on the expertise of a committee of architects that it retained, with Maxwell Fry taking the lead. They also appointed the housing consultant Elizabeth Denby to advise them, one of the earliest commissions of her career (Darling 2005b: passim). Under her direction, the scheme became much more than a means to promote gas. She had developed a housing theory that stressed the interconnectedness of material and social improvements in new working-class housing and placed great emphasis on the improvement of women's lives, not just as housewives and mothers but as individuals (in and of themselves) and as partners with their husbands in a modern companionate marriage. Only in this way could women become fully present in modernity.

Every aspect of the scheme was designed to this end. Befitting her and Fry's modernism, the maximum of technologies was used to construct well-built flats, planned on labour-saving lines and equipped with the most up-to-date gas equipment. Material needs met, the tenants' social lives were catered for through the provision of clubrooms (one for the adults and one for the children), the institution of a tenants' committee to run the estate on a daily basis, allotments and a playground for the children. An on-site nursery school was also provided for which all preschool residents were eligible. Denby intended that the resulting free time should be used for the mother's self-improvement and leisure rather than endless housework (already less likely given the efficiency of the design) if she did not work outside the home (Darling 2005a).

Amenities like the social clubs did not just enable a sense of community to develop across the estate, they also formed part of a range of devices to facilitate the evolution of the parents' relationship into a modern form, something prevented in the overcrowded slums from which most residents came. With the children entertained in their clubroom, mother and father

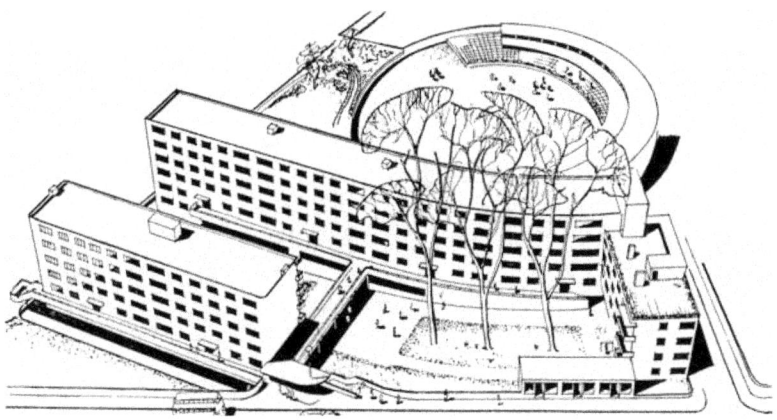

FIGURE 1.6 *Kensal House, Ladbroke Grove, West London, perspective.*

could enjoy time together in the adult club at the end of the day. Their flat was also designed to enhance a sense of companionship. The majority of the sixty-eight flats had three bedrooms, allowing parents, boys and girls to have their own bedroom. Moreover, as the plan shows, the children's rooms were accessed from the main hall (Fig. 1.7). Once they had gone to bed, the living room door could be closed, creating a space entirely for the parents, for their bedroom opened off this space. For the first time, probably in their marital life, they had a space for and to themselves.

A contemporary image shows a bedroom furnished on model lines (Fig. 1.8). Again, the choice of bed was meaningful. While the discourse of the companionate marriage permeated the scheme as a whole, a more complex symbolism was at play here. On a practical level, there was not room for twin beds but, in this context, the choice of a double bed served to reinforce the discreteness of the space. In the slum, at night the bed was a thing on which both parents and children would commonly sleep together and, if space was especially limited, during the day it might become a more general sitting surface. It was not a conjugal bed. Now enthroned in the centre of the Kensal House principal bedroom, its daytime emptiness hinted at pleasurable night-time activities at the same time as its doubleness connoted the pair (and only them) who would occupy it.

That Denby retained an affiliation to pro-maternalist politics is evident in the inclusion of the sling cot in the publicity photograph. She too believed that it was incumbent on the working-class woman to produce the children who would help Britain into the future, but that these should be wanted children whose upbringing was as good as possible. This explains the inclusion of a nursery school in the scheme, something highly unusual for the date. Even more remarkable is the fact that, in proximity to the flats, was a scheme

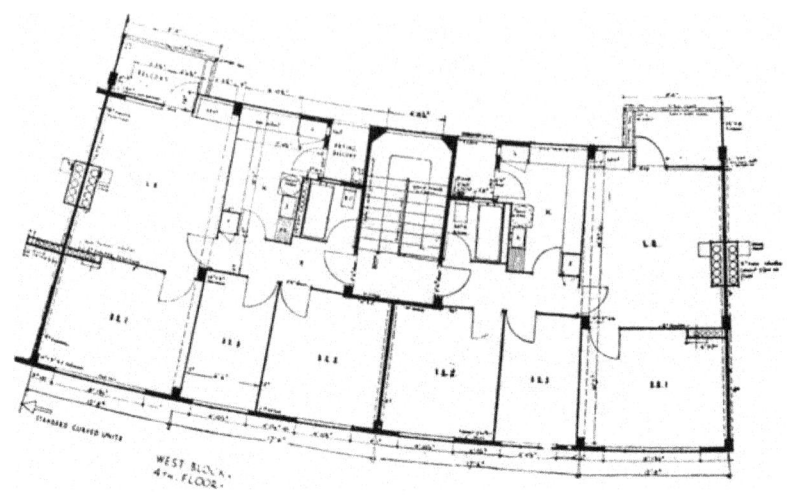

FIGURE 1.7 *Plan of the main floors at Kensal House.*

FIGURE 1.8 *The principal bedroom, with model furnishing, of a Kensal House flat, 1937. RIBA Collections.*

whose proponents shared Denby's interest in working-class women (and men) as sexual beings. This was the North Kensington Women's Welfare Centre, which had been opened in 1924 by a committee that included one of her closest friends (Leathard 1980: 31). Kensal House mothers were its direct constituents, being offered the birth control that had hitherto been more widely available to middle-class women and which could liberate them from endless childbearing. Both within and beyond Kensal House, therefore, the conditions were created in which working-class women could be modern wives, housewives and mothers. And as with the previous case studies, indeed all the more so, it was quickly harnessed into reformist narratives about the shape – both marital and architectural – of things to come, such as Marjory Spring Rice's 1939 social study *Working Class Wives* and, most visibly, as one of the schemes in the Army Bureau of Current Affairs poster series 'Your Britain – Fight for It Now' (Spring Rice 1939: 97/Moriarty 2003: 65–8).[2]

Conclusion

The rhetoric that surrounded the three examples discussed here formed part of the broader discourse that ensured that, after 1945, the conflation of romantic with conjugal love through the medium of the heterosexual marriage became the norm across the classes. By the end of the twentieth century, however, there were signs that this norm was faltering. As Gillis noted: 'Today … everyone loves a wedding, and the high rates of divorce guarantee an inexhaustible supply for a culture that cannot get enough of perfect couples, even as it encounters ever greater difficulty in maintaining marriage itself' (Gillis 1997: 151). How these shifts, and new forms of legislated relationship such as civil partnerships and gay marriage, might come to be embodied architecturally in the first decades of the twenty-first century is for another historian to explore.

Notes

1 All quotations from this, until signalled otherwise.

2 These are too numerous to list (Darling 2007: 167–74 offers a survey).

References

Callow, S. (1987). *Charles Laughton, a Difficult Actor.* London: Methuen.

Carrington, N. (1933). *Design in Modern Life* (Broadcast Talks Pamphlet). London: The BBC.

Coates, W. (1932a). 'Furniture today - furniture tomorrow – Leaves from a meta-technical notebook'. *Architectural Review* 34, no. 9 (July): 29–34.

Coates, W. (1932b). 'Specification for One Kensington Palace Gardens'. Canadian Centre for Archives, Montreal, Canada, Wells Coates Papers, Box 4.

Darling, E. (2005a). 'A citizen as well as a housewife: New spaces of femininity in 1930s London'. In *Negotiating Domesticity: Spatial Productions of Gender*, edited by H. Heynen and G. Baydar, 49–64. London: Routledge.

Darling, E. (2005b). '"The star in the profession she invented for herself": A brief biography of Elizabeth Denby: Housing Consultant'. *Planning Perspectives* 20 (July): 271–300.

Darling, E. (2007). *Re-forming Britain: Narratives of Modernity before Reconstruction*. London: Routledge.

Giles, J. (1995). *Women, Identity and Private Life in Britain, 1900–1950*. Basingstoke: Macmillan.

Giles, J. (2004). *The Parlour and the Suburb. Domestic Identities, Class, Feminity and Modernity*. Oxford: Berg.

Gillis, J. (1997). *A World of their Own Making. A History of Myth and Ritual in Family Life*. Oxford: Oxford University Press.

Hinds, H. (2010). 'Together and apart: Twin beds, domestic hygiene and modern marriage, 1890–1945'. *Journal of Design History* 23, no. 3: 275–304.

Holtzman, E. M. (1982). 'The pursuit of married love: Women's attitudes towards sexuality and marriage in Great Britain 1918–1939'. *Journal of Social History* 16, no. 2: 39–51.

Lanchester, E. (1938). *Charles Laughton and I*. London: Faber and Faber.

Lanchester E. (1983). *Elsa Lanchester Herself*. London: Michael Joseph Ltd.

Leathard, A. (1980). *The Fight for Family Planning*. London and Basingstoke: Macmillan.

Meynell, F. (1971). *My Lives*. London: Random House.

Miller, D. (1937). *Interior Decorating*. London and New York: The Studio Publications.

Moriarty, C. (2003). 'Abram Games: His work and its context'. In *Abram Games, Graphic Designer. Maximum Meaning, Minimum Means*, edited by C. Moriarty, J. Rose and N. Games, 38–120. Aldershot: Lund Humphries.

Offer, L. H. and S. H. Williamson (2015). 'Five ways to compute the relative value of a UK pound amount. 1270–Present'. Measuringworth.com.

Overend, A. B. (1932). Letter to family of 27 February, private collection.

Overend, A. B. (1935). 'The Bedroom'. Transcript of talk for 3LO radio, Melbourne, Australia, private collection.

Sigal, C. (1983). 'High life with Laughton'. *The Guardian* (10 September): 8.

Singer, K. (1954). *The Charles Laughton Story*. London: W. H. Allen.

Spring Rice, M. (1939). *Working-Class Wives*. Harmondsworth: Pelican.

Strauss Family. (2009). Interviews held June and July.

Woollcome, J. (1938). 'Background for talent'. *Woman's Journal* (October): 52–6.

2

Unhousing sexuality: Sexuality and singlehood in Singapore's public housing

Lilian Chee

Introduction

Looking at Singapore's ubiquitous and successful public housing, this essay will examine the perceptions and appropriations that subtly demarcate sexualized territories within these spaces. It is significant that state-sponsored architecture is outwardly concomitant with the needs and aspirations of the heteronormative nuclear family. Adding to human geography's critique of heteronormativity's limitations (Oswin 2010; Pilkey, Scicluna and Gorman-Murray 2015; Ramdas 2012; Wilkinson 2014), I will extend the discussions of 'alternate sexualities and subjectivities' through an architectural lens. I focus on 'other' spatial performances of such public housing architecture (administered by the Housing Development Board, or HDB) through the embodied perspectives of three single women who live alone in these flats.

The essay develops in two parts. The first highlights the problematics of considering sexuality as a critical category in Singaporean public housing. Here, I draw out the precariousness and absolute necessity of a feminist critique within the larger contours of a nationalistic programme, of which Singapore's public housing is exemplary. The second reprises insights gained from an architectural essay film *03-FLATS*[1], which I conceptualized in collaboration with Singaporean director Lei Yuan Bin. I discuss specific moments and spaces in the film and reflect on the alternative embodied narratives discerned from these filmic performances of public housing. The film hints at how the single women's use of their domestic spaces challenges the atomistic existence perpetuated by nuclear families. Ultimately, I ask how the frame of 'sexuality at home' might help to understand and intervene in this hegemonic housing environment.

'Shall we get married?': Housing the nation, unhousing sexuality

The family is the basic building block of our society. It has been so and, by policy, we have reinforced this and we want to keep it so. And by 'family' in Singapore, we mean one man one woman, marrying, having children and bringing up children within that framework of a stable family unit. (Lee 2007)

Public housing in Singapore is a peculiar architectural and sociopolitical phenomenon in its unprecedented success, not just in efficiently providing mass housing but in also continuing, from the 1960s on, to house over 82 per cent of the island state's resident population (HDB 2015: 6). As such, every housing block may be said to contain a microcosm of the nation (Goh 2003).

Installed as a state-controlled housing authority in 1960 to replace the colonial government's housing body, the Singapore Improvement Trust (SIT), the HDB's first task was to solve the housing shortage and modernize the public housing provision. This endeavour required not just an architectural investment in the most advanced building technologies, which included the use of prefabricated and modular building components, new sanitation services, passenger lifts systems and theories about environmental hygiene, it also involved a large-scale Haussmanian-like clearing of existing settlements that the state defined as urban 'slums' (Manderson 1996; Yeoh 2003). Here, communicable diseases like tuberculosis (Yeoh 2003: 93–101) had spread unchecked between densely packed dwellings holding multifamily households, single families with temporary lodgers, and groups of migrant bachelors who had travelled to Singapore for work from southern China. Characteristic of such household compositions was a loose interpretation of 'family', and social or economic alliances founded on kinship and pragmatic circumstance rather than through a marital contract.

By 1965, the fundamental problem of housing – in terms of sheltering the population – had been more than adequately addressed, and public housing continued to evolve from an architectural provision into a more sophisticated ideological instrument of the state (Chua 1997; Clancey 2003; Goh 2003; Kong and Yeoh 2003; Tremewan 1994). The act of modernization did not just involve the most up-to-date building technologies but essentially encompassed the development of a complex and fine-tuned state-sponsored apparatus – the public housing flat as a technology of governance – that enmeshed architecture and urban planning with public policy, finance, legalities and the reinforcement of societal norms around marriage and procreation.

To this day, legal ownership and tenancy rules of a new HDB flat, which are both state controlled, are structured around categories wherein 'eligibility' to purchase must satisfy specific requirements. For the purchase of new three-room or larger-sized flats, the main applicant, who must be a Singaporean citizen of at least twenty-one years of age, must first form a 'proper family nucleus'. This 'nucleus' may be achieved through several means: with a spouse, with one's fiancé or fiancée, between parents and children, between siblings (orphaned/single), or between a widowed or divorced applicant and children under his/her legal or custodial care (HDB 2015). It is also implicit that the engagements must be undertaken by heterosexual couplings.

Despite the multiple combinations, the geographer Natalie Oswin points out that the HDB's pro-family arrangements are ultimately restricted to heteronormative familial configurations – as this section's opening quote clearly articulates – that leave out many other possible groups such as 'unmarried persons, widowed/divorced persons without children, and single parents who have never been married' (Oswin 2010: 257). Oswin also argues for a link between Singaporean public housing's heteronormativity with a postcolonial 'desire for progress, modernization and development' (Oswin 2010). However, although SIT sought to regulate the composition of households, it did not strictly enforce these recommendations in the same way as the HDB (Oswin 2010: 262–3), whose policies made manifest the nation state's pre-independence modernizing efforts to place the 'married, monogamous, heterosexual, procreative couple' (2010: 263) at the heart of the public housing project: 'We believe that the state of our families, the building blocks of any society, determine not only the moral tone of the society but its economic health as well. As our families prosper, so does the nation' (Tarmugi 1995).

Without fulfilling the national responsibility of procreative coupling, the stakes for single women living in public housing, an institution undergirded by familial and nationalist proclivities, is precarious if also often unimaginable. Yet as the architectural historian Beatriz Colomina reminds us, 'The politics of space are always sexual, even if space is centred around mechanisms of the erasure of sexuality' (Colomina 1996: first page of intro). Indeed, Singaporean public housing has successfully naturalized heteronormative sexuality so as to make it already completely unremarkable. Moreover, with almost its entire population living in public housing, an alternate view of domesticity in the Singaporean context is problematic given that one's understanding is configured and determined by the politics of location, 'our mode of partisanship is an expression or function of our location: what that location includes or excludes' (Radhakrishnan 1992: 83). If public housing has housed a nation, it has succeeded by aggressively linking productive heterosexual coupling with rights to housing. The conservative view – that biological reproduction is only acceptable within a heterosexual relationship – is widespread and entrenched: 'The idealization of motherhood by the virile fraternity would seem to entail the exclusion of all nonreproducing-oriented sexualities from the discourse of the nation' (Parker et al. 1991: 6). As such, although the question of public housing has been broached through gendered terms, particularly in the discipline of human geography (Phua and Yeoh 1998; Yeoh and Huang 2010), the existing discourse has primarily focused on family-related entities such as married women, mothers and maids. The subject of single women in public housing has fallen by the wayside.

Bodies at home: Three single women in Singapore's public housing

Neither gender performances nor spatial typologies are fixed. As gender performances may be overdetermined by spatial contexts, spatial typologies can be subverted by those who fall outside heteronormative social matrices. (Baydar 2012: 702)

Recognizing this heteronormative stronghold, my architectural essay film *03-FLATS* (*03-FLATS* 2014) reacts against and attempts to critique the over-exhausted hegemonic representation of public housing as one catering exclusively to a 'family-centred heterosexism' (Blunt and Dowling 2006: 114), on the one hand, and as an architectural entity that is primarily examined from an urban or macro perspective, on the other. Filming was completed over ten months by Lei, who acted as the lone camera person. More than two hundred hours of footage was jointly edited by both Lei and myself over the course of one year.[2] The architectural theorist Gülsüm Baydar argues that 'heteropatriarchal understandings of space based on masculinist premises have largely ignored women ... who may subvert or alter normative spatial practices' (Baydar 2012: 699). Given this, the film addresses the under-sexualized or asexualized representations of Singaporean public housing through its three subjects by asking these questions: What if the HDB is imagined from the interior of the flat? What if the HDB is seen from the perspective of a single woman? What if the HDB's architectural space is reimagined from her body?[3] These questions revolve around issues of architectural representation, and more specifically, the consequences of architectural discourse and representation when architecture intersects with sexuality. How would sexuality play out in the representation of public housing? How does the sexuality of three single women affect how the architecture of public housing is discussed and visually portrayed?

The three flats featured in the essay film belong to, and are occupied by, three single Singaporean women whose ages ranged between early forties to mid-seventies at the time the film was made. Ling Nah and Amy purchased their flats from the open market after they were eligible (once they turned thirty-five years old), while Madam Sim inherited her property after her mother passed on. The decision to focus on three single women turned what was initially an aesthetic exercise in alternative visual representation into a politicized inquiry about the distinctly unremarked gender and sexual politics in architectural representation (Chee 2017). If the 'body' is evoked in architectural representation, it is the white male body which is implied (Bloomer 1995; Burns 1996; Wigley 1992). At the same time, this bodily reference is increasingly rendered discursive or metaphorical. It lacks materiality, or what Robyn Longhurst describes as the messiness of corporeal flesh and fluid (Longhurst 2004). And because 'bodies cannot be understood outside of place' (Longhurst 2004: 23), a reinscription of the single woman's body within the politicized space of public housing simultaneously counterposes a different value system to familial ownership and occupation of this architecture, while also pressing us to re-evaluate our understanding of such spaces through these 'new' bodies.

If public housing has been frequently portrayed as monumental and heroic in scale with a focus on its new, shiny outer forms and building technologies, *03-FLATS* produces a counternarrative by looking at the same architecture through the biographical, the mundane and the sexually differentiated life rhythms of these single women as they are positioned within the architectural interiors of the housing project. An attention to 'corporeal feminism' (Johnson 1990: 18) in public housing was never an explicit aim when I conceptualized the essay film. In fact, it was only through watching the footage many times over that I came to note the particularly nuanced ways in which these single women occupy and perceive public housing architecture. The women's appropriation of normative spatial typologies within the flat – and here I will focus on the common corridor, the bedroom and the living room – arguably disarm public housing's alienating culture of atomistic existence wherein nuclear families retreat into the security of their individual interiors, while domestic life becomes bound to, or limited by, these relatively static and homogeneous spaces.

So, as I rework the relationship between sexuality and public housing through this filmic material, it is not with the aim of using the film to explicate conclusively or propose that it represents generalized findings which may apply to all singles living in Singaporean public housing. Instead, what becomes clear is that through the body, 'the limits of experience and subjectivity' (Grosz 1992: 244) of each architectural space is fluid, with the flats being defined and redefined by the women as they move through different life stages and encounter the pleasures, and perils, of living alone.

... *Emerging through the corridor*

In the short story 'Corridor' by Singaporean writer and poet Alfian Sa'at (Sa'at 2015), a body with seven stab wounds is found at dawn, lying on the common corridor connected to a row of flats. The short story negotiates this corridor through a series of acrimonious encounters between neighbours and between these neighbours and strangers to the block, like the murdered man whom no one knew, 'no relatives found, dying words unrecorded, nothing to answer to but a ledge that blocked his view of dawn, and the fast-fading stars' (Sa'at 2015: 63). Conceptualized originally as a communal 'street' in the sky, the HDB's common corridor was designed for convivial gathering, for promoting chance encounters between residents, and in the ideal situation, for adoption by each household as an extended space of their individual flats. In some cases, corridors flourish as evidenced by the carefully tended gardens, children playing along its length, and neighbours checking up on each other on their way out or coming home. In other cases, such as Sa'at's 'Corridor', the corridor becomes an estranged space where the unknown lurks. The corridor becomes a fearful zone where the hazards of the outside threaten to spill inwards, disrupting the sanctuary of home.

In *03-FLATS*, however, Amy, who is a transgendered woman in her late 40s, spends as much time on her corridor as she does inside her flat. Amy

FIGURE 2.1 *The common corridor obstructed by a long table for* Hari Raya. *Courtesy of Lei Yuan Bin.*

openly acknowledges her alternate sexuality. She strongly self-identifies with the term 'transgender', perhaps as a way of making visible another community who have rights to public housing and are living in similar flats but remain unrecognized. This desire to become visible is translated to how she occupies such an open but deserted space like the corridor. Here is where she takes phone calls, plays with her cat, Dizzy, and pops out for a smoke. In the film, we see her watching television with Dizzy on their couch. The front door is left open, and at intermittent moments, this television scene is punctuated by her raucous laughter and gregarious greeting of neighbours walking in front of her flat. Instead of being placed in a private corner, the couch is situated immediately adjacent to the open door. The placement of the couch suggests that Amy does not perceive the space as an entrance hallway or a transition between the exterior and the interior of her flat. It is as if she has already entered the flat even before she opens the metal gate (a second layer of security installed by every resident, in addition to the wooden front door). While others keep their doors open for ventilation but the metal gate locked for security, Amy's gate and door are kept open whenever she is at home.

In another extended scene, Amy gets a council worker to clear large pieces of unwanted rubbish that others on the estate have dumped in the lift lobby connected to her corridor. She then begins to wash the floor herself with soap and water. This clearing and washing lead up to her appropriating the corridor and the lift lobby for the Muslim Hari Raya festival, a celebration held after the fasting month of Ramadhan (Fig. 2.1). She decorates the lift lobby as one would a room, putting up red streamers on the ceiling and setting up tables covered with starched linen cloths. Against the outside wall of her flat, along the narrow corridor, she places a long table laden with traditional Malay dishes for her guests, who number over eighty persons and are barely contained by her modest sixty-square-metre flat.

FIGURE 2.2 *Dizzy the cat waiting at the threshold of the flat and the corridor. Courtesy of Lei Yuan Bin.*

In both these instances (on her couch and at her Hari Raya party), Amy distinguishes herself from the heteronormative family norms of what to do and where to be. She emerges as the fun-loving, loud, cheerful, cat-loving, middle-aged, transgendered single woman – a complex 'Other' persona in this cautiously regarded context of the shared corridor space. Her unguarded behaviour here correlates with the notion that the overscripted communitarian roles and ideologies of 'family' have failed to resonate in such in-between zones. The 'open spaces' of the HDB block, made exemplary by the ground-level 'void deck' and the common corridors on each floor, were indeed meant to have the kind of liveliness and spontaneity that made the slums and play-areas of their back lanes so attractive to the early HDB settlers (Seng 2012: 153). Through her generous, excessive and 'spectacular' acts of friendship,[4] Amy converts the fringe site of the corridor into a carnivalesque space in which the rules of use and conduct are made ambiguous and porous (Stallybrass and White: 1986), overturning the 'aesthetic of containment' (Seng 2012: 152) that the public housing block has so successfully deployed.

In her exacting occupation of that potentially alienating space, Amy has domesticated the corridor and made it contingently social in purpose. She has reactivated the corridor's self-surveillance capacity, that of opening every flat on it to public scrutiny, for a more benign function. Turning the visibility of her premises to her advantage, she uses this modern Panopticon to safeguard her own vulnerability. As the sexuality of her transgendered body renders Amy's position in the family-centric space fluid and uncertain, how her body destabilizes some of the spatial and architectural norms attached to the corridor and her flat within the institution of public housing are also made more complex by her relationship to her cat Dizzy. Through the film, we also view the spaces of the block through Dizzy as she goes in and out of the flat (Fig. 2.2). Or more accurately, we are left to imagine where Dizzy might go, how this cat might roam the corridors, staircases, lift lobbies and void decks as she slips in and out of the camera's frame at her own will. Significantly, while dogs are allowed as pets in HDB households, cats are prohibited. This is probably because it is hard to restrain them indoors, and also because they tend to multiply quickly and prolifically. The sexed body of the cat must be controlled. Yet, like Dizzy, many cats continue to freely roam public housing estates. Their domestic geographies overlap with the hostile, interstitial and disregarded corners of these estates.

... From the sewing machine

The oldest flat is owned by Madam Sim, who is in her late 70s. She has lived in the same apartment since 1974, when she jointly purchased the

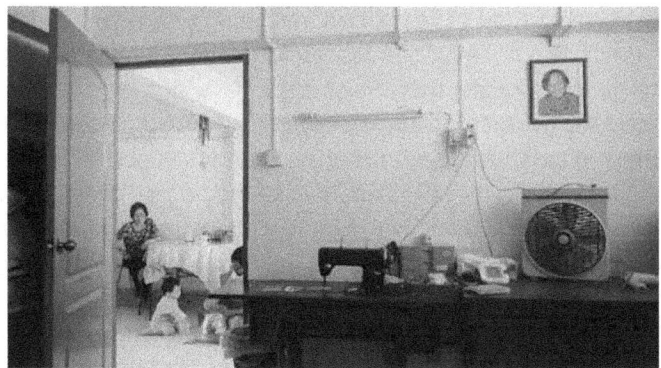

FIGURE 2.3 *From the vantage point of the sewing machine. Courtesy of Lei Yuan Bin.*

FIGURE 2.4 *Creative activity in the bedroom. Courtesy of Lei Yuan Bin.*

newly built two-bedroom flat with her mother. Growing up at a time when women's education was not prioritized, much of her young adult life was spent babysitting her infant nephews and nieces who were left in her care at their Holland Close flat. She cooked and cared for her mother, whom she resided with, and worked as part-time domestic help at several households. In recent years, she was the sole carer for her ageing mother who passed on in 2011.

In *03-FLATS*, there is an extended scene of Madam Sim cutting and stitching a child's garment before finally presenting this garment to a toddler, who is her grandniece (Fig. 2.3). The child is seen trying on the garment in the living room. The scenes were shot from the doorway of Madam Sim's bedroom, where the sewing machine is placed. This is Madam Sim's vantage point. Her frail and severely arthritic seventy-year-old body is positioned at the fringe between bedroom and living room. Here, she hones a craft she loves, one which also maintains a family tradition that this older woman has established through the years she has lived in this flat.[5]

In Daniel Miller's study of retrofitted kitchens in London council flats, he noted that the householders needed to 'enter into creative strategies of consumption to appropriate that which they have not themselves created' in order to achieve a sense of fulfilment (Miller 1988: 370). In Madam Sim's case, her most prized possession is a heavy, old-fashioned Singer sewing machine. It was purchased in 1970 and was carried over from her rental flat in Tanglin Halt to the new property at Holland Close when she and her mother first moved here. The sewing machine is extremely heavy, weighing at least twice the weight of its owner. A self-taught and skilled seamstress, Madam Sim still enjoys sewing. Often asked by relatives and friends to create clothes or upholstery for special occasions, sewing is an important part of her creative life. Like her cooking, Madam Sim's sewing is socially motivated. She does it for leisure rather than out of need. The sewing machine is placed in her bedroom, which is adjacent to the common corridor, or the first room flanking the living room that one encounters upon entering the flat (Fig. 2.4). It was put there so it could be worked on without disturbing her mother, who used to sleep in the other room. The sewing machine faces a blank wall that separates the bedroom from the living room, and is placed just next to the bedroom door. This door is always kept open. From her sewing machine, Madam Sim has a commanding view of the living room.

The introduction of the sewing machine at the boundary of these adjacent spaces – one private and the other one more public – suggests a revised understanding of the sexually differentiated idea that the home should be a private space for family and not a public space of labour. Recent historical research on the typology of live/work spaces by Frances Holliss suggests that the enforced separation between living and working may not have been as dominant as is assumed (Holliss 2012, 2015). Holliss's study ultimately challenges the convention of home being reserved for private familial reverie. It might also support the critique that this concept of privacy is intrinsically motivated by a conservatism that views home as the primary site of biological reproduction, and consequently that this kind of privatization is sexually rather than socially constructed. In Madam Sim's situation, such normative spatial relationships are complicated. The bedroom is private, not just for sleep, but for setting aside quiet space for Madam Sim's creative work on the sewing machine. A bedroom traditionally reserved for sex – procreative sex in the eyes of HBD – has become a bed-sewing room that maintains Madam Sim's position as the family's elected seamstress. The bedroom is still private but it is active. It is a place of production – its output materially creative rather than biologically so.

In his exposé of the bourgeois interior, Walter Benjamin espouses the importance of being a collector who has a 'connoisseur's value' on the objects of the home as opposed to one who 'tak(es) possession' of things as mere commodities, defining these objects only through their usefulness (Benjamin 1999: 19). The old-fashioned sewing machine – simultaneously useful equipment and useless relic – at the edge of the bedroom with a perpetually open door challenges the normative boundaries and conduct assigned to this single woman's private sphere. The living room, which is traditionally the most 'active' and most public space in the flat, is here suspended between a productive kitchen and a creative sewing room, between the stove and the sewing machine; the activity and presence of the living room is here completely reliant on the flows of food and clothing produced in these two other feminized spaces.

... Drawing, dressing, dwelling

The last flat is the biggest and newest of the three featured in the film. It is owned by Ling Nah, a prominent Singaporean artist in her early forties who is known for her large-scale charcoal drawings of the city's transitory spaces.

Unlike Amy and Madam Sim, Ling Nah's domestic space is completely inseparable from her professional work as an artist. It is not unusual nowadays for someone to work from or at home. However, here, the separation between what is work and what is home is often ambiguous. It is as though by working from home, work cannot help but be inflected by the rhythms and forms of domestic life. Here, the boundaries between home and studio are constantly challenged and broken down by numerous newspaper clippings, postcards, notes, books and drawings which collide and mix with 'cute' collectable soft toys, sentimental mementoes and household paraphernalia.

The film begins by scrutinizing the view from Ling Nah's window. We see an old shipyard and a new port in the making. There are vast strips of land in the horizon, fading into the sea. The industrial landscape outside her flat is evidence of the economic foundations on which Singapore was first built and continues to prioritize. As the camera turns towards the interior, we see Ling Nah working at home, oscillating between making art and keeping house: pinning huge

FIGURE 2.5 *The studio in the living room. Courtesy of Lei Yuan Bin.*

pieces of blank canvas on the walls and collecting wastewater from the washing machine to clean the toilet; drawing and cleaning; drawing and cooking.

The living room is the epicentre of this flat. Here, faint but discernible traces of charcoal residue are visible everywhere – on the floor, the walls, the ceiling, the furniture, the curtains and, we might imagine, in the air. By normal domestic standards, this soot-stained space would fare miserably. But it is not quite a standard living room. It has an industrial, workaday air, as if summoning up the landscape glimpsed through the window. It is a restless space of production. There is nowhere to sit and relax. In the centre of the space, there is a big table with a computer and two chairs. They are chairs for working from. The living room-studio was created by gutting out two bedrooms (Fig. 2.5). By HDB standards, it is a big space. It is surrounded on one end by the last remaining bedroom and on the other end by ceiling-high shelving.

The studio is distinguished by its organized clutter. The space lacks the permanence associated with domestic architecture. It is always changing – walls are continually covered and uncovered with newspaper, newsprint, canvas, charcoal, pencil; shelves slide open to reveal a toilet, a wardrobe of clothes and another window hidden behind the wardrobe; piles of stuff migrate from one side to another to make space for work. The walls are not decorative as much as they are confused with impermanent coverings (charcoal, canvas, mementoes, clothing, souvenirs). The studio is made of walls that are constructed around or conceal what is superfluous to the wall and to the architecture. It is continually dressed and undressed. The wall is undermined and obfuscated by layer upon layer of coverings and accessories.

Significantly, the architectural theorist Mark Wigley describes modern architecture as having a 'dresslike quality' (Wigley 1995: xxv). Its 'whiteness' refers not only to the white paint that is used on the walls, but also to the denial of any kind of coating or accessory that would diminish the structural integrity of modern architecture. Whitewashing, argues Wigley, may be said to be another kind of fashionable accessory and thus comparable to the categories which modern architecture ghettoizes as 'supposedly inferior, as "feminine", domains of "ornament", "accessories", "interior decoration", "art nouveau", "architect's partner", "homosexual", "woman", and so on' (Wigley 1995: xxv).

In Ling Nah's studio, this dress-like quality is taken to another level. Not only is the whitewash contaminated by charcoal residue so that the white wall becomes increasingly obvious and must be conscientiously kept clean, the accessorized walls also clearly need to be worked on – dusted, wiped, polished, painted, arranged and rearranged – so that they do not collapse. Here, the whitewashed wall and the accessories it carries are all artifices of domestic labour. There is no 'clear and naked emergence of the Essential' architecture, borne of an efficient, modern and functional body which Le Corbusier in *Towards a New Architecture* attests can be had by 'rejection, pruning, cleansing' (Le Corbusier 1931 [1923]: 138). Here, the demand for the white, undecorated wall can only be achieved through housework, a domestic undertaking which is usually assigned to and performed by a female body. As such, the white wall becomes sexualized by the housework which enables it.

Adjacent to the studio is Ling Nah's bedroom. It is separated from the studio by a beaded curtain and its interior is visible from the studio. The feature of the bedroom is yet another wall. This is a wall of shelves holding all kinds of collectable vintage toys and trinkets that jostle for space among some books on politics and biographies. The toys are colourful, furry, cute, soft and plush. Even when lined up neatly row upon row, they are tactile, sensual. The bedroom is purposefully dressed in childlike clothes. It might be an escape for the artist whose work is frequently seen in black and white.

The studio is, in effect, very much like the bedroom. If the latter's childlike contents are disciplined by strict arrangement, the former's monochromatic contents are disrupted by an urge to endlessly collect and hoard. The consequence is that architecture disappears into and is displaced by stuff, by decoration, by ornament. The ornamental is the only architecture left. The promiscuities between architecture and ornament, art and domesticity, the artist and the homeowner are everywhere visible. They resist the whitewash.

Conclusion

In this essay, I have pressed the question of embodied sexuality into the re-evaluation of Singaporean public housing, giving first a 'big picture' of this conceptual blind spot, and then reflecting on the architectural essay film *03-FLATS* to viscerally and vicariously think through this quandary. In particular, I have examined the category of sexuality in public housing through the perspectives of three single Singaporean women. Given the cultural, familial and national pressures to marry and procreate, coupled with the public housing programme's outwardly pro-family stance, this group has unsurprisingly received little attention in terms of research. I draw on the essay film to discuss the women's embodied spatial negotiations of their flats.

The body is affective, and architecture seen through such a body is also affective. This is where the film is able to bring out the nuances of sexuality and space, showing architecture as always entangled with something else, continually suspended in 'the midst of' time, rhythms, rituals, routines, atmospheres, textures brought about by ageing, weathering and use. Here, the sexualized bodies are marked by physical frailties, gendered proclivities, emotional attachments and social relationships. These bodies are eccentric, fleshy, storied, historicized, politicized and socialized. The reading of the spaces in *03-FLATS* is both complicated by and enmeshed with the physical, social, psychological and emotional dimensions that surround the three single women who have also chosen to live alone.

The film's effects cannot be duplicated by textual discourse. But as the theorist, artist and filmmaker Trinh T Minh-Ha argues, 'It is important not to confuse the film with the discussion around it or with the theoretical work that comes out of it' (Minh-Ha 2013: 143). Because it is never 'the truth' or objective fact, the film should not be seen as unquestionable evidence. Rather, this essay has done what Minh-ha advocates, which is to 'not speak about' but only to discuss what the film impresses upon me, what is 'nearby' and to use it to 'theorize with' (Minh-Ha 2013).

I began by asking if sexuality could matter as a critical category within a hegemonic housing environment. The visual narratives woven by the three single women in the architectural essay film *03-FLATS* suggest that the recognition of sexual difference opens up new ways of understanding the degree by which public housing – an entity shaped through policy, design and habit, as suited to heterosexual families – might accommodate other ways of being and living. More importantly, it also offers glimpses of how these spaces may be creatively occupied by others outside the heterosexual familial norm.

Notes

1 *03-FLATS* is a film conceptualized by myself (as principal investigator), directed by Lei Yuan Bin and funded by the Ministry of Education, Singapore and the National University of Singapore. For more information on the film and research project, see Chee 2014.

2 Filming started in September 2012 and was completed in July 2013. The editing was completed in May 2014. The film was officially released at the Busan International Film Festival in October 2014, where it was chosen to compete in the Wide Angle Documentary competition. *03-FLATS* won the Best ASEAN Documentary in the Salaya International Documentary Film Festival in February 2015.

3 It is of no coincidence that Lei and myself share a fascination for Chantal Akerman's *Jeanne Dielman* (1975), a film whose plot is bound to the architectural confines of one flat and structured around the domestic routines taking place within this limited setting. *03-FLATS* is very much influenced by and indebted to Akerman's technique of giving value to women and housework, with the film transforming such mundane gestures into what may be described as 'hyperreal', that is, that these denigrated aspects acquire their own sociopolitical and aesthetic value in the film (see Margulies 1996).

4 In 2012, Amy shared her home with a family of six and their helper for nine months as the family was unable to find suitable housing.

5 For activist potential of domestic maintenance and preservation, see Young 2005.

References

03-FLATS (2014). [Film] Directed by Y. B. Lei. Concept and research by L. Chee. Singapore: National University of Singapore and 13 Little Pictures.

Baydar, G. (2012). 'Sexualised productions of space'. *Gender, Place & Culture* 19, no. 6: 699–706.

Benjamin, W. (1999 [1939]). 'Paris: Capital of the nineteenth century'. Translated by H. Eiland and K. McLaughlin. In *The Arcades Project*, edited by R. Tiedemann, 77–88. Cambridge, MA: Harvard University Press.

Bloomer, J. (1995). 'The matter of the cutting edge'. *Assemblage* 27: 106–11.

Blunt, A. and R. Dowling (2006). *Home*. London: Routledge.

Burns, K. (1996). 'Architecture/discipline/bondage'. In *Desiring Practices: Architecture, Gender, and the Interdisciplinary*, edited by K. Rüedi, S. Wigglesworth and D. McCorquodale, 73–87. London: Black Dog Publishing

Chee, L (2014). 03-FLATS: Domesticity, home and its representations. 03-Flats research project. Available at: http://www.03-flats.com/.

Chee, L. (2017). 'Reimagining domesticity in 03-FLATS: Entering Singaporean domestic space through the essay film'. In *Making Visible: Architecture Filmmaking*, edited by H. Campbell and I. Troaini. London: Intellect Books.

Chua, B. H. (1997). *Communitarian Ideology and Democracy in Singapore*. London: Routledge.

Clancey, G. (2003). 'Toward a spatial history of emergency: Notes from Singapore'. *Singapore Asia Research Institute Working Paper*.

Colomina, B. (1996). 'Introduction'. In *Sexuality and Space*, edited by B. Colomina. New York: Princeton Architectural Press.

Goh, R. B. H. (2003). 'Things to a void: Utopian discourse, communality and constructed interstices in Singapore public housing'. In *Theorizing the Southeast Asian City as Text*, edited by B. S. A. Yeoh and R. B. H. Goh, 51–75. London: World Scientific.

Grosz, E. (1992). 'Bodies-cities'. In *Sexuality and Space*, edited by B. Colomina, 241–53. New York: Princeton Architectural Press.

Holliss, F. (2012). 'Space, buildings and the life worlds of home-based workers: Towards better design'. *Sociological Research Online* 17, no. 2: 24.

Holliss, F. (2015). *Beyond Live/Work: The Architecture of Home-based Work*. London: Routledge.

Housing and Development Board (2015). Eligibility to buy new HDB flat. HDB InfoWEB. Available at: http://www.hdb.gov.sg/cs/infoweb/residential/buying-a-flat/new/hdb-flat.

Johnson, L. (1990). 'New courses for a gendered geography: Teaching feminist geography at the University of Waikato'. *Australian Geographical Studies* 28, no. 1: 16–28.

Kong, L. and B. S. A. Yeoh (2003). *The Politics of Landscapes in Singapore: Constructions of 'Nation'.* Syracuse, NY: Syracuse University Press.

Le Corbusier (1931 [1923]). *Towards a New Architecture.* Translated by F. Etchells. London: John Rodker.

Lee, H. L. (2007). Speech to Parliament on Reading of Penal Code (amendment) Bill, 22 October.

Longhurst, R. (2004). *Bodies: Exploring Fluid Boundaries.* London: Routledge.

Manderson, L. (1996). *Sickness and the State: Health and Illness in Colonial Malaya, 1870–1940.* Cambridge, UK: Cambridge University Press.

Margulies, I. (1996). *Nothing Happens: Chantal Akerman's Hyperrealist Everyday.* Durham: Duke University Press.

Miller, D. (1988). 'Appropriating the state on the council estate'. *Man* 23, no. 2: 353–72.

Minh-Ha, T. T. (ed.) (2013). 'The politics of forms and forces (with Eva Hohenberger)'. In *D-Passage: The Digital Way*, 141–67. Durham: Duke University Press.

Oswin, N. (2010). 'The modern model family at home in Singapore: A queer geography'. *Transactions of the Institute of British Geographers* 35, no. 2: 256–68.

Parker, A., M. Russo, D. Sommer and P. Yaeger (1991). 'Introduction'. In *Nationalisms and Sexualities*, edited by A. Parker, M. Russo, D. Sommer and P. Yaeger, 1–18. London: Routledge.

Phua, L. and B. S. A. Yeoh (1998). 'Everyday negotiations: Women's spaces and the public housing landscape in Singapore'. *Australian Geographer* 29, no. 3: 309–26.

Pilkey, B., R. M. Scicluna and A. Gorman-Murray (2015). 'Alternative domesticities'. *Home Cultures* 12, no. 2: 127–38.

Radhakrishnan, R. (1992). 'Nationalism, gender, and the narrative of identity'. In *Nationalisms and Sexualities*, edited by A. Parker, M. Russo, D. Sommer and P. Yaeger, 77–95. London: Routledge.

Ramdas, K. (2012). 'Women in waiting? Singlehood, marriage, and family in Singapore'. *Environment and Planning A* 44, no. 4: 832–48.

Sa'at, A. (2015). 'Corridor'. In *Corridor: 12 Short Stories*, 51–64. Singapore: Ethos Books. Available at: http://www.ethosbooks.com.sg/products/corridor-12-short-stories.

Seng, E. (2012). 'Politics of greening: Spatial constructions of the public in Singapore'. In *Non West Modernist Past: Architecture and Modernities*, edited by W. S. W. Lim and J.-H. Chang, 143–59. London: World Scientific.

Stallybrass, P. and A. White (1986). *The Politics and Poetics of Transgression.* Ithaca, NY: Cornell University Press.

Tarmugi, A. (1995). *Statement by Singapore, HE Mr. Abdullah Tarmugi Acting Minister for Community Development.* United Nations Department of Economic and Social Affairs (DESA). World summit for social development by the United Nations Development Programme. Available at: http://www.un.org/documents/ga/conf166/gov/950310074254.htm.

Tremewan, C. (1994). 'Public housing: The working class barracks'. In *The Political Economy of Social Control in Singapore*, edited by C. Tremewan, 45–73. London: St Martin's Press.

Wigley, M. (1992). 'Untitled: The housing of gender'. In *Sexuality and Space*, edited by B. Colomina, 327–89. New York: Princeton Architectural Press.

Wigley, M. (1995). *White Walls, Designer Dresses: The Fashioning of Modern Architecture*. Cambridge, MA: The MIT Press.

Wilkinson, E. (2014). 'Single people's geographies of home: Intimacy and friendship beyond the family'. *Environment and Planning A* 46, no. 10: 2452–68.

Yeoh, B. S. A. (2003). *Contesting Space in Colonial Singapore: Power Relations and the Urban Built Environment*. Singapore: NUS Press.

Yeoh, B. S. A. and S. Huang (2010). 'Sexualised politics of proximities among female transnational migrants in Singapore'. *Population, Space and Place* 16, no. 1: 37–49.

Young, I. M. (ed.) (2005). 'House and home: Feminist variations on a theme'. In *On Female Body Experience: 'Throwing Like a Girl' and other Essays*, 123–54. New York: Oxford University Press.

3

Negotiating sexual relationships and alternative domesticities in shared households in England

Sue Heath and Rachael M. Scicluna

Introduction

Living in close everyday contact with non-family members (non-kin) in shared living arrangements necessitates an often extraordinary degree of physical and emotional intimacy, whether actively sought or not. In this chapter, we explore some of the ways in which sexual intimacy plays out in shared households, including how these may change at different points in a relationship or at different life stages. Our focus is on the ways in which relationships that are more commonly conducted in private are negotiated and managed when conducted under the gaze of non-kin, and what this suggests about the possibility of creating alternative forms of domesticity that, whether intentionally or not, challenge the widespread conflation of home with family.

Regardless of motivation, the sharing of domestic space with unrelated others inevitably brings co-residents into close spatial proximity with each other. Referring to such proximity, British sociologist David Morgan (1996) uses the term 'bodily density', noting the consequent monitoring, control and knowledge of each other's bodies that occurs when individuals live communally. In family households, these practices may be taken-for-granted aspects of everyday intimacy, yet may be more problematic in shared households, especially where housemates are, at least initially, relative strangers to each other. The nature of sharing a roof means that co-residents may generally know rather more about each other's bodies and bodily practices than is usual among non-kin. They may, for example, regularly see each other in states of (un)dress not usually seen by non-household members, be aware of each other's standards in relation to bodily and household hygiene and be intimately acquainted with the state of each other's sexual relationships (Gurney 2000; Procupez 2008). Relationships with co-residents in shared households hence constitute 'critical associations' (Davies and Heaphy 2011): critical in the dual sense that these relationships both provide a significant backdrop to everyday domestic life yet are often viewed with ambiguity.

In what follows, we discuss data from two complementary studies of shared living arrangements conducted in England, one focusing on under-35-year-olds living mostly in shared households in the private rented sector, the other focusing on sharers of all ages living in diverse forms of shared accommodation.[1] The first consists of data from twenty-five group interviews held with the members of twenty-five different shared households and individual interviews with sixty-seven of the housemates living in those households, based in and around a coastal city in southern England and conducted between 1998 and 2000. The second consists of data from interviews with sixty-five sharers, (mainly one-to-one interviews, although a small number involved two or more co-residents), living in towns and cities across England – albeit with a clustering in the north – and conducted between 2013 and 2015. This second study included both 'intentional' forms of sharing (co-housing; cooperatives) and less intentional forms (shared rentals; private lodgings). In considering the time difference between these two studies, it is important to note the changing patterns of sharing in the broader UK context. At the time of the first study, sharing was a common living arrangement among graduates and young professionals. It was widely viewed as a time-limited arrangement prior to living alone or living with a partner within a foreseeable, usually relatively short-term, time frame (Heath and Kenyon 2001). In the years since, rising housing costs and welfare reforms mean that shared housing has become a common feature of young adulthood, almost regardless of background, with many unable to imagine a time when they can afford not to share. These same factors have also impacted on older people, with many taking in lodgers to cover their housing costs or becoming lodgers or tenants in shared rentals following a change of circumstances. Living with others is rarely the first choice of these 'new' sharers. There is nonetheless a small core of sharers for whom living with others represents at least some degree of preference, and the more recent study includes both 'intentional' and 'non-intentional' sharers.

We first consider how sharing beyond young adulthood challenges widespread assumptions in the UK regarding the link between home and family and the place of non-kin in domestic settings. We then present our findings, highlighting a range of issues linked to the formation, maintenance and renegotiation of sexual relationships with non-resident partners. These include how much time partners spent in the shared house and in what ways they spent that time; the desire to create safe and accepting home settings for sharers with non-heterosexual/queer identities; and the possibilities afforded by shared households for the renegotiation of couple relationships on new footings, whether existing or 'ex' relationships. In our concluding discussion, these various scenarios are conceptualized through the lens of 'alternative domesticities', which embraces alternative family formations that are not necessarily exclusive to LGBT relations, while taking into consideration the multiple domestic experiences that are shaped by power relations within and beyond the household.

Shared living, home and family

In the recent history of the UK, shared living arrangements, whether in domestic or more institutional contexts, have often been specific to particular moments in the life course: boarding schools and student halls of residence, for example; the peer-shared households of single young adults; and residential care homes in later life. These typically occur for most people prior to 'settling down' with a partner or following a relationship breakdown when one or both parties may have to move house; relatively few people live with a partner on a permanent basis while also sharing their home with non-kin (Heath and Cleaver 2003; Beer and Faulkner 2011). Yet shared living arrangements are generally on the rise in the UK as well as in many other globalized cities with high living costs (Heath 2016). Sometimes this reflects an element of choice, for example the growth of housing schemes including communal provision – the communal lounges, restaurants and leisure facilities of 'new style' retirement villages, for instance, and the 'common house', which is an integral part of co-housing developments – but more commonly it reflects some degree of constraint, such as taking in a lodger to cover rising housing costs or sharing with friends due to the unaffordability of living on one's own.

Within Western neoliberal societies such as the UK which are dominated by privatized notions of housing, home and domesticity, sharing beyond young adulthood still tends to confound normative expectations of the place of non-kin in most people's lives (i.e. that it is preferable to share domestic space with family members and not with those to whom one is unrelated). This is despite nearly two decades of sociological and anthropological research on 'families of choice', indicating how non-kin can form 'family-like' relationships through their own distinct ethics, practices and displays (Weston 1991; Weeks et al. 2001), yet such networks are often presumed to exist above the level of the domestic spaces of home. Living communally seems then to exemplify sociologist Brian Heaphy's observation of a perception that 'alternative or critical displays of family are weak displays within our culture', with potential audiences 'unwilling to receive, interpret and validate them as desirable or viable alternatives to family' (2011: 37). The British anthropologist Daniel Miller (2007) offers an alternative suggestion, arguing 'that flexibility and negotiation are a direct result of the struggle people have in trying to retain clear principles and formal expectations in kinship in the face of the complexity of modern family lives. It is an instrument of conservatism in kinship' (ibid: 540). Miller argues that we live in a society with clear, normative expectations of a series of familial roles and relationships that continue to matter. Therefore, the flexible negotiations that people use aim to achieve this consistency found within kinship.

The possibility that a sense of homeliness might be created within households consisting largely or solely of non-kin also immediately destabilizes normative understandings of the nuclear family home. Home is largely described in 'Western' academic literature as a 'private, secure location, a sanctuary, a locus of identity and a place where inhabitants can escape the disciplinary practices that regulate our bodies in everyday life' (Johnston and Valentine 1995: 100). As feminist literature suggests, this specific perspective of home is a nineteenth-century invention with class, work and leisure implications and differences (Hayden 1985; Davidoff 1995; Blunt and Dowling 2006). It was a reaction to the serious changes that agricultural capitalism brought about in English society. Further, the cultural historian Matt Cook, in his book *Queer Domesticities: Homosexuality and Home Life in Twentieth-Century London* (2014), takes the argument that the family has always been a flexible phenomenon further by showing that queer domestic arrangements were just as common in the Victorian period and earlier. We propose, then, to think of 'domestic pluralities' (Scicluna 2015) and move away from the monolithic understanding of home as the place of the heteronormative family. Instead, we will illustrate the varied and multiple experiences of home through the theoretical framework of alternative domesticities (Pilkey, Scicluna and Gorman-Murray 2015).

The negative connotations popularly attached to communal living are also related to idealized understandings of what a good home ought to be. Sociologist Diana Leonard (1980: 49) famously noted that making a home alone or with peers 'is a contradiction in folk terms and difficult in practice'. In a similar vein, Lewin (this book) contends that the family still holds as a 'key marker of adulthood and citizenship', which in turn manifests as a reality that creates 'the foundation for the formation of a *home*'. According to Lewin, obtaining the status of family and having children enables a claim to the cultural performances and benefits associated with full adulthood. The family thus confers more than 'moral normativity on parents; it can also be seen as the foundation of citizenship in the sense of an individual being a visibly contributing member of society' (ibid). Hence, straying away from this normative understanding of home is perceived as strange, especially when it confounds expectations of the appropriateness or otherwise of age-specific living arrangements. Interestingly, reinforcing this, many older sharers in our study, for instance, indicated their discomfort in letting others, especially work colleagues, know of their shared living arrangements.

The dominance of the linked ideologies of heteronormativity and familialism and their influence on the meaning and practices of what constitutes a home tends to obscure alternative household formations. Experiences of home are nonetheless multiple and complex, and aside from the assumption that the presence of a family is one of the key markers in the foundation of a 'good' home, the idea and meaning of home is also forged through the material form of the house and its possessions. We also note that the domestic entails relations with those who are not necessarily formally resident in the house but who nonetheless play a significant part in domestic arrangements as frequent guests and visitors. The concept of alternative domesticities (Pilkey, Scicluna and Gorman-Murray 2015) is useful as it embraces the multidimensionality of identity across the life course while encapsulating different domestic scenarios that do not solely refer to the domestic sphere,

> or a set of normative domestic relations and domestic practices, which are often understood through a set of relationships bound to marriage, family, religion and economy. Instead, it also encapsulates the multiple experiences founded in emotions, kinship, friendship, homelessness, care, and different flows of power within and beyond the household. (ibid: 129).

Additionally, this concept asks us to think of the domestic in the plural. It is the varied intimate experiences and practices that people share that bring out important differences in the meaning of home and the domestic. It is the combination of these assemblages that infuse a home with a domestic quality. Hence, the element of openness in the theoretical framework of alternative domesticities is ideal for understanding the meaning of shared living, while at the same time challenging normative concepts of the home.

In what follows, we consider shared households as places for the negotiation and renegotiation of sexual and bodily intimacy. Central to our findings are the themes of *boundaries* and *the preservation of distance*, and these tend to operate in different ways according to age and life stage. For younger sharers, in particular, living with peers offers the freedom to live a single lifestyle away from the parental gaze while also offering the opportunity to initiate and maintain intimate sexual relationships with partners who are semi-resident at most, most typically prior to eventually 'settling down' with a partner in a couple household. For others, particularly older sharers, who in many cases may be moving into shared accommodation following the breakdown of a long-term couple relationship, shared living arrangements offer the possibility to reshape normative ideas of the couple/family household as the primary site of sexual intimacy while providing the space in some contexts to negotiate relationship breakdown and the subsequent reformulation of relationships with former partners.

Negotiating intimacy in shared housing

In our research, most of the tensions surrounding physical intimacy in shared households did not arise from sexual relationships occurring between existing housemates. Indeed, there is something of a taboo concerning the formation of sexual relationships between housemates in shared contexts. This is not to suggest that they never happen, but that they are generally considered to be ill-advised because of their ability to destabilize the household and cause unwanted tensions between housemates, especially if a relationship subsequently goes wrong. More commonly, then, concerns arise around the conduct of relationships between housemates and their non-resident sexual partners, whether one-night stands or long-term partners, and most notably with regard to the *amount* of time they spend in the shared house and the *way* in which that time is spent. These issues matter because the shared house constitutes the main home space, however transitory, of those residing there, and the presence of non-residents can easily disturb the often delicate balance that can be achieved between privacy and communality in shared households.

These issues are particularly pronounced among younger sharers, who may be engaging in sexual relationships, including casual sexual encounters, for the first time in the context of the shared household. Just over half of the sharers involved in our first study, focusing on under 35-year-olds, had a non-resident partner, most of whom lived locally and were frequent visitors to the shared house. If the non-resident partner still lived with his or her parents, then most of a couple's domestic time together occurred in the shared household. If the non-resident partner lived alone, more time would tend to be spent away from the shared house, while if both partners were sharers, one of the two houses often proved to be more conducive to spending time together than the other, for example because housemates were more welcoming or because one house offered greater opportunities for privacy than the other. In some shared households, there was very little tolerance for the presence of partners and consequently, the most easy-going households tended to be the most crowded, with partners and friends coming and going at regular intervals. Nonetheless, even in these households, it was important to strike the right balance in terms of the amount of time that partners spent in the shared house, as their presence could be seen as diverting the energies of a housemate away from the collective elements of shared living (through spending too much time in their own room, for example), or the non-resident partner could be seen as a freeloader who took advantage of the household's goodwill (regularly staying over, for example, but not contributing to household finances). Trying to avoid these problems by spending more time in the home of the non-resident partner could be equally problematic, though, as this too could be seen as a rejection of one's housemates.

Many of these manoeuvrings related to a desire to secure the privacy necessary to conduct sexual relationships, and most households in both studies had very clear boundaries in place regarding appropriate and inappropriate sexual behaviour in shared households. Most housemates respected each other's right to privacy in this regard, for example not barging into a housemate's bedroom if their partner was known to be around, as well as each other's right not to be embarrassed by displays of sexual behaviour in the shared areas of the household when others were around. One household of six women in their early twenties responded with humour when asked about the limits of physical intimacy in shared spaces:

> Daisy: If you're in the lounge, as long as they're not slobbering on each other it's alright. Or they'll go to their room if they want to slobber.
> Jane: I don't mind someone putting their arm around their boyfriend.
> Daisy: Yeah, sitting and having a cuddle and that.
> Ray: Holding hands. On top of each other might be going a bit far.
> Jane: Removing each other's clothes.
> Daisy: Kissing.
> Jane: Nibbling at the ears, yeah.
> Daisy: Fondling breasts and things is out.
> Jane: Whispering sweet nothings whilst you're trying to watch *ER*.
> Ray: Being a bit pukey is a bit of a no-no, isn't it?

Nonetheless, even where housemates respected these boundaries, the noise of housemates having sex in their bedrooms was a perennial cause of complaint in even the most tolerant of households, although as in the example above it was invariably treated with humour by younger sharers. Older sharers in our second study also referred to the potential discomfort caused by the intense proximity that sexual relations brought within the household, but often expressed this with less tolerance. Several older participants living with much younger housemates, for example, spoke about their dislike of sexual partners being brought into the house without advance warning, noting the awkwardness of bumping into strangers in the night or over breakfast.

At their most extreme, tensions surrounding new partners could sometimes lead to the breakdown of sharing relationships. Samantha, whom we interviewed in the more recent study, recounted a particularly traumatic experience involving a former housemate, Claire, who was seven years her junior. Claire would often bring 'male friends' back to the house on one-night stands, often the boyfriends of mutual friends, which Samantha described as 'a bit awkward' but 'I just kept my mouth shut'. However, when Samantha met her current boyfriend, the household dynamics changed overnight. Claire tried to prevent her from bringing her boyfriend home, which made Samantha's life very difficult, to the extent that she became very ill due to anxiety caused by Claire's frequent tantrums. Things got progressively worse: Claire took to locking Samantha out of the house or would lock herself into the bathroom to prevent Samantha from using the toilet. The situation came to a head on Christmas day, when Samantha and her boyfriend believed they had the house to themselves. However, Claire turned up unexpectedly and went into a rage,

> She started going on, running in the room, grabbing everything she owned out of the living room, candles, picture frames, everything, everything she owned, she grabbed in her arms and stormed out of the room, stormed upstairs crying. Then she came downstairs, threw all her stuff back in the living room and said, this is my room, I pay for the Sky, you get out.

In the subsequent weeks, the two women effectively split the house in two and lived completely separate lives until Samantha eventually moved out with her boyfriend. This household scenario, although extreme, nonetheless highlights the intensity of living in close proximity with non-kin and the sometimes unexpected reactions of housemates to non-resident partners.

Another important issue in both studies related to the need of some sharers to be able to create a home that was accepting of their non-heterosexual or queer identity (Gorman-Murray 2007). This was easiest for those able to exercise some control over the selection of potential housemates, either because they owned the property or because they were effectively 'lead tenants', for example by virtue of having lived in the house the longest. Two households involved in our earlier study were headed by gay men who owned their properties, and both spoke of the importance of ensuring that new housemates were aware of and comfortable with their sexual orientation before they moved in. Jamie, for example, would advertise for 'broad-minded tenants', hoping that this would attract 'people who are sort of relaxed and comfortable with things' and would filter out potentially homophobic applicants. Similarly, a housing cooperative involved in the second study consisted of a group of young adults with a strong identification with queer politics, and a rainbow flag was hung in one of the front windows as a way of proudly signifying their politics to the wider world as well as a reminder of their commitment to creating a home where they could feel comfortable and accepted. In contrast, ensuring a gay-friendly home environment was potentially more difficult for sharers looking to join existing households and where residents' views were an unknown quantity. Joe, a 23-year-old sharer involved in our more recent study, spoke for example about his potential concerns with respect to sharing with people who might have religious objections to homosexuality. Although this had never actually been an issue for him in practice, he nonetheless spoke about the need to be 'a little bit more guarded with that individual as opposed to being open with them'.

For many sharers, living in a shared household provided the opportunity to deliberately create new ways of negotiating their sexual relationships, away from the expectations of conventional couple relationships based on co-residence. Some sharers, for example, noted their personal discomfort concerning the undesirable intensity of their own sexual relationships and preferred to keep their intimate relationships at arm's length. Linda, a woman in her sixties, lived in a housing cooperative that had started out as a single household but that had subsequently been converted into separate apartments, albeit still managed cooperatively. Linda found it difficult to live with a partner, preferring them to have their own bedroom or ideally their own flat. She noted that she liked her own company and had 'never really liked the idea of living with somebody as a, you know, a relationship … the idea of having to sleep with someone night in, night out, just, I just couldn't do it, I like to sleep on my own'. Emily, a woman in her late forties who had lodged with the same landlady for eighteen years, had a similar view. She had been in a relationship for the previous two years. However, her partner also lived in a shared household and they had opted to continue living communally in their respective house shares. She explained that 'you get used to it … . I mean I like being with people, and I like people around, but I know that I also need that time and space on my own, and living in a one-bedroomed flat [which is all they would be able to afford], you know where you're in each other's pockets all the time can become quite stressful I think'. In both cases, living in shared buildings provided them with the company of others when they needed it and afforded them privacy – both from partners and co-residents – at other times.

These kinds of concerns were often directly addressed in the context of intentional shared living arrangements, where there was frequently an overt questioning of the assumed primacy of couple relationships and where space was quite literally made to accommodate other possibilities. Members of the various shared housing cooperatives involved in our second study spoke of the prohibition on moving a partner into a co-op without them first having to go through the process of applying to become a fully fledged member of the co-op and, if accepted, each partner would be expected to have their own room rather than moving into one room together. In one co-op, it transpired that two existing members had conducted a clandestine relationship, which was only revealed after it had ended. Other co-op members spoke of how living in large shared properties with multiple bedrooms and hence the potential for 'space moves' made it possible to renegotiate not just existing relationships on a new footing, but failed relationships too. Tony, for example, a man in his late fifties, had lived in communal settings for many years, and at the time of the research was living in a shared housing cooperative in the north of England. Tony first experienced communal living as a young father, moving with his then wife into a community of sixty people with 'a nearly-two-year-old and a pregnancy, and that was quite a shock'. While living in this community, his marriage had broken down, yet instead of having to go through the ordeal of moving home, Tony and his ex-wife had the possibility of moving to separate rooms. Something similar had happened in his present co-op, which consists of several connected properties. A couple had separated and had moved to different parts of the co-op, enabling the couple's children to spend time with each parent in different parts of the co-op while retaining their own bedrooms. In Tony's experience, 'co-op space moves' were a periodic occurrence, which were prompted either by relationship breakdowns or by an interest in occupying a different room. Despite the situation being tough in case of breakdowns, things would eventually settle down and allow people to start again. It seems then that the ways in which domestic space in housing co-ops were arranged and conceptualized, and the liberal attitudes that co-op members often had to intimate relationships, meant that members were able to accommodate change over time in group dynamics and family settings.

Towards multiple meanings and experiences of home and sexuality

While the above scenarios are unique, the themes of jealousy, privacy, sexuality, control and homeliness are common to the sharers interviewed, and they illustrate some of the ways in which sexuality is negotiated within shared households. For some, sharing puts a huge strain on intimate relationships, while for others, their shared housing arrangement provides the right balance between privacy and intimacy. For others, living communally and having a relationship is unthinkable. In other cases, the intense proximity of sharing a home can lead to disastrous situations, as was clear in Samantha's story. However, this is not always so, as illustrated by Tony's story, where the degree of flux that can occur within a cooperative and the malleability of the domestic architecture made it possible to accommodate ephemeral relationships and changes in family dynamics such as divorce. Many of these scenarios can also be better understood through applying Morgan's (1996) concept of bodily density, which we referred to earlier. He notes that bodily density can operate 'across and between households linked through ties of marriage or descent including reconstituted households' (ibid: 132), yet we have demonstrated how the knowledge and monitoring of intimate bodily relations between co-residents, and the power dynamics that can flow from these, are by no means exclusive to family relationships. In the case of Samantha's story, for example, Claire's knowledge of Samantha's bodily rhythms became a technique of control that Claire used in order to upset Samantha, and Samantha's sexual relationship, despite being conducted discretely – in contrast to Claire's one-night stands – led to the breakdown of their friendship.

Following on from this point, there is also much in these accounts about the importance of boundaries and the preservation of distance, both of which can be particularly difficult to achieve in shared housing contexts, whether in their literal sense or in a more metaphorical sense. Housing philosopher Peter King (2009: 4) writes of how 'in the case of dwelling, privacy helps us to separate and seclude ourselves from unwelcome attention', yet this is often impossible or difficult to achieve in relation to sexual intimacy in shared households. He notes further that private dwelling, in the context of more conventional living arrangements, is not about being solitary but about allowing space for intimacy, again something that can be challenging when living with non-kin. Nonetheless, for some sharers (including the small minority in our two studies whose partners were co-resident in the shared household), the presence of others provided a welcome refuge from the intense emotional intimacy of their exclusive sexual relationships.

The perspective of alternative domesticities is, then, a productive point of departure, which illustrates that there are multiple meanings of home that are not necessarily tied to normative understandings of kin-based household composition. For some sharers, the conduct of their relationships in shared contexts represents a deliberate attempt to trouble these normative understandings, while for others (probably the majority) this is a necessary consequence – sometimes welcome, sometimes not – of living in a shared context. Both positions nonetheless present a challenge to orthodox views of how sexual relationships should ideally be conducted. This is an important shift in the way we theorize the relationship between home and sexuality, and especially within a *shared domestic context* with non-kin. The varied house-settings described in this chapter illustrate the nuanced experiences of how people live and why they live where they do. These are very important assertions which illustrate the heterogeneity of society, while simultaneously they challenge the more dominant ideologies associated with homeownership, domestic space and living arrangements.

Acknowledgements

We would like to thank all the participants in both studies who were willing to share their life and housing stories with us. We would also like to thank Brent Pilkey, Ben Campkin and Barbara Penner for their insightful comments, which undoubtedly led to the improvement of this chapter.

Note

1 The first study is entitled *Single Young Adults and Shared Household Living* and was funded between 1998 and 2000 by the UK's Economic and Social Research Council (ESRC; award reference R000237033). The second study is entitled *Under the Same Roof: The Everyday Relational Practices of Contemporary Communal Living*. It was also funded by the ESRC, between 2013 and 2015 (award reference ES/K006177/1).

References

Beer, A. and D. Faulkner (2011). *Housing Transitions Through the Life Course: Aspirations, Needs and Policy*. Bristol: Policy Press.

Blunt, A. and R. Dowling (2006). *Home*. London: Routledge.

Cook, M. (2014). *Queer Domesticities: Homosexuality and Home Life in Twentieth-Century*. London: Palgrave Macmillan.

Davidoff, L. (1995). *Worlds between: Historical Perspectives on Gender and Class*. Oxford: Polity Press.

Davies, K. and B. Heaphy (2011). 'Interactions that matter: Researching critical relationships'. *Methodological Innovations Online* 6, no. 3: 5–16.

Gorman-Murray, A. (2007). 'Contesting domestic ideals: Queering the Australian Home'. *Australian Geographer* 38, no. 2: 195–213.

Gurney, C. (2000). 'Transgressing public/private boundaries in the home: A sociological analysis of the coital noise taboo'. *Venereology* 13: 39–46.

Hayden, D. (1985). *The Grand Domestic Revolution*. Cambridge, MA: The MIT Press.

Heaphy, B. (2011). 'Critical relational displays'. In *Displaying Families*, edited by E. Dermott and J. Seymour, 19–37. Basingstoke: Palgrave Macmillan.

Heath, S. (2016). 'Young, free and single: Alternative living arrangements'. In *Handbook of Youth and Young Adulthood: New Perspectives and Agendas*, second edition, edited by A. Furlong, 211–16. London: Routledge.

Heath, S. and E. Cleaver (2003). *Young, Free and Single? Twenty-Somethings and Household Change*. Basingstoke: Palgrave Macmillan.

Heath, S. and E. Kenyon (2001). 'Single young professionals and shared household living'. *Journal of Youth Studies* 4, no. 1: 83–100.

Johnston, L. and G. Valentine (1995). 'Wherever I lay my girlfriend, that's my home: The performance and surveillance of lesbian identities in domestic environments'. In *Mapping Desire: Geographies of Sexuality*, edited by D. Bell and G. Valentine, 88–103. London: Routledge.

King, P. J. (2009). 'Using theory or making theory: Can there be theories of housing?' *Housing, Theory and Society* 26, no. 1: 41–52.

Leonard, D. (1980). *Sex and Generation: A Study of Courtship and Weddings*. London: Tavistock.

Miller, D. (2007). 'What is a relationship? Is kinship negotiated experience?' *Ethnos* 72, no. 4: 535–54.

Morgan, D. H. J. (1996). *Family Connections: An Introduction to Family Studies*. Oxford: Polity Press.

Pilkey, B., R. M. Scicluna and A. Gorman-Murray (2015). 'Alternative domesticities: A cross-disciplinary approach to home and sexuality'. *Home Cultures* 12, no. 2: 127–38.

Procupez, V. (2008). 'Beyond home: Forging the domestic in shared housing'. *Home Cultures* 5, no. 3: 327–48.

Scicluna, R. M. (2015). 'Thinking through domestic pluralities'. *Home Cultures* 12, no. 2: 169–91.

Weeks, J., B. Heaphy and C. Donovan (2001). *Same Sex Intimacies. Families of Choice and other Life Experiments*. London: Routledge.

Weston, K. (1991). *Families We Choose: Lesbians, Gays, Kinship*. New York: Columbia University Press.

4

Making a house a home: Children and the meanings of home among gay men in the United States[1]

Ellen Lewin

I was visiting with Tyrone Landon and Thomas Palmer[2] at their Chicago flat shortly after they adopted their son, Damian, from the foster-care system. Tyrone and Thomas, both African American, explained that having a child allowed them to establish a good home, one that they expected to become the 'focal point' for holiday celebrations in their extended families. What did they mean when they talked about 'a good home'?, I asked. Tyrone explained.

> It should be warm and inviting. I had a wonderful experience growing up [with] extended family, church family. It felt very warm and right. I've always cherished that and wanted to pass it on. I want to create that here. Christmas with a tree and the fire going, and the dogs, you know, running back and forth. That's family, that's home. That's what I like. It's so traditional … like a picket fence and those types of things.

The picture that Tyrone and Thomas painted was attractive, invoking the ubiquitous American image of a picket fence, despite their residence in a south side Chicago flat. But I understood 'picket fence' to be an image that simply meant 'home' in a very deep way, one that pointed to comfort, safety and affection as the hallmarks of what it meant to have a family. In this construction, home emerges as the moral centre of these men's lives, either as they aspire to live them or in ways they feel they have achieved.

Stories like Tyrone and Thomas's demand explanation, as having children may seemingly not be a very rational choice, at least from a strictly economic perspective, in the twenty-first century. Parenthood is expensive and rarely yields the material rewards that impelled reproduction in earlier generations. Most of us no longer need children to herd our cattle or help plant and harvest our crops. Children can no longer be counted on to care for their elderly parents or to produce any sort of monetary pay off; in fact, the recent phenomenon of children returning to their parents' home after college or even later in adulthood suggests a lifelong pattern of dependence that may undermine parental financial security. Even thinking of the possible financial benefits of having children threatens to violate the dictum that children are (or ought to be) 'priceless', and not to be thought of as conferring measurable rewards on their parents (Zelizer 1985). Is the symbolic weight of the picket fence enough to defuse these disincentives?

In my research, one of the commonly cited reasons gay men offer for seeking to become fathers is the desire to create a *home*, a goal that requires achieving recognition and legibility as a *family*. In this chapter, I will discuss the cultural linkage between parenthood, family and home, and using the narratives of gay fathers, examine the ways in which these domains, hallmarks of adulthood, are co-constructed in gay men's personal accounts. American cultural imaginaries of both biological and social reproduction loom large in these narratives, and gay men's explanations of the allure of domesticity often depend on distancing themselves from representations of gay male life that emphasize frivolous pleasure seeking – in effect, recreating themselves as something other than *just* gay men.

The narratives I present are drawn from among nearly one hundred open-ended interviews I conducted with gay fathers, including both couples and single fathers. I carried out my research between 2002 and 2003, mostly in the Chicago metropolitan area, and connected with interlocutors in institutional settings, such as churches, and through referrals from other fathers or community members. As a cultural anthropologist, my approach places narrative at the centre of my inquiry: I draw on the approaches to narrative used by such scholars as Faye Ginsburg (1989) and Cheryl Mattingly and Linda Garro (2000) that seek to understand what is *said* about a cultural phenomenon rather than on what can be documented as being *done*. As Mattingly and Garro point out, narratives offer useful sites for teasing out the relationship between the individual and the culture and focus on the ways in which meanings are made on an ongoing basis. Anthropologist Renato Rosaldo has commented that 'narratives often reveal more about what can make life worth living than about how it is routinely lived' (1986: 98). Not surprisingly, the stories fathers told me about the meaning of parenthood in their lives depend on their views of their circumstances, not necessarily on depictions that might be interrogated for accuracy. My interlocutors rarely produced narratives that would pass muster among proponents of a queer politics, understood to consist of resistance (see, for example, Duggan 2003; Halberstam 2013; Warner 1999), nor do they exemplify the chosen or alternative family models proposed by scholars who have mostly worked with lesbians and gay men who are not parents (Weston 1991).[3]

Many scholars have tried to explain the continuing importance of children as their arrival appears to be more and more irrational. Famously, sociological economist Gary Becker advanced the argument that both the wish for children and the size of completed families must be seen as analogous to consumer desire. Assuming that the family in places like the United States has 'perfect control over the number and spacing of its births' (Becker 1960: 210) because of the availability of birth control, he claimed that the desire for children was no different from any other economic motive. According to his calculations, couples with higher incomes will seek higher-quality but smaller numbers of children (i.e. by providing more education, healthcare and other advantages), while those with lower incomes will have larger numbers of children but invest less in assuring their 'quality'. According to Becker, because children cost more than they produce, they are analogous to consumer durables (like cars), though 'since children cannot be bought and sold they are less "liquid" than ordinary durables' (ibid: 227).

In 1968, demographer Judith Blake's now-classic article 'Are Babies Consumer Durables?' challenged the notion that reproduction and fertility could be understood in the same terms as the acquisition of durable goods like cars and refrigerators. Instead, she highlighted the non-economic forces that influence parents to desire children. The importance of children exists, she explained, in 'the goals to which children are intrinsically related' (Blake 1968: 22). She went on, 'One can become a "parent", "have a family", or be a "mother" or "father" only by acquiring children. That one should desire these statuses is the final result of complex institutional control, but *given this desire,* children and only children can satisfy it' (Blake 1968: 23, emphasis in original).

Another way of thinking about these motivations is that the addition of children to a household enables it to enact particular kinds of cultural performances – that is, to claim the status of 'family', and thus to access an array of cultural benefits, particularly those associated with full adulthood and moral standing. Indeed, as sociologist Brian Powell and his colleagues have demonstrated, the inclusion of children in households, whether they consist of heterosexual or same-sex couples, or even of single adults, is widely seen to transform such households into 'families' (Powell, et al. 2010); in contrast, couples without children rarely get to make such claims. Powell and his co-investigators were interested in these entitlements in relation to public opinion about marriage equality, but there are other, perhaps less tangible, benefits that come with being able to present oneself as part of a family.

So having a family, by which we usually mean family of orientation, at least when discussing adults, leaves those without children languishing in a kind of social wilderness. Nor is this a neutral status: according to Smith (1993), adults without children, without families, may seem or feel inadequate, as not having completed a developmental process that is mandated for everyone, at least in the US context. Nervous jokes about people who have seemingly substituted pets for children speak to the pervasiveness of these ideologies (Grier 2006).[4]

But having a family confers more than moral normativity on parents; it can also be seen as the foundation of citizenship in the sense of an individual being a visibly contributing member of society. Historian Nancy Cott (2000) has shown that being married, and by extension having a family, serves as a critical marker of citizenship as well as constituting evidence of the achievement of full adulthood, a demonstration that one is contributing to the wider society (see also Cherlin 2004; Edin and Kefalas 2005). This is particularly marked when one looks back in history at the condition of slaves, who could not marry, and some immigrant groups, whose marital status was also constrained; the desire for full citizenship has been the driving force behind the marriage equality movement as well, both in terms of material benefits that accrue to married couples and less tangible cultural advantages that marriage makes it possible to claim (Lewin 1998). Marriage has long placed men at the head of their households and thus provided a legal avenue to the production of more citizens (Cott 2000: 133). Therefore, the symbolic imagery of the picket fence evoked by Tyrone and Thomas becomes powerful when understood in relation to the above, and especially as a widely recognized symbol of 'home' in this cultural complex of heteronormative and patriarchal domesticity.

Gay men and parenthood

Given these diffuse cultural benefits, perhaps it is not surprising that some gay men would want to join the ranks of those who wish to become parents. From my research, it emerged that gay men's familial ambitions are still treated as peculiar and sometimes unreasonable. Many of those whom I interviewed in the project told me stories not only of having faced practical obstacles posed by reproductive gatekeepers, but also about having experienced disbelief and hostility, even from other gay men. That is, they not only face all of the disincentives that other potential parents must manage – the seeming economic irrationality of having children, as I outlined above, including the financial challenges of raising children successfully – but also must contend with widespread gendered assumptions that men are 'naturally' less motivated to parent and that they are biologically and temperamentally less suited to raising children. Fathers are conventionally thought of as being less engaged with the business of parenting and far less eager to become parents, even when they actually do yearn to be fathers (Greil 1991). While motherhood is on many levels the defining attribute of womanhood, the single activity that fuels the system of gender that characterizes most Euro-American cultures, fatherhood is not conventionally mandated for the formation of manhood in American culture. Marsiglio (1998) argues that impregnating women may be a source of pride for men in that it signals their virility, but fulfilling the caring role of a father may not be what men are often stereotypically believed to desire (Marsiglio 1998). And as Nicholas Townsend (2002) shows in his study of suburban Californian men, fatherhood is understood to be well executed if men provide their children with good mothers.

But for some men, despite the expectation that fatherhood is not the focus of passionate yearning, having a child may come to seem absolutely essential to a meaningful life. As Jesse Green (1999) explained in his moving account of his struggle to become a father as a gay man, not achieving fatherhood would rob him of the hope of living a meaningful life.

> On a twigless branch of the family tree, merely an uncle, I would never achieve that kind of adulthood; I'd just keep aging. My hair might fall out, my gums might retreat to the bone and beyond, but all it would make me is old. Without a child you were always a child: a hanger-on, an exile, a zero (ibid: 96).

But becoming a father is not an easy matter for a gay man. Aside from being subject to views of men and women that assign parenting to women, gay men must deal with daunting practical obstacles if they do want access to fatherhood. Here I am referring not to gay men who have children from prior heterosexual unions – and they are probably the majority of gay fathers – but to the array of difficulties faced by gay men who seek out fatherhood *as* gay men. These are formidable impediments and can only be negotiated by those who are strongly motivated.

First, and most obvious, pregnancy is not an option for them, as it might be for lesbians. The next possibility, the domestic foster parent/adoption system, though low-cost, is often difficult to navigate, with social workers and other gatekeepers patrolling the boundaries of parenthood to be sure that only the worthy make it through the thicket of bureaucratic challenges. In the United States, at least, its accessibility to gay men is disparate and idiosyncratic, with individual agencies making specific policies depending on their views of homosexuality and how many children they are trying to place for adoption. That is, pragmatic concerns with finding good homes for children who have been languishing in the foster-care system may trump reluctance to make placements in gay-parent homes (Pertman 2000). Still, a kind of market system tends to rule these transactions, with 'less desirable' gay parents more likely to be matched with the 'less desirable' older, non-white or disabled children. As Pertman (2000) shows, in this system, healthy, newborn Caucasian infants (to the extent that any are available) tend to be matched with heterosexual married couples in the United States.

International adoption is rarely open to gay men (unless they can successfully conceal their sexual identity) as nearly all countries that permit children to be adopted by non-nationals have established barriers intended to keep out same-sex partnerships, and often single prospective parents (Briggs 2012). In the United States, domestic private adoptions, which involve agreements with pregnant women to relinquish their babies at birth, are notoriously unreliable, with birth mothers sometimes waiting until long into the process, even after giving birth, to decide that they do not want to give up their infants after all. This is a process that may have prospective parents paying large sums of money and ultimately being disappointed. Still, such adoptions offer the promise of getting a child who is newborn and whose racial background is known ahead of time.

Finally, surrogacy (in the United States) is phenomenally expensive (typically over $100,000 per birth) and also requires extensive negotiations with surrogates and, where necessary, egg donors, before it can be completed.[5] Surrogacy offers prospective parents the possibility of getting a child (or children, if in vitro fertilization [IVF] yields multiples) who is biologically related to one of the intended parents. For those whose dream of establishing a family is intertwined with images of children who resemble them physically, surrogacy has a strong appeal. Biological relatedness, usually imagined in terms of resemblance, is a key element of how Americans understand the foundation of kinship, and becoming the parents of a child who does not resemble its parents presents constant challenges to the authenticity of the family unit (Becker et al. 2005).

Yet even in the face of these challenges, growing numbers of gay men are seeking fatherhood, either as couples or as single parents, and gay dads are becoming an increasingly visible population in the United States, showing up in popular media, advertising and other locations that offer them visibility unimaginable just a few years ago (Cavalcante 2015). Indeed, the importance of legal rights for gay fathers and lesbian mothers has assumed prominence in legal discourse about marriage equality, often serving as the primary justification offered for approving proposals to open marriage to same-sex couples.[6] For those of us who have been following the situation of gay and lesbian parents over the past three or four decades, this visibility is nothing short of astounding, as the possible existence of such parents was long treated as oxymoronic at best, and criminal at worst.

It turns out that achieving that key marker of adulthood and citizenship is having a family, a reality that then creates the foundation for the formation of a *home*. Achieving this objective is central to making claims for citizenship across the spectrum, but its urgency is amplified for gay men, whose ability to make such claims has historically been impeded. Gay men are popularly portrayed in the media as exceptionally well-dressed, occupying exquisitely decorated homes and being loath to settle into committed relationships for any length of time, which some may see as at odds with typical foundations of parenthood.

Do the right thing

Creating a home through parenthood is, above all, a moral quest. These kinds of parental discourses are familiar aspects of motherhood, and while they are less conventionally expected for fathers, they are equally central to what gay fathers have to say when they reflect on parenthood.[7] For example, fatherhood puts pressure on gay men to disclose their identity, particularly in situations where people they encounter assume that they are minding their children for their wives or 'babysitting'. Such situations confront gay fathers with moral choices of 'doing the right thing', which emerges from the morality of heteronormative parenting. Being seen in the company of a child commonly erases their homosexuality, and even when they are out with their partners, they tend to be read as a heterosexual dad and his pal filling in for a mother.[8] Although deciding how to handle such situations can be exhausting – how important is coming out in a particular situation? – fathers often see their honesty as a significant moral lesson for their children, an opportunity to remind them that their family is as good as any other.

Enrique Morales, the single gay father of three children, explained that having children had radically changed his relationship with his parents and the wider heterosexual world.

> So I told them at one point, 'I'm no longer willing to be apologetic for my life to you. You need to stop calling me and saying, "Why don't you move down here? Why don't you do this and that?" You need to realize that I'm a

grown man, I have a family. My family is just as valid as my brother's family. Yes, there's no wife in this family. Yes, we don't have the same look. But it is as legitimate a family as my brother's and I don't feel that you give me that.' And I don't think they did. I think they still saw me as my younger brothers at the time who were still single.

Narratives such as Enrique's that situate honesty or 'doing the right thing' as a central feature of personal morality also draw on wider discourses about coming out that have circulated since the early days of gay liberation. These basically hold that both outright lying about being gay and the more passive dishonesty that comes with passing as straight by not correcting heteronormative assumptions are at least morally suspect – if not clearly reprehensible – both because such deception obviates the need to challenge popular misconceptions about gay people and, probably more importantly, because it requires a gay person to disown what they believe to be naturally the essence of his or her identity.[9] Enrique's narrative also parallels the situation of gay families and those of members of ethnic minorities or other stigmatized populations in that he draws on a discourse of group pride as an antidote to discrimination and situates self-acceptance as a key element of good parenting.

Enrique has made other choices that speak to the moral strength of his parenting. He and his children live in a modest Victorian house in San Francisco's working-class Bernal Heights neighbourhood, a move he made shortly after adopting his first child. By living in a neighbourhood with lots of children from diverse kinds of families rather than in the indexically gay (and mostly childless) area around the Castro district, where he formerly lived, Enrique has established the foundation of a home that he understands as appropriate for his three children and clearly demonstrates his commitment to putting his children's welfare ahead of his own personal preferences.

Erving Goffman's concept of 'moral career', though developed to describe quite a different situation – the struggle of psychiatric patients to establish themselves as honourable members of society (1961) – may be productively applied here. Gay men, like other members of stigmatized populations, face the task of managing what Goffman called their 'spoiled identities' (Goffman 1963). My reading of the narratives of many of the gay fathers I interviewed shows how these men approach the challenge of establishing 'moral careers': they stress their altruism, departing in some ways from conventional images of fathers and instead embracing a maternal model of parenthood. The emphasis on honesty, as expressed by Enrique, represents one such pattern. But a moral agenda also emerges in the accounts of fathers who see themselves as having contributed to wider goals of fostering justice.

Randall Johnson and Trent Williams, an African American couple who adopted their son shortly before I met with them, explained how becoming parents has shaped their lives. Randall is firm in expressing his commitment to spiritual values on which his life is centred, disavowing the material goals he achieves through his success as a professional.

> Let's really remember what I'm really here on this earth for and how I'm here on this earth. ... I think I'm on this earth to create justice, ... to celebrate life, to celebrate God. And to make the world a better place. we buy a good bottle of wine once... That piece of it comes from your house and home and to raise [our son] the way I'd like to raise him.

Trent's answer about why he is on earth is more concise. 'I'm a serving kind of person. I'm a servant.' While both men see their desire for a child as selfish on some levels, as having a child enabled them to establish themselves as a family in a way that eluded them when they were a childless couple, they also understand that adopting their son meant that he would be saved from a life in the foster-care system, the fate of most black male children who don't get adopted when they are young. Having a child, and having a home, enables them to strike a blow for justice, and also to overcome the spiritual limitations of affluence, to make themselves more substantial citizens.

'We're not gay anymore'

I was enjoying Sunday brunch in the Chicago suburban home of Paul O'Hara and Keith Michaels while their two adopted sons ran in and out of the room. The two men, both white and successful professionals, had adopted the two African American boys through a private agency when they were infants. I asked, 'How has becoming parents affected what it means to you to be gay?' Paul and Keith exchanged a knowing look, and then Paul said, 'Oh, we're not gay anymore. We pick our friends by what time their kids' nap time is.'

What did this tongue-in-cheek comment mean? Paul and Keith are clearly still gay; they are active in a gay fathers' organization and have chosen to raise their kids in a particularly gay-friendly suburb of Chicago. But they referred to something else: the notion that gay identity is embedded in a set of practices and pastimes that are conventionally associated with being gay and, more importantly, organizing one's life around adult activities undertaken in the company of other gay men. Popular images of gay male life have it that they have few concerns beyond attending parties, engaging in constant sexual activity and pursuing other forms of entertainment, be they patronizing restaurants, attending cultural events like the opera (Koestenbaum 2001) or sculpting their bodies in gyms. Implicit in such stereotyping is an assumption that non-parents think of no one except themselves but that parents must put their children's welfare first, that many of the activities that would have absorbed their time and money before having kids would now be impossible either because they are time-consuming or cost too much when one also has the expenses of parenthood to manage.

In contrast to the rather toxic images of gay men that circulate in popular representations and were remarked upon by my interviewees, not only among homophobes or persons hostile to homosexuality but among gay men themselves, parenthood provides an opportunity for moral improvement through the formation of a *home,* a space that is dedicated to the care of children and the pursuit of the kinds of endeavours that mark one as being *ordinary* and even *normal.* Another Chicago-area couple, Russ Anderson and Jason Williams, find that having a child put them in contact with people they characterized as 'normal'. What made them normal? These people are parents and their values seem to resonate with those held by Russ and Jason. Bar-hopping and gay nightlife receded in importance, finally disappearing altogether as they set up their suburban home and adopted their son. Other parents in their neighbourhood have become the source of most of their friendships, as they set up playgroups and cooperate on childcare. I maintain that these perspectives do not constitute *emulation* of heteronormative family forms; rather, they show how gay fathers respond to the same exigencies that face other parents on both material and cultural levels.

For some gay fathers, parenthood presents an opportunity to withdraw from forms of gay sociability that feel inauthentic or morally questionable. Lawrence Lock, a deeply religious single gay dad who lives in a working-class Chicago suburb, had long struggled with his realization that he was gay, a condition he linked with superficial pastimes and self-indulgence. He had never succeeded in forming a meaningful relationship with another man, though he still felt a yearning to express his love to another human being. Becoming the father of two disabled brothers enables him to do something 'important' with his time rather than 'wasting time on entertainment things', which he not only can no longer afford, but which also seem decidedly frivolous and morally compromised. He assumes that being a father makes the formation of an intimate relationship with another man totally impossible, but feels that God had brought these two boys into his life so that he could care for them and help them through the challenges imposed by their disabilities. The home he has made for these boys is the site of a sort of redemption; he no longer has to cope with the shame associated with his gay identity and can make a life that will be a source of goodness for children who had no other options.

When I first met with Dennis Caruso and Harvey Stone, they were in the process of completing the adoption of their Guatemalan-born daughter. They lived in a charming Victorian cottage on the Far North Side of Chicago and were able to undertake an international adoption because Dennis was going to travel to Guatemala with his mother, playing the part of a single father. Both men come from small towns. While these towns are in different parts of the country, they share blue-collar backgrounds with large, stable, extended families. While education has meant that their options are different from those of their parents and siblings, they connect their desire to be parents with the values by which they were raised, in which parenthood looms large. Having children is something that both men always assumed they would – and could – do. They never really wrestled with the question of whether to have children but did have to figure out how they would achieve parenthood. Both men were driven by images of creating a *home* that included children and was founded on a set of family-driven values. They expressed these to me when they spoke at length about their commitment to 'social responsibility', something they understood to be far more meaningful than achieving goals of personal gratification. Harvey explained:

> We've worked hard. We have a great life, and resources, and this nice thing going, and what a cool thing to share with a kid that might not otherwise get that. … There's this want of doing good.

Not only is the focus on doing good and replicating family traditions important to Dennis and Harvey, but both men locate these impulses at some distance from being gay men. While they share these desires with other potential parents, they had to go to greater lengths to convince those who control access to children that they deserved the same consideration as heterosexual parents. The theme of social responsibility was linked to their being gay, as they felt that having this moral centre allowed them essentially to opt out of the superficiality they see as deeply implicated in gay life. Dennis said,

> At the end of the day, at the end of our lives, do I want to say, 'Wow, we had some great trips to Key West, and wasn't the Pottery Barn fabulous when we furnished our house, and wasn't my garden cute?' I mean, is that what I want the essence of my life to be? Yes, there was career and friends, and all that stuff that was important, but then there's also that bigger legacy that's important. When you think about importance, it ties to social responsibility and making a difference and growing and raising this hopefully happy, and well-adjusted, and productive and caring human being.

Both men felt that these values situated them outside of 'gay life'. Harvey explained,

> We're always going through, like, 'When do we start the gay life?' Well, there's laundry, then we go to the grocery store, and then we get up for work, and then we rent movies, and we have some friends over for dinner, and we buy a good bottle of wine once in a while, and got a new cat. ... Because what's this gay thing? ... It gets into identity issues with us in terms of, like, that whole set of White Party, muscle boy, gym boy. That subculture is something that really doesn't appeal to us on a lot of levels. ... As we've both matured as gay men, finding authenticity and real down-to-earth people has been a huge thing to us.

They further explained that they had many lesbian friends and saw them as being less caught up in the pretensions of being gay than gay men they have known. Having a home, and having that home become fully realized as a moral centre, means having children. This will assure that they will have less time for the frivolity they associated with gay male life. Their alignment with 'ordinary people' demands that they devote their time to the kinds of things such people value, not coincidentally much the same as the central values with which they were raised.[10]

Home as a moral centre

These narratives often refer to 'home' tangentially, as a basic element of a good life that does not require elaboration. It is clear, however, from the narratives of the fathers I interviewed, that for a home to be authentic, it must share key qualities with people in the wider society who are not necessarily gay. Indeed, the construction of gayness that many gay fathers express place gay life and rewarding family life at some distance from one another, not coincidentally replicating the discourse of anti-gay rhetoric in the culture. In this construction, family is associated with parenthood, and parenthood depends on unselfishness to be fully realized. On the other hand, the fathers who told me their stories tended to characterize gay life as self-indulgent and irresponsible. They embrace a view that circulates among opponents of gay rights: that without dependent children to care for, gay men can do whatever they please in pursuit of entertainment and personal gratification. They cannot achieve a morally satisfying life under such conditions.

Let us return to the story told by Tyrone and Thomas at the beginning of this chapter. The image of the 'white picket fence' invokes a conventional scene, one that is imbued with tradition and that has continuity across time. Having children facilitates the creation of this sort of social unit, one that recalls family holiday celebrations, deep involvement with church (the 'church family') and the inculcation of moral values that will carry over to future generations. These are all domestic elements that gay men are at some pains to reproduce. They are largely seen as inappropriate candidates for the status of parent, and are assumed to be preoccupied with a range of frivolous pastimes and to exhibit a level of narcissism that negates their familial aspirations. Yet they aspire to a kind of moral solidity that will allow them to claim cultural citizenship. Such aspirations ought not to be seen either as futile (as they might be in the view of anti-gay actors) or as craven assimilation that repudiates the special differences proponents of queer culture would seek to elaborate. They are simply part of being members of a wider culture that valorizes nurturance and responsibility and that questions the morality of self-indulgence, and as such, situate themselves as gay fathers squarely in American life.

Notes

1 Portions of this chapter appeared in *Gay Fatherhood: Narratives of Family and Citizenship in America* (Lewin 2009).

2 All names used in this chapter are pseudonyms.

3 See Lewin 2009 for a more detailed discussion of this issue.

4 Some respondents in Powell et al. (2010) thought that couples and even single persons who lived with a pet constituted a family.

5 India has been a particularly active site of overseas surrogacy, with some agencies even specializing in providing services for Western gay men. See, for example, Frank, Z. B. dir. (2009); Pande (2014).

6 Rather than assuming that lesbians and gay men cannot (or should not) have children, those adjudicating demands for marriage equality often use the status of children to justify ruling in favour of legalizing same-sex marriage. For example, in his majority opinion striking down most provisions of the Defense of Marriage Act (DOMA) in *US v. Windsor* (2013), Supreme Court justice Anthony Kennedy said that DOMA 'humiliates tens of thousands of children now being raised by same-sex couples. The law in question makes it even more difficult for the children to understand the integrity and closeness of their own family and its concord with other families in their community and in their daily lives.' The presence of children in these families was not a source of controversy for Justice Kennedy; he simply took their existence for granted and thus was able to raise their well-being as an issue that the Court needed to address. Justice Kennedy used similar arguments in the 2015 decision that made same-sex marriage legal in the United States.

7 I found strikingly similar accounts of the moral foundation of parenthood among lesbian mothers with whom I worked in the late 1970s and early 1980s (Lewin 1993). Mothers often saw their status as grounded in kind of

self-sacrifice and moral goodness that led them to characterize non-mothers as selfish and self-indulgent, cut off from the 'important' things in life.

8 Dan Bucatinsky's book, *Does This Baby Make Me Look Straight?* (2012), offers a humorous account of how such cases of mistaken identity can work.

9 While scholars in LGBT and queer studies eschew the relevance of essentialism in discussing gender, sexual and other dimensions of identity, the research I and others have done point to widespread popular acceptance of such ideas. Essentialist constructions of gender and sexuality are also pervasive in legal arenas, where they are often employed to argue that, for example, gay people have no choice in their sexual orientation (Lancaster 2003).

References

Becker, G. (1960). 'An economic analysis of fertility'. In *Demographic and Economic Change in Developed Countries*, edited by N. B.o.E. Research, 209–40. Princeton, NJ: Princeton University Press.

Becker, G., A. Butler and R. D. Nachtigall (2005). 'Resemblance talk: A challenge for parents whose children were conceived with donor gametes in the US'. *Social Science and Medicine* 61, no. 6: 1300–9.

Blake, J. (1968). 'Are babies consumer durables? A critique of the economic theory of reproductive motivation'. *Population Studies* 22, no. 1: 5–25.

Briggs, L. (2012). *Somebody's Children: The Politics of Transracial and Transnational Adoption*. Durham, NC: Duke University Press.

Bucatinsky, D. (2012). *Does this Baby Make Me Look Straight? Confessions of a Gay Dad*. New York: Touchstone.

Cavalcante, A. (2015). 'The representation of gay parenting on *Modern Family* and *The New Normal* and the management of cultural anxiety'. *Television and New Media* 16: 454–71.

Cherlin, A. (2004). 'The deinstitutionalization of marriage'. *Journal of Marriage and Family* 66, no. 4: 848–61.

Cott, N. F. (2000). *Public Vows: A History of Marriage and the Nation*. Cambridge, MA: Harvard University Press.

Duggan, L. (2003). *The Twilight of Equality? Neoliberalism, Cultural Politics, and the Attack on Democracy*. Boston: Beacon Press.

Edin, K. and M. Kefalas (2005). *Promises I Can Keep: Why Poor Women Put Motherhood before Marriage*. Berkeley: University of California Press.

Frank, Z. B. dir (2009). *Google Baby*. Filmmakers' Library.

Ginsburg, F. (1989). *Contested Lives: The Abortion Debate in an American Community*. Berkeley: University of California Press.

Goffman, E. (1961). *Asylums: Essays on the Social Situation of Mental Patients and Other Inmates*. Garden City, NY: Anchor Books.

Goffman, E. (1963). *Stigma: Notes on the Management of Spoiled Identity*. New York: Simon & Schuster.

Green, J. (1999). *The Velveteen Father: An Unexpected Journey to Fatherhood*. New York: Villard.

Griel, A. L. (1991). *Not yet Pregnant: Infertile Couples in Contemporary America*. New Brunswick, NJ: Rutgers University Press.

Grier, K. C. (2006). *Pets in America: A History*. Chapel Hill, NC: University of North Carolina Press.

Halberstam, J. J. (2013). *Gaga Feminism: Sex, Gender, and the End of Normal*. Boston: Beacon Press.

Koestenbaum, W. (2001). *The Queen's Throat: Opera, Homosexuality and the Mystery of Desire*. Cambridge, MA: Da Capo Press.

Lancaster, R. (2003). *The Trouble with Nature: Sex and Science in Popular Culture*. Berkeley: University of California Press.

Lewin, E. (1993). *Lesbian Mothers: Accounts of Gender in American Culture*. Ithaca, NY: Cornell University Press.

Lewin, E. (1998). *Recognizing Ourselves: Ceremonies of Lesbian and Gay Commitment*. New York: Columbia University Press.

Lewin, E. (2009). *Gay Fatherhood: Narratives of Family and Citizenship in America*. Chicago: University of Chicago Press.

Marsiglio, W. (1998). *Procreative Man*. New York: New York University Press.

Mattingly, C. and L. Garro (2000). *Narrative and the Cultural Construction of Illness and Healing*. Berkeley: University of California Press.

Pande, A. (2014). *Wombs in Labor: Transnational Commercial Surrogacy in India*. New York: Columbia University Press.

Pertman, A. (2000). *Adoption Nation: How the Adoption Revolution is Transforming America*. New York: Basic Books.

Powell, B., C. Blozendahl, C. Geist and L.C. Steelman (2010). *Counted Out: Same-sex Relations and Americans' Definitions of Family*. New York: Russell Sage.

Rosaldo, R. (1986). 'Ilongot hunting as story and experience'. In *The Anthropology of Experience*, edited by V. W. Turner and E. M. Bruner, 97–138. Urbana-Champaign, IL: University of Illinois Press.

Smith, D. E. (1993). 'The standard North American family: SNAF as an ideological code'. *Journal of Family Issues* 14, no. 1: 50–65.

Townsend, N. W. (2002). *The Package Deal: Marriage, Work and Fatherhood in Men's Lives*. Philadelphia: Temple University Press.

Warner, M. (1999). *The Trouble with Normal: Sex, Politics, and the Ethics of Queer Life*. New York: Free Press.

Weston, K. (1991). *Families We Choose: Lesbians, Gays, Kinship*. New York: Columbia University Press.

Zelizer, V. (1985). *Pricing the Priceless Child: The Changing Social Value of Children*. Princeton, NJ: Princeton University Press.

PART TWO

Queering home

Introduction: Queering home

Ben Campkin and Brent Pilkey

Through everyday tactics, ordinary homemakers and dwellers have the possibility to rewrite home as a space liberated from the structures that otherwise impinge on them, and to incrementally challenge those structures from within. We can think of these negotiations in the spirit of Michel de Certeau's understanding of the potential inherent in the quotidian to 'reappropriate the space organized by techniques of sociocultural production' (de Certeau 1984: xiv). Everyday practices, therefore, can work to subvert the construction of heteronormativity through home spaces. The chapters that follow explore a range of subtle and defiant ways that homes have been queered, both through historical examples of rather exceptional home lives and through recent research on contemporary, everyday gay and lesbian domestic scenes.

There is a growing body of work on LGBTQ domesticities by scholars, theorists and practitioners within the wider field of gender and sexuality-focused home studies in spatial disciplines (Bonnevier 2005; Carrington 1999; Cook 2014; Dines 2010; Ellwood 2000; Gorman-Murray 2006a, b; Johnston and Valentine 1995; Pilkey 2015). This work has, for example, uncovered previously untold herstories and histories of sexual minorities' lived realities, and through ethnographic and other forms of empirical evidence it has challenged and problematized the notion of home as a de facto heterosexual and patriarchal space. This body of work has to date focused more on gay and – to a lesser extent – lesbian experiences over those of others with bisexual, trans, queer or non-binary identities. However, moving away from essentialist understandings of identity, it creates the possibilities for more inclusive approaches, open to multiple, dynamic and intersecting characteristics shaped in and by the domestic spaces people inhabit. Furthermore, this literature places emphasis on empowering nonconforming domesticities – through the ways that subjects actively queer home. To think in this verb form opens up queering as an everyday political act that anyone of any sexual or gender identity can partake in. The queering of home, and of studies of home, takes its place among other strategies in transgressing and dismantling oppressive heteronormative and patriarchal imaginaries and institutions – those firmly entrenched in views and practices that convene domestic space only through the performance of sanctioned hegemonic gendered and sexed identities.

Scholars in this section demonstrate a range of tactics through which domesticities have been queered historically. They attend to both widely known and obscure figures from the past and their distinctive and subversive practices and performances. Alice T. Friedman's chapter focuses on the pioneering lesbian domesticities of North American expat writer Janet Flanner and her Parisian circle of friends. Rejecting stereotypes of lesbian homemaking, Friedman shows how Flanner's home life in a left-bank hotel challenged convention in the first half of the twentieth century. Flanner refused contemporary social norms; she travelled as a 'hermit crab' with few possessions and never 'settled down' with family or became rooted in a conventional sense by domestic ties. Friedman shows how, through her deliberately unconventional approach to domesticity and identity, Flanner lived an intimate queer life within an extended circle of close female friends.

In his chapter, Matt Smith also explores the intertwining histories of minority sexualities and domesticity, this time in England. Smith reflects on two artistic interventions he worked on, in historic stately homes owned and curated by the UK heritage organization the National Trust. These site-specific installations disrupted conventional curatorial narratives within the historic buildings in which they were sited, drawing attention to queer life stories through images constructed in assemblages of material artefacts. Intervening in their domestic settings, the works highlight the methodological and ethical challenges of historical commentaries on the sexual orientation and gender identities of the historical subjects they invoke (Mills 2006). They also demonstrate the potential of telling complex histories of queer kinship and domesticity through spatial strategies that open possibilities for multiple interpretations. The focus on heritage – both in the built structures of the houses in which Smith intervened, and their material fixtures and fittings – connect with discussions of inheritance and reproduction elsewhere in this book.

Like Friedman and Smith, Matt Cook explores a domestic scene, attending to a specific building and the tactics through which it was materially queered, as well as its adaptation and inhabitation by a particular social set. His chapter focuses on the playwright Donald Howarth and his

London riverside home, which is equally illuminating for showcasing the intersection of sexuality and domesticity alongside friendships and long-lasting relationships. Cook records a decades-long history of this previously undocumented home and the ways in which it shaped and was shaped by Howarth's milieu. He frames this within a discussion of the tangible and intangible qualities of heritage. Through the architecture and the objects within it, Howarth's home was and continues to be a place where convention is queered.

Queering, of course, is an elusive political act open not only to privileged elites who are given exceptional status in the historic and archaeological record, but to anyone and to everyday spaces. It is important to show how ordinary lives, both in the past and in the contemporary moment, perform identity through queerness at home. Highlighting the everyday queering of homes can go a long way in reimagining domesticity and associated lifeworlds. Rachael M. Scicluna's chapter on the domestic experiences, politics and transgressions of a group of lesbians in Brighton and Hove, in the south-east of the UK, further draws attention to how the home operates as a contested space, a zone in which the messiness of everyday social and political discourse unfolds. Scicluna uses ethnographic methods, including participant observation, informal conversations and biographical interviews, as a way of gathering insights into the lives of a group of older lesbians who are connected through an analogue – pre-Internet – social network. Such approaches reveal how these individuals respond to subtle hostility within and outside of the domestic context. Scicluna's respondents' social practices and narratives, are shown to be generation specific. This group of older lesbians are seen to make alternative domestic meanings, addressing the oppressions they otherwise experience, through the subversive practice of collectively socializing in each other's homes.

Andrew Gorman-Murray's chapter similarly engages an everyday politics of home. Specifically, it interrogates right-leaning critiques that see home as a place of 'homonormativity'. Radical queer critiques, Gorman-Murray argues, denigrate sexual minorities who embrace domesticity and home life; this view sees investment in the home as an aspiration towards conservative, middle-class and not-very-queer mainstream assimilation. Through challenging this as well as the too-often misread meaning of homonormativity, and by recognizing that homes and the lives that inhabit them are incredibly diverse, heterogeneous and nuanced, the chapter argues that home is anything but private, depoliticized or un-empowering. Gorman-Murray reimagines home as a contested space for the performance of multiple, alternative lived realities. With his extensive scholarly output on home and queer sexualities (see, for example Gorman-Murray 2006a, b, 2007, 2008, 2009, 2012, 2013; Waitt and Gorman-Murray 2011), rather than produce an empirical piece, Gorman-Murray takes the unique opportunity to reflect and position his work, and the themes in this section, within contemporary queer debates.

There is political power in the ways in which diverse individuals and groups make home. Simply because these political actions are, for some, seemingly internal and private does not mean the affective power to destabilize oppressive ideologies remains muted indoors. Interior domestic space is an active representation of public, private and personal notions of subject and self. The divide between inside and outside is therefore often porous when it comes to how we shape both our homes and family identities. If public regimes like heteronormativity have infiltrated the home from the outside in, then arguably the everyday actions of countless other domestic realities might work in some small way towards rewriting home from the inside out. While recent media have presented society with a new, typical, non-heterosexual home and family (Gorman-Murray 2006b; Pilkey 2015), this has often reinforced alienating homonormative values. An exception might be the recent critically acclaimed television hit, *Transparent*, in its more nuanced representation of complex queer domestic scenes and lives in mutual and ongoing processes of becoming (see Villarejo 2016). Through drawing attention to queer domesticities through close spatial and historical analyses, the five chapters in this section offer a window into the multiple and complex ways that queering at home unfolds. They suggest the power in understanding and more widely celebrating the queering of home by people with diverse sexual and gender identities. The challenge is to find ways to turn these thriving and diverse domesticities inside out, to maximize the social potential that can be derived from the rejection and reconfiguration of restrictively normative spaces and relationships.

References

Bonnevier, K. (2005). 'Queer analysis of Eileen Gray's E. 1027'. In *Negotiating Domesticity: Spatial Productions of Gender in Modern Architecture*, edited by H. Heynen and G. Baydar, 162–80. Abingdon: Routledge.

Carrington, C. (1999). *No Place Like Home: Relationships and Family Life Among Lesbians and Gay Men*. Chicago: University of Chicago Press.

Cook, M. (2014). *Queer Domesticities: Homosexuality and Home Life in Twentieth-Century London*. Basingstoke: Palgrave Macmillan.

de Certeau, M. (1984). *The Practice of Everyday Life*. Berkeley: University of California Press.

Dines, M. (2010). *Gay Suburban Narratives in American and British Culture: Homecoming Queens*. Basingstoke: Palgrave Macmillan.

Elwood, S. A. (2000). 'Lesbian living spaces'. *Journal of Lesbian Studies* 4, no. 1 (May 26): 11–27.

Gorman-Murray, A. (2006a). 'Gay and lesbian couples at home: Identity work in domestic space'. *Home Cultures* 3, no. 2 (July 1): 145–67.

Gorman-Murray, A. (2006b). 'Queering home or domesticating deviance?: Interrogating gay domesticity through lifestyle television'. *International Journal of Cultural Studies* 9 (June): 227–47.

Gorman-Murray, A. (2007). 'Rethinking queer migration through the body'. *Social and Cultural Geography* 8, no. 1: 105–21.

Gorman-Murray, A. (2008). 'Queering the family home: Narratives from gay, lesbian and bisexual youth coming out in supportive family homes in Australia'. *Gender, Place and Culture: A Journal of Feminist Geography* 15, no. 5: 31–44.

Gorman-Murray, A. (2009). 'Intimate mobilities: Emotional embodiment and queer migration'. *Social and Cultural Geography* 10, no. 4: 441–60.

Gorman-Murray, A. (2012). 'Queer politics at home: Gay men's management of the public/private boundary'. *New Zealand Geographer* 68: 111–20.

Gorman-Murray, A. (2013). 'Liminal subjects, marginal spaces and material legacies: Older gay men, home and belonging'. In *Queer Presences and Absences: Time, Future and History*, edited by Y. Taylor and M. Addison, 93–117. London: Palgrave-Macmillan.

Johnston, L. and G. Valentine (1995). '"Wherever I lay my girlfriend, that's my home": The performance and surveillance of lesbian identities in domestic environments'. In *Mapping Desire: Geographies of Sexualities*, edited by D. Bell and G. Valentine, 88–103. London: Routledge.

Mills, R. (2006). 'Queer is here? Lesbian, gay, bisexual and transgender histories and public culture'. *History Workshop Journal* 62: 253–63.

Pilkey, B. (2015). 'Reading the queer domestic aesthetic discourse: Tensions between celebrated stereotypes and lived realities'. *Home Cultures* 12, no. 2 (special issue 'Queer domesticities: Sexuality, identity and politics at home'): 213–39.

Villarejo, A. (2016). 'Jewish, queer-ish, trans, and completely revolutionary: Jill Soloway's *Transparent* and the new television'. *Film Quarterly* 69, no. 4 (Summer): 10–22.

Waitt, G. and A. Gorman-Murray (2011). '"It's about time you came out": Sexualities, mobility and home'. *Antipode: A Radical Journal of Geography* 42: 1380–1403.

5

F the U-Haul: Janet Flanner's Paris and the varieties of lesbian domesticity

Alice T. Friedman

Some people have never heard the phrase 'U-Haul Lesbian', but a lengthy definition can be found on Wikipedia.

> *U-Haul lesbian* or *U-Haul syndrome:* a stereotype of lesbian relationships, referring to the joke that lesbians tend to move in together on the second date. It suggests an extreme inclination toward monogamy or committed relationships. It can be considered both complimentary and pejorative, depending on context.
>
> Psychologists note that the U-Haul joke epitomizes the perceived phenomenon of lesbians to form intense emotional connections, referred to in [North American] gay slang as an *urge to merge*. Critics of this alleged tendency suggest that it is used by lesbians to avoid the risks involved with dating. In their view, an aversion to the risks of dating is linked to a stunted development of intimate relationships during the teenage years when most gays and lesbians are in the closet. With the freedom of adulthood, lesbians become drawn to the 'U-Haul' relationships, appreciating their intensity and intimacy. (U-Haul Lesbian 2016)

When it comes to mainstream stereotypes – or at least to the ways in which these are represented in the admittedly limited scope of the Internet – it seems that even today, as so often in the past, lesbians just can't seem to catch a break: even our efforts to create stable homes with other women are viewed as a twisted expression of 'stunted development of intimate relationships during the teenage years', or 'unhealthy' efforts to avoid the 'risks of dating', and the 'urge to merge'. Although for well over half a century, psychologists, historians and political activists have gone to considerable lengths to show that lesbians have always made lots of *different* choices about how to live, still the image of the merged and inseparable lesbian couple persists.

Nevertheless, as with all stereotypes, this one seems to be the result of a lack of first-hand knowledge, grounded in the very small sample that most people can call to mind – if indeed they know of any lesbians at all. Some think perhaps of that most famous (and now better known than ever, thanks to the 2011 film *Midnight in Paris*) of all lesbian couples, Gertrude Stein and Alice B. Toklas, whose immediate and passionate intimacy and highly visible 'marriage' in Paris before the First World War was indeed a 'U-Haul' relationship *avant la lettre* (Friedman 2015).[1] Yet Gertrude and Alice are simply the most visible in a long line of highly educated, upper- and middle-class couples whose private lives and public demeanour defied categorization by outside observers, puzzled by what it was – feminism? friendship? sex? – that kept them together for so long.[2] These women, whose partnerships were sometimes described as 'Boston marriages', may have been admired for their loving commitment to each other, to art or to literature, but they were also deliberately and persistently marginalized as lesbian eccentrics.

Stein herself made her outsider status clear in her *Making of Americans* (1925) when she described herself as one of the 'queer people' – using a term that even in her own time had a variety of connotations, including sexual orientation (OED). As readers, we fill in the blanks to define that word – expatriate, woman, artist, lesbian, Jewish, all of the above – although Stein forbears to specify: 'It takes time to make queer people', she wrote.

> We flee from the disapproval of our cousins, the courageous condescension of our friends who gallantly sometimes agree to walk the streets with us, from all of them who never any way can understand why such ways and not the others are so dear to us, we fly to the kindly comfort of an older world accustomed to take all manner of strange forms into its bosom. (Stein 1925: 21)

Stein returned to the themes of place and identity throughout her career: as she famously wrote in *The Making of Americans*, 'America is my country and Paris my home town ... so I am an American and have lived half my life in Paris, not the half that made me but the half that made what I made (Stein 1925, quoted in Weiss 1998: 47–8). In the years between 1907, when Stein and

Toklas met, and her death in 1948, the couple were a visible presence.[3] Stein 'walked the streets' and parks of Paris daily, alone, with Toklas or with 'Basket', their large white poodle (Corn and Latimer 2011). Everything about her – her shape, her choice of companions and her increasing notoriety as a modernist writer – highlighted her queerness, but her wanderings on foot in Paris also staked her claim to the city. As the couple became more recognizable, and more deliberate about their appearance and actions, these public displays became more and more akin to a queer performance that insisted on their right to public space. In matching 'butch' and 'femme' costumes, stitched up by a Parisian tailor to Toklas's designs, they insisted on their right to be seen as a couple in an enduring and visible marriage.

Janet Flanner and Solita Solano: Friends and lovers

Despite the courageous and visually compelling image of lesbian marriage created by Stein and Toklas in the first half of the twentieth century, alternative ways of living clearly existed among lesbian expatriates. This is why a close examination of the life of Janet Flanner (1892–1978), a writer whose bimonthly 'Letter from Paris' – written under the gender-neutral name 'Genêt' – appeared in the *New Yorker* magazine between 1925 and 1975, is so historically significant.[4] A generation younger than Stein and Toklas and a denizen of lesbian Paris throughout her adult life, despite being closeted both in print and in public, Flanner embraced a very different notion of lesbian domesticity: in an interview with *People* magazine in February 1975, she described herself as a 'hermit crab' who travelled light with 'few possessions and fewer clothes', insisting that she had lived in Paris hotels for her entire life because she 'never wanted a home' (O'Higgins 1975). In response to the interviewer's question about whether she had ever been married, Flanner surrounded her answer in a characteristic miasma of ambiguity: 'Oh yes, but it was so long ago that the details of the union escape me. I am essentially a single woman who has, on occasion, enjoyed lasting friendships.' The complexity of this statement, the evasions, distortions and outright lies it contains – along with the unassailable kernel of truth that Flanner was indeed nominally 'single' despite a lifetime of committed lesbian partnerships – speaks volumes both about her own ambivalence and about the fun-house distortions that a life inside the closet creates.

Born in Indianapolis in 1892, Flanner was the daughter of an undertaker: she married young, fled to New York City, quickly divorced and then travelled to Europe with her lover, Solita Solano (1888–1975), who was born Sarah Wilkinson in Troy, New York, arriving in Paris in 1921 (Wineapple 1989: chaps 1–5; see also Haggerty and Bonnie Zimmerman 2000; and Streitmatter 2012).[5] As the *New Yorker*'s Paris correspondent, Flanner was known for her brilliant style, her light-hearted panache and her distinctive ability to remain at a certain remove from people and events. Indeed, Flanner's 'Letter from Paris' shaped an impression of the Parisian avant-garde for a generation of readers – educated, aspirational, mostly middle-class and suburban – for whom gay and lesbian life remained off-limits. Adopting the magazine's signature breezy and cosmopolitan tone, Genêt offered brief glimpses of street-corner cafés, bustling flower markets and glittering celebrities – Picasso, Josephine Baker, Hemingway, Stein – whose lofty conversations, good taste and pleasurable existence aroused curiosity and envy. The queer and lesbian Paris that she inhabited in her private life – the small Hotel St German des Prés, where she and Solano lived together for nineteen years; the bookshops on the Rue de l'Odéon run by her friends, Sylvia Beach (Shakespeare and Company) and Adrienne Monnier (La Maison des Amis des Livres), one of the Left-Bank Paris's most influential and enduring lesbian couples; the lesbian literary salons/hook-up socials held on Friday evenings by Natalie Barney and on Saturdays by Gertrude and Alice; and the many bars,

FIGURE 5.1 *Janet Flanner. Photograph by Berenice Abbott, 1927. Courtesy of Elizabeth Jenks Clark Collection of Margaret Anderson, Yale Collection of American Literature, Beinecke Rare Book and Manuscript Library.*

FIGURE 5.2 *Solita Solano. Photograph by Berenice Abbott, 1927. Courtesy of Elizabeth Jenks Clark Collection of Margaret Anderson, Yale Collection of American Literature, Beinecke Rare Book and Manuscript Library.*

dance halls, *bals musettes* and small boîtes where she and her friends danced until dawn – formed only a shadowy background world in these texts, which added a hint of danger and glamour to the literary cityscape (Wineapple 1989: xxii–xxiii, 85–6).[6] The tension between these realms, as described in Flanner's Paris letters – which often ended abruptly, with the force of a closet door being slammed shut – and her own private experiences, underscored the allure of the knowing, ironic and sometimes even campy tone that was her trademark.[7] A consummate literary stylist, Flanner cracked open the door of her literary closet a bit in later years, creating profiles of Sylvia Beach, Colette, Alice B. Toklas and Margaret Anderson between 1959 and 1975, but for the most part her literary persona remained neutral, distant and detached (Drutman 1979: 309–42).

Berenice Abbott's well-known portrait of Flanner as Uncle Sam, in striped trousers, a dark jacket and a tall, white top hat adorned with two masks (Figure 5.1), suggests some of the facets of her multiple identities. Seated next to a steamer trunk, she is an American traveller who can switch from one role to another, a lesbian in an elegant drag costume who can choose to reveal or

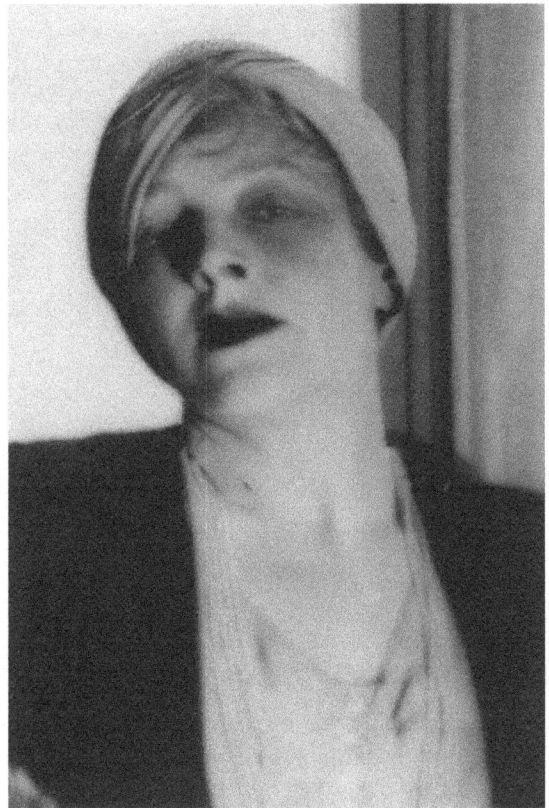

FIGURE 5.3 *Margaret Anderson. Photograph by Berenice Abbott, 1927. Courtesy of Elizabeth Jenks Clark Collection of Margaret Anderson, Yale Collection of American Literature, Beinecke Rare Book and Manuscript Library.*

conceal her many 'faces' behind the masks that she holds at the ready. For both Abbott (who was part of Flanner's lesbian circle) and Flanner herself, this portrait – one of a series showing members of the gay and avant-garde communities in Paris in the 1920s – was a form of performance (Weissman 2011: chapter 2). According to Abbott scholar Terri Weissman, the photographer allowed each sitter to be 'framed by her own terms of definition': using her own clothes, her pose and her relationship to the camera to shape her image. Abbott further believed that her portraits revealed 'each person's uniqueness' through a process of 'exchange' that occurred between the photographer and the sitter (Weissman 2011: 39). Such elements highlight the differences between Abbott and her mentor Man Ray, for whom she had worked as an assistant and printer when she arrived in Paris in 1923 (Weissman 2011: 53).

What would we know of lesbian Paris in the 1920s were it not for Abbott's photos? Her portrait of Solita Solano (Figure 5.2) preserves the style and

FIGURE 5.4 *Jane Heap. Photograph by Berenice Abbott, 1927. Courtesy of Elizabeth Jenks Clark Collection of Margaret Anderson, Yale Collection of American Literature, Beinecke Rare Book and Manuscript Library.*

energy of a fashionable young woman who played only a minor role in the literary society of the time, but whose role in Flanner's life – and in the social and cultural world of lesbian Paris – was central. Solano had been an actress, newspaper woman and writer before she first met Flanner in New York in the early 1920s, and the two shared a commitment to freedom, as they put it, in love and art (Wineapple 1989: 47–89).[8] Even when they were tied to other lovers, the two women maintained an intimate partnership, both emotional and professional. Indeed, in the 1930s, when both were romantically involved with other women and Solano had immersed herself in the work and teaching of Gurdjieff, the mystic philosopher, they saw each other regularly: always the caretaker, Solano edited Flanner's work, kept her accounts, boosted her spirits, cared for her when she was sick and ran interference with other women (Streitmatter 2012: chapter 8).

At Solano's insistence, Abbott photographed the glamorous Margaret Anderson (Figure 5.3), who had founded the *Little Review* in Chicago in 1914 and published Joyce's *Ulysses* in 1918 (Ford 1987). With her long-time partner and co-editor, Jane Heap (Figure 5.4), Anderson arrived in Paris in 1923 along with her new lover, Georgette Leblanc. Solano was drawn to her immediately

(Anderson briefly became her lover in the late '20s) and the two joined forces in creating an affective queer space by sitting for Abbott, as did many others in the lesbian circle, including Eileen Gray, Djuna Barnes, Sylvia Beach and the Princess Eugene Murat.[9] Since a number of Abbott's portraits decorated the walls of Shakespeare and Company, these photographs served as a visual reminder of the ties that created a sort of 'lesbian archipelago' of people and places that connected with one another across the virtual space of the city (Weissman 2011: 64).

Berenice Abbott's photographs serve to document the early years of a durable network of lovers, ex-lovers and friends that would survive to span a half-century: young women committed to a life of freedom (both sexual and artistic), they toughed out periods of jealousy and disappointment to preserve their community. This was as true for friends as it was for lovers; indeed, among the closest members of this group, the distinction was often rendered meaningless. As Solano put it when writing about the enduring relationship between herself, Flanner and their close friend, the writer and philanthropist Nancy Cunard, the three 'became a fixed triangle … [which] survived the spring quarrels and the sea changes of forty-two years of modern female fidelity' (Wineapple 1989: 78, quoted in Ford 1968: 76).

Abbott's photos and the stories surrounding them thus form an invaluable corrective to the fictionalized Paris – normatively heterosexual, rich in sensations, mysterious, fashionable, sophisticated – created by mainstream evidence like Flanner's *New Yorker* letters and her *Paris Was Yesterday*, which appeared in 1972. True to her own inclinations and to the customs of the time, there was barely a trace of lesbian life – except, of course, for the mention of Gertrude and Alice – in these writings. On the contrary, as Flanner looked back across the span of years, she not only romanticized her experience – like Hemingway before her in *A Moveable Feast* (1964) – but also glossed over the question of *difference*: 'Memories are the specific invisible remains in our lives of what belongs in the past tense', she wrote,

It is now more than half a century ago, back in the opening of the 1920s, that for the first time Paris began to be included in the memories of a small contingent of youngish American expatriates, richer than most in creative ambition and rather modest in purse. For the most part we had recently shipped third class to France across the Atlantic, at that date still not yet flown over except by migratory sea birds. We had settled in the small hotels on the Paris Left Bank near the Place Saint-Germain-des-Prés, itself perfectly equipped with a large corner café called Les Deux Magots and an impressive twelfth-century Romanesque church, with its small garden of old trees, from whose branches the metropolitan blackbirds sang at dawn, audible to me in my bed close by in the rue Bonaparte. Though unacquainted with each other, as compatriots we soon discovered our chance similarity. We were a literary lot. (Flanner 1972: vii)

This sort of reverie was no doubt responsible for inspiring a post-war influx of young American tourists, hungry for an authentic, non-American Paris filled with great food, great art and creativity that they hoped would rub off if only they approached the city with the appropriate spirit of adventure and diffidence. The door to that world was all but closed, Flanner warned: 'Paris then seemed immutably French. ... The quasi-American atmosphere which we had tentatively established around Saint-Germain had not yet infringed onto the rest of the city. In the early twenties, when I was there, Paris was still yesterday (Flanner 1972: xxiv).'

As is well known, Flanner, Solano, Gerald and Sara Murphy and F. Scott Fitzgerald and his wife Zelda were, among many others, part of a well-documented migration of young, middle- and upper-class Americans to Paris that began in earnest soon after the turn of the century and continued until the outbreak of the Second World War (Stein and Toklas were among the pioneers, arriving at the beginning of the century). Thanks to the rise of both middle-class tourism and foreign study as socially acceptable forms of education, and especially to low prices and a very favourable exchange rate on the dollar, the relationship of young Americans to Paris – 'an older world accustomed to take all manner of strange forms into its bosom', as Gertrude had put it – proved deep and enduring. Living cheaply in Left-Bank hotels, these aspiring artists, writers and – more importantly for our purposes here – young tourists, both gay and straight, seeking an alternative to American social conservatism, flocked to the city, putting down stakes for weeks or months: during the 1920s, Flanner, Solano, Jean Cocteau, Margaret Anderson, Jane Heap, Djuna Barnes and a host of others stayed, at various times, in the Hotel Saint Germain des Prés (formerly the Hôtel Napoleon Bonaparte); Ernest and Hadley Hemingway, Man Ray and later Margaret Anderson and Georgette Leblanc lived in the Hôtel Jacob (formerly Angleterre) nearby; James Joyce was at the Hôtel Lenox on Rue de l'Université; Ezra Pound was at the Hôtel du Pas-de-Calais – and the list goes on and on until the outbreak of the Second World War. When the war ended, the parade began again with the arrival of writers like James Baldwin, who moved into the Hôtel du Rome on the Boulevard Saint-Michel for a time before decamping to the Hôtel Verneuil and, in 1949, to the Grand Hôtel du Bac. In the mid-1950s, Allen Ginsberg and his lover Peter Orlovsky and their friends camped out for a winter at the so-called 'Beat Hotel' on Rue Git-le-Coeur: the hotel was a run-down establishment where the proprietors cultivated their young, artistic and mostly male clientele by allowing them to cook in their rooms and bring home guests, as long as they signed the visitor's book.[10]

For gay men and lesbians, these small hotels had obvious advantages: they were inexpensive short-term alternatives to apartment living, they were close to cafés and restaurants, they offered freedom and relative anonymity, and they possessed the allure of the *vie bohemè* that many came to Paris to experience. Yet in the case of Flanner and Solano, the reality was different: unlike other visitors, they remained in the Hôtel Napoleon Bonaparte for seventeen years, only leaving when the city became too dangerous for Americans in the late 1930s. Solano's extraordinary reminiscence of their life together in the hotel, partially published in the 1970s, provides many details: each of the five floors of the hotel had only four rooms, and while she and Flanner originally occupied one room each on the fourth (US fifth) floor, their domain expanded over time to include the other two, one for 'overflow', as Solano put it, and the other as a common space, which Solano described – perhaps unsurprisingly – as 'a room of constant dramas, marital and otherwise' (Solano n.d.; Broderick 1977). Other guests came and went, but the two women stayed: it was their 'ideal all-purpose hotel – no domesticity, privacy for work and study, all delights free and within walking distance'. About the 'Persian-style amenities', she added, the less said the better – but the place suited them perfectly. Providing an unusual balance of freedom and familiarity, a place to call home and to entertain their friends without the burden of cooking or cleaning, the Hôtel Napoleon Bonaparte was like a college dormitory without rules.

The hotel formed a stable base, but these women rarely stayed in one place for very long. Regular stays at country inns in spring and summer extended the lesbian archipelago beyond the confines of homes and hotels. Indeed, Flanner and Solano both developed strong ties to the village of Orgeval, where Noel Murphy, Flanner's lover from the 1930s on, had lived in a sprawling compound in the village of Orgeval since the 1920s. For Flanner, Solano, Anderson and others, including fellow Gurdjieff follower Kathryn Hulme (who would publish *The Nun's Story* in the 1950s [Hulme 1954]) and the sculptor Elizabeth Jenks Clark (Solano's lover from the 1940s until her death in 1975), this town, and especially their own houses and gardens served as a refuge and social centre; even Gertrude and Alice played a role in the making of this lesbian pastoral as frequent guests of Noel's before the war. When Flanner chose to take up residence at the Hôtel Continental in Paris in the late 1940s, Noel's home at Orgeval became more than a retreat: she may have 'never wanted a home' as she put it, but she certainly availed herself of her girlfriends' domesticity (Wineapple 1989: 120ff).[11]

Flanner's habit of maintaining close ties to past lovers, even as she acquired new romantic partners, clearly made things more complicated. In the early 1940s, while visiting the gay enclave at Fire Island, New York, she fell in love with Natalia Danesi Murray (1901–94), a prominent Italian journalist and publisher who had a home there, and began living with her, off and on, in New

York City (Flanner 1985).[12] Murray was recently divorced and had a young son, William; Janet was enchanted not only by her glamour and beauty – still evident in photos taken some thirty years after they met – but also by the Upper East side world in which she lived (Krementz 2011). Though their relationship was often fraught with struggles over Janet's frequent trips to Paris and Orgeval to see Solita and Noel – and, of course, by her lifelong unwillingness to settle down – Natalia Murray would remain another anchor of Flanner's life and work until she died in November 1978.

By the 1960s, Solano could welcome Flanner, Anderson and others to her own Orgeval home, a cluster of buildings and lovingly tended gardens that she shared with Clark, shrugging off the many love triangles in her circle to maintain the bonds of friendship (Wineapple 1989: Chap. 7).[13] As Solano's diary records, at Orgeval, women came and went, staying for days or even months, working, talking and comforting each other in times of distress. Thanks to a series of Kodak snapshots, taken in the early 1960s and preserved at Yale, we can glimpse these women and the relaxed social life they enjoyed as they grew older. In one group of photos, perhaps taken in the United States, we see Solano, with permed hair and sensible shoes, resting on a bench with Clark (Figure 5.5), who is as usual nattily dressed in a mannish dress shirt

FIGURE 5.5 *Elizabeth Jenks Clark and Solita Solano with a cat, ca. 1950. Photographer unknown. Courtesy of Elizabeth Jenks Clark Collection of Margaret Anderson, Yale Collection of American Literature, Beinecke Rare Book and Manuscript Library.*

and pressed trousers; in another, we see Solano at work at the desk in the small stone cottage she used as a workspace on the grounds of the home she and Clark shared (Figure 5.6). In group photos, we can always recognize Flanner – bright-eyed and angular – with her ever-present cigarette (Figure 5.7) as she chats with Noel Murphy and other friends in the garden of Murphy's

FIGURE 5.6 *Solita Solano in her study at Les Hiboux, Orgeval, ca. 1960. Photographer unknown. Courtesy of Elizabeth Jenks Clark Collection of Margaret Anderson, Yale Collection of American Literature, Beinecke Rare Book and Manuscript Library.*

FIGURE 5.7 *Janet Flanner, Noel Murphy (foreground left and right) and friends at Les Hiboux, Orgeval, ca. 1960. Photographer unknown. Courtesy of Elizabeth Jenks Clark Collection of Margaret Anderson, Yale Collection of American Literature, Beinecke Rare Book and Manuscript Library.*

FIGURE 5.8 *Margaret Anderson and Solita Solano in the garden at Orgeval, ca. 1960. Photographer unknown. Courtesy of Elizabeth Jenks Clark Collection of Margaret Anderson, Yale Collection of American Literature, Beinecke Rare Book and Manuscript Library.*

home. In another, we see Margaret Anderson, still vamping for the camera (Figure 5.8), sitting on the terrace on a warm spring day: even late in her life, when she was isolated, ill and mourning the death of her beloved partner Dorothy Caruso, she called herself the 'happiest person I know' (quoted in Flanner 1979: 332).

Flanner, on the other hand, remained a restless and peripatetic figure throughout her life. As a reporter for the *New Yorker* and a writer of international standing, she was required to travel, but this clearly suited her temperament and her independent spirit: safely absent from one life or another, she could put on or remove the masks that her multiple identities required. In her private letters to Murray, Flanner was candid about the many questions she had about work, sexuality and the choices she had made. In one letter, written in June 1946, she wondered whether her own ambivalence and the homophobia in which she remained so thoroughly steeped had been worth all the pain it had caused her and others:

> Do you think that being a woman loving women has also helped tear me and my life and my brain to bits? Tell me. … I wish I did not remember what mother said, almost the last thing, to me: 'Oh my darling, protect yourself, even late in life, from all that which can destroy you, your precious talent …' She always knew, of course, what my life was, though only once did she mention it, years ago. … I swear I would rather see a young girl dead

than go through the struggles against society, for self-control, for peace and for the mad kindly tender joy only such love brings; it is a love which truly understands the beloved because there is no different ratio of reaction or character as between men and women. I feel it is the most equal and therefore the most powerful in its imaginative bliss and pain; each truly shares. I share, you share. I pay, you pay, my body is yours in our struggle for survival, at a distance of a few more months, as it is in love when we are alone. (Flanner 1979: 171–2)

Juggling her relationships with Solano, Murphy and Murray for over thirty years, Flanner got into the habit of packing up and moving from one loving woman to another, shuttling between her comfortable hotel (she spent her last years in Paris at the Ritz) and the old farmhouses of Orgeval or Natalia's elegant, New York apartment. She continued to publish her Paris 'Letter' throughout the 1960s and early 1970s, observing the changing streets of Paris with her habitual posture of detachment, yet there is something increasingly dated and off-key about her ability to turn everything into a series of pictorial vignettes. And she developed an old person's querulousness: she wrote that while she admired the student revolutionaries who 'fought like young heroes' in May 1968, she had no patience for the 'adolescent public nightly violence' that had caused so many sleepless nights in the increasingly upscale neighbourhoods of the Left Bank (Flanner 1968). Although she had danced 'til dawn and caroused on these same streets as a young woman, she now prized a good night's sleep more highly than a night on the town. If she knew or cared about the Gay Liberation Movement of the late 1960s, she certainly never mentioned it, preferring to manage her public persona behind her mask and to remain in constant motion until it became physically impossible for her to do so.

Thus it was only after Solita's death, and as a result of Noel's increasing infirmity, that Flanner consented to establish a permanent home in New York. She arrived at Natalia's in the fall of 1975, finally settling down at age eighty-three. By all reports, Flanner enjoyed her new-found domesticity, once she gave in to it. She was now old enough to enjoy (and need) the daily contact of a stable relationship: she could remove her masks and she lived quietly with her lover in New York. Although the ever-present enforcers of homophobia would again make an appearance in these women's lives, denying Murray and Flanner the comfort of being together in the emergency room and hospital – because they were not family – in the moments before Flanner died, she never lost her pleasure in life, in beautiful women, in well-chosen words, in drinking or smoking (Flanner 1985: 486; Krementz 2011). Like Toklas, Anderson, Natalie Barney and Romaine Brooks, Flanner survived well into our own modern era, but she remained very much a creation of the past. Sustained by her lovers, her ex-lovers and her many devoted readers, she retained her distinctive style, never giving up the belief that she could live in a world of love and intimacy as a 'hermit crab', free from the restrictive bonds of home and marriage that she had come to Paris to escape.

Notes

1 For Stein, see Mellow 1974 and Wineapple 1996: 1–2, 263–5, 300–15 and *passim*. Recent work, focusing on Stein and visual culture, includes Corn and True Latimer 2011.

2 See the classic essay by Smith-Rosenberg 1975, as well as Deegan 1996.

3 For 'lesbian Paris', see the classic study by Weiss 2013.

4 For Flanner, see Wineapple 1989.

5 The papers of Janet Flanner and Solita Solano are in the Library of Congress.

6 Flanner noted that Barney's salons often resulted in 'a new rendezvous among ladies who had taken a fancy to each other or wished to see each other again' (Wineapple 1989: 86).

7 Janet Flanner's 'Letter from Paris', appeared in *The New Yorker* from 1925 to 1975.

8 Solita moved to New York in 1918. Born in 1888, she married in 1904 at the age of sixteen, leaving town with her husband, Oliver Filley to travel in China and Japan and to live, for a period, in the Philippines.

9 For women's fashion and gender-bending codes, see Doan 2001: 95–125; Roberts 2003; and Latimer 2003.

10 For these and many other examples, see Miles 2000: 8–17; Hansen 1990; and Leeming 1994: 57–9. Baldwin's *Giovanni's Room* (1956) is particularly relevant in this context.

11 See also Solita Solano's diary in the Elizabeth Jenks Clark Collection of Margaret Anderson, Beinecke Library, Yale University.

12 The letters are contained in the archive of Janet Flanner and Natalia Danesi Murray Papers, Library of Congress.

13 The activities of this group of Gurdjieff's followers, known as 'The Rope', (including Anderson, her lover Georgette Leblanc, Jane Heap and Kathryn Hulme) are documented in the second volume of Anderson's autobiography (1951). See also Lappin 2004.

References

Anderson, M. (1951). *The Fiery Fountains: Continuation and Crisis to 1950*. New York: Hermitage House.

Baldwin, J. (1956). *Giovanni's Room*. New York: Dell Publishing.

Broderick, J. C. (1977). 'Paris between the wars: An unpublished memoir by Solita Solano.' *Quarterly Journal of the Library of Congress* 34 (October): 306–14.

Corn, W. and T. Latimer (2011). *Seing Gertrude Stein: Five Stories.* Berkeley: University of California Press (selections available online: http://www.npg.si.edu/exhibit/stein/intro.html).

Deegan, M. J. (1996). 'Dear love, dead love: Feminist pragmatism and the Chicago female world of love and ritual'. *Gender and Society* 10, no. 5: 590–07.

Doan, L. (2001). *Fashioning Sapphism: The Origins of Modern English Lesbian Culture.* New York: Columbia University Press.

Drutman, I. (ed.) (1979). *Janet Flanner's World: Uncollected Writings 1932–1975.* New York: Harcourt, Brace, Jovanovitch.

Flanner, J. (1968). 'Letter from Paris.' *The New Yorker* (May 25: 79–82); (June 22: 62); (July 20: 52).

Flanner, J. (1972). *Paris Was Yesterday: 1925–1939.* New York: Harcourt Publishers.

Flanner, J. (1979). 'Life on a cloud.' In *Janet Flanner's World: Uncollected Writings 1932–1975*, edited by I. Druttman. New York: Harcourt Brace Jovanovich.

Flanner, J. (1985). *Darlinghissima: Letters to a Friend.* New York: Random House.

Ford, H. (ed.) (1968). *Nancy Cunard: Brave Poet, Indomitable Rebel, 1896–1965.* Philadelphia: Chilton.

Ford, H. (1987). *Four Lives in Paris.* San Francisco: North Point Press.

Friedman, A. (2015). 'Queer old things'. *Places* (February). Available online: https://placesjournal.org/article/queer-old-things/.

Haggerty, G. and B. Zimmerman (eds.) (2000). *Encyclopedia of Lesbian and Gay Histories and Cultures.* New York: Garland.

Hansen, A. J. (1990). *Expatriate Paris: A Cultural and Literary Guide to Paris of the 1920s.* New York: Arcade Publishers.

Hemingway, E. (1964). *A Moveable Feast.* London: Vintage Books.

Hulme, K. (1954). *The Nun's Story.* London: Little, Brown and Company.

Krementz, J (2011). 'Jill Krementz covers Rosamond Bernier's 95th birthday'. *New York Social* (Tuesday October 11). Available online: http://www.newyorksocialdiary.com/guest-diary/2011/jill-krementz-covers-rosamond-berniers-95th-birthday.

Lappin, L. (2004). 'Jane Heap and her circle.' *Prairie Schooner* 78, no. 4 (Winter): 5–25.

Latimer, T. T. (2003). 'Looking like a lesbian: Portraiture and sexual identity in 1920s Paris'. In *The Modern Woman Revisited: Paris between the Wars*, edited by W. Chadwick and T. T. Latimer, 127–44. New Brunswick: Rutgers University Press.

Leeming, D. (1994). *James Baldwin, a Biography.* New York: Alfred A Knopf.

Mellow, J. (1974). *Charmed Circle: Gertrude Stein and Company.* New York: Praeger.

Miles, B. (2000). *The Beat Hotel: Ginsberg, Burroughs and Corso in Paris, 1957–1963.* New York: Grove Press.

O'Higgins, P. (1975). 'Janet (Genet) Flanner on her "pets" from 50 years in Paris (de Gaulle wasn't one of them)'. *People* 3, no. 7 (February 24). Available online: http://www.people.com/people/archive/article/0,20064994,00.html.

(OED) Oxford English Dictionary. 'Queer'. Available online: http://www.oxforddictionaries.com/definition/english/queer.

Roberts, M. L (2003). 'Samson and Delilah revisited: The politics of fashion in 1920s France'. In *The Modern Woman Revisited: Paris Between the Wars*, edited by W. Chadwick and T. T. Latimer, 65–94. New Brunswick: Rutgers University Press.

Smith-Rosenberg, C. (1975). 'The female world of love and ritual: Relations between women in nineteenth-century America'. *Signs* 1, no. 1: 1–29.

Solano, S. (n.d). 'Hotel Napoleon Bonaparte.' Flanner-Solano Papers, Box 16, Folder.

Stein, G. (1925). *The Making of Americans*. Paris: Contact Editions.

Streitmatter, R. (2012). *Outlaw Marriages: The Hidden Histories of Fifteen Extraordinary Same-Sex Couples*. Boston: Beacon Press.

U-Haul Lesbian. *Wikipedia*. Available online: https://en.wikipedia.org/wiki/U-Haul_lesbian.

Weiss, M. L. (1998). *Gertrude Stein and Richard Wright: The Poetics and Politics of Modernism*. Jackson, MS: University Press of Mississippi.

Weiss, A (2013 [1995]). *Paris Was a Woman: Portraits from the Left Bank*. Berkeley: Counterpoint.

Weissman, T. (2011). *The Realisms of Bernice Abbott: Documentary Photography and Political Action*. Berkeley: University of California Press.

Wineapple, B. (1989). *Genêt: A Biography of Janet Flanner*. Lincoln, NB: University of Nebraska Press.

Wineapple, B. (1996). *Sister Brother: Gertrude and Leo Stein*. Lincoln, NB: University of Nebraska Press.

6

Queering the historic house: Destabilizing heteronormativity in the National Trust

Matt Smith

Unravelling the National Trust was a three-year project organized by Unravelled Arts. It comprised three curatorial interventions in historic properties owned by the National Trust in the south-east of England: at Nymans House and Gardens in 2012, The Vyne in 2013 and Uppark in 2014. At each house, the directors of Unravelled – Polly Harknett, Caitlin Heffernan and myself – commissioned between ten and twelve contemporary artists to respond to the house and its histories. These new commissions, including pieces by Heffernan and myself, resulted in new, site-specific work that examined some of the multiple stories contained in the properties.

Rather than impose an exhibition theme or idea, we were keen that the site itself was the core of each exhibition. Artists were commissioned whose interventions revealed some of the multitude histories inherent in the houses, allowing the properties their place as 'sites of contradiction' (Taylor 1997: 8). This resulted in a disruption of any sense of a unified, homogenous narrative into multiple, diverse and discordant histories. Two of the properties had histories that included men who never married and whose intimacies fell outside of heterosexual norms. I created interventions about these two men and the discussion of these forms the core of this chapter.

Alison Oram (2012: 533) argues that 'the presentation of historic houses in Britain generally reflects dominant ideas about the national past, and mobilizes family narratives about aristocracy, class, lineage and family in order to forge a sense of stability and national identity'. This presentation is undertaken by the house custodians who choose what is and is not suitable for public consumption. With a few notable exceptions, LGBT sexualities are seldom included in that mix. This creates an interesting paradox since at the heart of most visitor guides is the family tree, which records the sexual relationships and procreation of members of the family, tracing the inheritance of the house through the generations and thereby making reproduction and heteronormative sexuality a core part of the curatorial narrative. Family trees provide a sanitized history of heterosexual intimacies while at the same time usually silencing all same-sex relationships, which until recently could not be recorded through marriage or civil partnerships and are therefore seldom included.

Both Nymans and The Vyne have historic links to men whose lives and intimacies ran in contradiction to social norms and did so openly in society. While it may be tempting to retrospectively attach labels such as homosexual or gay to these men, the historical specificity of these terms makes this problematic. By contrast, queer 'and the imprecise way it signals sexual difference but not necessarily in the way we think about such difference now' (Cook 2014: 8) enable the exploration of these alternative intimacies, allowing contemporary visitors to identify with the past and for empathetic attachments to form between ourselves and these men.

The two interventions that will be considered queered those sites in two distinct ways: by disrupting the normative curatorial methods and by exploring LGBT histories. The interventions, *Piccadilly 1830* at Nymans House and Gardens and *The Gift* and *Dandy* at The Vyne, allowed me to interrogate how the houses dealt with their queer histories and the complexities that this might entail. The use of art interventions, and their openness to multiple and ambiguous readings, enables the histories of these houses to be opened up while circumnavigating some of the problematic issues of utilizing contemporary, didactic language to discuss intimacies that do not conform to heterosexuality.

Nymans House and Gardens

Nymans House is sited in East Sussex, South East England, and benefits from a particular microclimate, making it ideal for horticulture. It was with this in mind that Ludwig Messel bought the country estate in 1890 and began developing one of the foremost English gardens. The house that Ludwig Messel bought was an early Victorian villa, which he added to and modified. However, as the architectural historian Christopher Hussey notes, this was not to the taste of his daughter-in-law, Maud, who on inheriting the house, rebuilt it as a 'medieval' manor house 'begun in the 14th century and added to intermittently till Tudor times' (quotes in The National Trust 1997: 10). Maud made her way around the Cotswolds, picking up historic architectural fragments and incorporating them into her new vision, a vision she shared with husband Leonard and their three children: Linley, Anne and Oliver. In 1947, as a result of warming a frozen water pipe with a blow lamp, a plumber set fire to the house, leaving most of it in ruins, resulting in a 'ruined house with an even greater air of romantic antiquity' (The National Trust 1997: 10). This has left the property with a haunting quality: a small, habitable core of a building within much larger ruins.

The house was last lived in by Anne Messel who moved there when she was widowed, and the house is preserved as it was when she lived there. Traces of the solitary existence of this elderly woman still pervade the house. Going around the house, there is an uneasy mixing of elderly isolation with youthful, camp theatricality, for within the house there is a television set that was customized by her brother, the stage designer Oliver Messel, into a theatre with red curtains and gold tassels.

Anne and Oliver and their brother Linley are discussed in the property's 2007 guidebook, *The Nymans Story*. Anne and Linley both married twice. Both Linley's marriages and his divorce are written about in a paragraph in the guidebook (Brown 2007: 19). Anne's first marriage is covered in a paragraph and her divorce and second marriage gets its own section and two paragraphs. Their brother Oliver has three paragraphs devoted to him. All three paragraphs talk about Oliver's professional career as a theatre and interior designer and his connections with other members of the family. Oliver had a very public relationship with another man, Vagn Riis-Hansen, who was also his business partner, for nearly thirty years. This is not mentioned in the guidebook. Anne and Linley's heterosexual relationships are therefore treated very differently in the guidebook compared with Oliver and Vagn's same-sex relationship, which is omitted.

Elsewhere, Oliver's personal life and relationship with Vagn has been dealt with in different ways by a range of authors. Oliver has been described as 'a homosexual' (Beaton et al. 1983: 18) and Vagn has been called a 'manager and friend' (Pinkham 1983: 15), a 'life-long companion and administrator' (Castle 1986: 124) whom Oliver would call 'Vagnie dear' (ibid: 125). More recently, Oliver's great-nephew Thomas Messel described Vagn as 'Oliver's companion [with whom he had] ... a devoted friendship, lasting twenty-seven years until Vagn's death' (Messel 2011: 25). During the course of the book, Vagn's status moves from 'companion' to 'partner', by the time they moved to Barbados in 1964 (Messel 2011: 146). This ambiguity creates difficulty for contemporary curators. Labelling the two men as lovers could be argued to be, on the one hand, a retrospective outing of them, and on the other, a reasonable assumption based on the information we have. Terms like 'partner' have enough ambiguity to ensure that no one is clear (see also Friedman, this book).

This lack of clarity raises interesting and difficult questions for curators and visitors alike, and it is possibly unsurprising that the interpretation provided in the Nymans House guidebook bypassed their relationship completely, effectively excluding and erasing the relationship between these two men. However, the importance of Vagn, and also Nymans, in Oliver's affections is demonstrated in his wish that 'following his [Oliver's] meticulous instructions, his and Vagn's ashes were buried together at Nymans, in the walled garden which he had loved so much from childhood' (Messel 2011: 26).

There is something particularly challenging and poignant about omitting or erasing these relationships from the curation of their domestic spaces – one of the few spaces where same-sex desire might be acted out safely before it was decriminalized in Britain in 1967. I was therefore interested in how an intervention at Nymans could speak of this relationship. We were interested in the house because of the theatricality of Oliver's designs, so it seemed sensible to start looking at the Oliver Messel material held at the Victoria and Albert Museum (V&A), which holds many of his stage designs and costumes. I was drawn to the costume for a highlander that Oliver designed for the dancer Serge Lifar, the former lover of the Russian ballet impresario Sergei Diaghilev (Jennings 2010), to wear in a dance piece called *Piccadilly 1830*, which formed part of Charles B. Cochran's stage production called *1930 Revue*. Oliver obviously had an affinity for this costume since he had it either 'remade or adapted' (V&A 2013) so that he could wear it to a party given by Daisy Fellowes, the editor-in-chief of French *Harper's Bazaar*. The camp theatricality of the costume provides a pastiche of masculinity, taking military dress and exaggerating it to the point of parody, with the exuberance of the feather headpiece speaking more to cabaret than the military.

Messel's original costume for *Piccadilly 1830* compressed two dates into one location – the Piccadilly of 1830 as a haunt for upper-class men was 'a distant cry from what (it) had become by 1930 ... a cruising ground for the working-class Dilly Boys' (Jobling 2012: 52). It is unlikely that Messel would not have been aware of Piccadilly's reputation in 1930 and that this could have acted as an 'in joke' for those in the know: fusing the adoption of military dress with a site known for casual sex.

This colliding of temporalities is echoed in historic house curation that relies on a dynamic, lived environment being presented as a static space and the compression and juxtaposition of multiple historical times being experienced in a single visit. Lord ascribes this bringing 'together of disparate objects from different times in a single space that attempts to enclose the totality of time' to a heterotopia (Lord 2006: 3). By adopting this theoretical framework in practice, I used one installation in order to collapse numerous separate moments of occupation: Anne Messel's solitary final days as a widow at the house, Oliver Messel's 1930s heyday and the Nymans of Anne and Oliver's childhood with its make-believe, dressing up and play – a time alluded to by Oliver's customized television. In doing so, I hoped that this costume could also speak to the silence about Oliver and Vagn's relationship that currently existed at the property.

The jacket that I made for the installation *Piccadilly 1830* at Nymans was hand cut and sewn (Fig. 6.1). It was then embellished with thousands of mirror-backed glass beads, each one individually sewn on, a labour-intensive process that involved repetition over a long period of time. During the making process, I entered into what Marcia Tucker calls *polychronic time* (Tucker 1996: 68). Tucker argues that, unlike the 'evolutionary, progressive, monochronic sense of time that informs the high art tradition' (Tucker 1996: 68), polychronic time, which is 'experienced in the long and complex processes of embroidery, lace-making, knitting and quilting … weaves the past and present together' and through these objects 'communal values and practices are brought forward into the present' (Tucker 1996: 68). It was this weaving of past and present that underpinned the intervention.

In the installation, the jacket was paired with an oversized feather bearskin. The cage and feathers were commissioned from a feather wholesaler who undertakes work for the Ministry of Defence. The bearskin band and rosette were made out of ceramic. The feathers and wool of the intervention are relatively fragile materials, prone to decay. In contrast, the ceramic band and rosette, unless smashed, provided an almost permanent element to the intervention. I was drawn to the idea of a future curator trying to include a ceramic band sewn onto a metal cage into any (hetero)normative interpretation of the house.

As Messel had replaced bearskin with ostrich feathers, I had replaced the cotton braiding used in the original stage costume with mirrored beads. Both these substitutions 'betray many of the characteristics and tropes of the Camp sensibility that Susan Sontag enumerated in her seminal essay of 1964, namely: exaggeration, artifice, aestheticism' (quoted in, Jobling 2010: 54). The use of camp is fitting. Sontag suggests that 'Camp taste turns its back on the good-bad axis of ordinary aesthetic judgment. Camp doesn't reverse things. It doesn't argue that the good is bad, or the bad is good. What it does is to offer for art (and life) a different – a supplementary – set of standards' (Sontag 1999 [1964]: 61). Sontag is therefore suggesting that camp allows a space for difference to exist. Here, the overlap between camp as a means of opening up debate and questioning norms fulfils a similar purpose to artist interventions.

FIGURE 6.1 *Matt Smith,* Piccadilly 1830, 2012, *turkey and ostrich feathers, ceramic, wool, linen, mirror-backed beads, dimensions variable, Nymans House and Gardens. Photography by Sussie Ahlberg,* © *Unravelled Arts.*

To reduce the intervention down to a simple 'outing' of Oliver Messel is to miss the point. The intervention plays with those subtle sleight of hands that shine light on how fragile performances of masculinity are: a feather too high allowing it to slip between military butch and showgirl effeminacy.

The jacket and bearskin were placed on an existing Roman sculpture, *The Antique Youth,* at the property. The interaction between the new intervention and the existing object was a key consideration, since 'juxtaposition queerly challenges and contests both accepted codes and a system of values that implies oppression and silencing, not only within sexuality but also within cultural institutions' (Mathieu 2003: 132). This juxtaposition directly responded to the institutional silencing that was in place at Nymans.

As previously mentioned, *Piccadilly 1830* aimed to compress the time between when Oliver first wore the jacket and when his sister lived at the house, merging a high point for Oliver with a low point for Anne. By the time Anne moved to Nymans, both Oliver's relationship with Vagn and Anne's with the Earl of Rosse had ended, since they had both been widowed. Artwork and

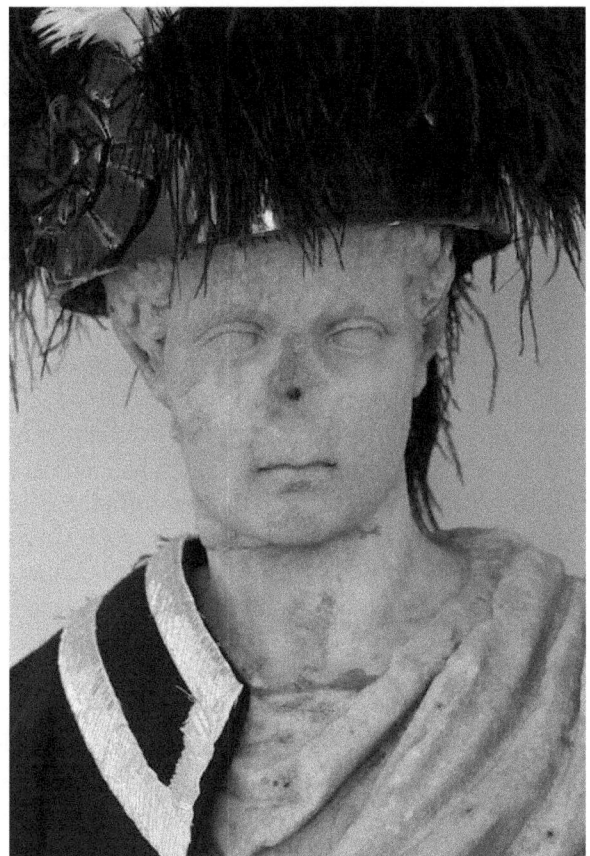

FIGURE 6.2 *Matt Smith,* Piccadilly 1830, *2012, turkey and ostrich feathers, ceramic, wool, linen, mirror-backed beads, dimensions variable, Nymans House and Gardens. Photography by Sussie Ahlberg, © Unravelled Arts.*

site came together when the piece was placed in location on *The Antique Youth*. The sculpture, which now exists without a nose or genitals, both lends the intervention a sense of the cadaverous and also comments on the de-sexing of Oliver (Fig. 6.2). It both signposts something queer and acts as a memento mori. It is to the credit of the house team at Nymans that, following the *Unravelling Nymans* exhibition, Vagn was put on the Messel family tree and linked to Oliver Messel, unravelling Oliver's previous status as a 'bachelor uncle'.

The Vyne

The Vyne is a large, adapted Tudor property near Basingstoke in Hampshire. Unlike Nymans, which has a relatively short history and whose interpretation by the National Trust is specifically focused on the period when the last resident lived there, curation at The Vyne presents the visitor with numerous histories ranging from the 1500s to the 1950s. The slicing of time at the Vyne therefore becomes that much more complex to navigate. Between 1754 and 1776, The Vyne was owned by John Chute. According to the guidebook:

> John Chute as the youngest of Edward Chute's ten children and, as he was unlikely to inherit the family estates, spent many years travelling in Italy. ... He was never to marry, but surrounded himself with younger men, including his handsome, wealthy and deaf cousin, Francis Whithead. ... In Italy the two inseparable cousins were called the 'Chutheads'. (Howard 2010: 53)

This is an odd paragraph and it is unclear what we are meant to make of it. It is hard to think that linking his unmarried status with handsome younger men can be anything but a thinly veiled indication that something queer is going on. Raymond Bentman is more explicit, arguing that 'John Chute and Francis Whithead made no secret of their intimacy. They were inseparable ... Chute referred to Whithead as "my other half"' (John Chute quoted in Bentman 1997: 277). The unpicking here becomes difficult, Bentman goes on to state:

> We may debate what to call these men and we will never know what they did in bed. But when we survey all the information, the explanation that makes the most sense of the material is that these men were strongly interested in other males for sexual and emotional gratification and that they formed some kind of group around this common interest. (1997: 278)

Francis Whithead died in his early thirties, about ten years after he and John Chute had met Horace Walpole in Florence on the Grand Tour. It was the relationship between Chute and Walpole that the intervention explores. We are fortunate that Horace Walpole was one of the most prodigious letter writers of the eighteenth century, providing us with insight into the intimacies between these two men.

'Other half' was also to be used by Walpole, many years after Chute had used it to describe Whithead. This time, it was used by Walpole following the death of John Chute: 'I am lamenting myself, not him! – no I am lamenting my other self. Half is gone; the other remains solitary' (Walpole 2011: 14). While I am not arguing that this term is being used to signify a queer sexual relationship, it does suggest a strong homosocial intimacy. Walpole's letters have been used to argue, on the one hand, that Walpole was a homosexual (Bentman 1997: 278) and, on the other, that he was celibate and confined himself to epistolary relationships with both men and women (Haggerty 2011: 111).

Regardless, Walpole's non-normative masculinity did not go unnoticed. A contemporary, George Hardinge, referred to Walpole's 'effeminacy of manner', adding that 'some of his friends were as effeminate in appearance and in manner as himself and were as witty. Of these I remember two, Mr. Chute and Mr. George Montagu. But others had effeminacy alone to recommend them' (George Hardinge quoted in Bentman 1997: 277). Chute chose language that would today be linked to gay culture, particularly gender reversal, as this excerpt from a letter to Walpole about a Raphael painting in Rome makes clear: 'Such a Christ, as beautiful, as graceful, and we may suppose, if his petticoats were off, as well made as his elder brother of the Belvidere' (John Chute quoted in Bentman 1997: 277).

This gives us an insight into the social expectations of male and female gender norms and the policing of their transgression. George Haggerty suggests that we concentrate less on what might be happening sexually and instead think 'about the bachelorism, amicability, intimacy, and wit, then we will start to understand this man [Walpole] and his circle' (Haggerty 2011: 13). While I agree with Haggerty, I think there is enough evidence of nonconformity to create tentative, historical links between Chute and Walpole and behaviour that we might now associate with queer identity.

What I was particularly interested in at The Vyne, though, was how this queer subculture responded to and adapted their houses. Alongside Richard Bentley, Walpole and Chute had formed the 'Committee of Taste'. This committee supervised the enlargement and decoration of Strawberry Hill, Walpole's London villa. Taste occupies a very specific place here; according to Haggerty, 'taste became a code for a certain mode of shared sensibility that was often understood to suggest something about sexual predilection, or at least qualified masculinity' (2011: 15). Haggerty continues to argue:

> Walpole and his closest friends … understood taste as a definitive arbiter, something that they shared and that defined them. Like the later concept of identity, taste, for Walpole and his friends, is a shared predilection for the artistically sophisticated, for the idiosyncratic. (ibid: 73)

Haggerty is here linking a domestic visual sensibility and taste with identity politics. Therefore, I would argue that to understand how these men self-identified, we need to look at how they used, decorated and filled their homes, as the two are intrinsically linked. To continue the conflation started by Haggerty, these are queer men and they designed queer houses. I was interested in using two more contemporary queer visual strategies, camp and kitsch, to inform the interventions at The Vyne.

Both Walpole and Chute were avid collectors, both during and after the Grand Tour. I would suggest that Walpole and Chute's collections were used by the two men as a way of visually presenting themselves and also as a way of socializing and bonding, since 'objects for Walpole are what bring him in to closer touch with the men he loves' (Haggerty 2011: 85). Michael Camille has argued that 'collecting is a performance' (2001: 2) and that collecting has a specific role in queer identity formation: 'It is not just that the unmentionable nature of same-sex desire has often meant that the subject had to communicate the "secret" in a coded language, but the fact that this language was a system of objects. What could not be said could be spoken through things' (2001: 2). Connecting with this idea, I decided to use this love of collecting as the starting point for the first intervention at The Vyne: *The Gift* (Fig. 6.3). While Walpole and Chute obviously influenced each other, there seems to have been some inequality, to the point that Walpole, writing to George Montagu, comments: 'I don't guess what sight I have to come in Hampshire, unless it is Abbotstone. I am pretty sure I have none to come at the Vine [*sic*], where I have done advising, as I see Mr. Chute will never execute anything' (Walpole quoted in Bentley 1840: 314).

Not wanting to further hurt Walpole's feelings, *The Gift* sees Chute bundling all of Walpole's rejected suggestions together and hiding them out of sight behind the main staircase. Unable to throw away the unwanted tokens and trinkets, Chute masses the divergent objects gifted to him, objects that map Horace's travels and magpie-like search for beauty.

By recasting the discordant objects in the same material and firing them together, they have been reworked to create '*family resemblances* between objects' (Davis 2011: 310). Davis (2011: 309–29) has proposed the idea of queer family romance, where collections of objects can come together to form substitute queer family groups. He has suggested that this can work with the collector becoming either an inheritor – placing himself within a group of historical objects or queer biographies – or as a progenitor, creating new links between objects, sometimes physically as in the Walpole Cabinet in the V&A's collections and the pietra dura casket at The Vyne to which John Chute added the later rococo stand. Queer family romance offers an interesting counterargument to the heteronormativity of historic house histories based around family trees. If we are to accept Davis's suggestions, then *The Gift* in some way acts as Walpole and Chute's love child – admittedly one created via immaculate conception and surrogate delivery. That the installation visually resembles a contemporary wedding cake further visually seals the relationship between the two men.

The second intervention, *Dandy*, looks solely at John Chute and his self-presentation (Fig. 6.4). *Dandy* is cast from a relatively contemporary, mass-produced figurine of a dandy with a dog. In and around the late 1890s – the time of Oscar Wilde's fame – the dandy was positioned as aristocrat-cum-effeminate man with a keen interest in aestheticism, and likely same-sex desire (Cook 2003: 22). This figure is placed on a tower of cast objects, formed from classical vases

FIGURE 6.3 *Matt Smith,* The Gift, *2013, white earthenware, freshwater pearls, wire, 60 cm tall, The Vyne. Photography by Sussie Ahlberg, © Unravelled Arts.*

and plinths with neoclassical additions and pearls. The piece is placed on the central staircase at The Vyne, one of the areas of the house that Chute remodelled.

Figurines based on eighteenth-century dandies were ubiquitous, cheap and mass produced in the twentieth century and aimed at the mass market. They occupy an interesting place in popular culture since they refuse to moan original object of questionable taste wase with popular taste and are often imbued with nostalgia. Working with them 'raises questions about high and low culture, class, taste and value in general' (Britton 2011: 33). Similarly, the eighteenth century itself has been a recurring motif in interiors, going in and out of fashion, oscillating between being a source of good taste and of bad taste. Referencing the work of Lisa Dowling, Jasmine Rault (2010: 196) suggests that it is a period synonymous with decadence and gender abnormality. The ceramic dandy therefore fuses two sensibilities affiliated with queer: camp and licentious freedom.

FIGURE 6.4 *Matt Smith,* Dandy, *2013, white earthenware, enamel, decals, freshwater pearls, wire, 130 cm tall, The Vyne. Photography by Sussie Ahlberg, © Unravelled Arts.*

The figurine from which the cast was taken was specifically chosen for the installation since it echoes 'the cruising style that has come to be known as 'stand-and-pose' – a decidedly self-contained form of cruising that telegraphs something like 'I am indicating that I want you only to the extent that I am showing how desirable I am by demonstrating that I am capable to complete indifference to you' (Crimp n.d.: 52). This work therefore places John Chute as a queer, cruising man and also shows him presenting himself to the world, propped up on a collection of classical vases and plinths, which brings us back to the notion of camp:

Theatrical self-presentation and the establishing of subcultural taste are central factors in the manifold concept of camp. The collecting of objects, artworks, interiors, clothes, and memorabilia, and the ways that they are displayed, can be considered as two practices that allow for camping both as the objects are collected and as they are appreciated. (Steorn, 2010: 131–2)

The decision to use an original object of questionable taste was a conscious one. Exploiting camp, where 'an engaged irony which (as the best definition of camp puts it) allows one a strong feeling of involvement with a situation or object while simultaneously providing one with a comic appreciation of its contradictions' (Butt n.d: 91–2), charges the installation with a queer sensibility. For although John Chute is placed in prime position as the emperor of all he surveys, it is a slightly comic emperor at best. In addition to it being part of the house that Chute remodelled, there is another reason for the installation to be placed in the Staircase Hall, since it forms a queer triangulation with the busts of Caligula and Antinous at the base of the staircase.

Whitney Davis has discussed the idea of queer family romance (2011: 309–29), where objects are used to develop a 'queer self-genealogy' (2011: 316). In this case, the intervention sees the representative *Dandy* piece placing John Chute at the apex of three queer-associated historical biographies: drawing on Chute's biography, the indiscriminate sexual activities of Caligula and the adoption of Antoninus by Hadrian following the death of Hadrian's lover Antinous. The three objects resonate with queer once the installation is in place, fulfilling Whitney Davis's idea of queer family romance, 'a romance that might make such family socially possible' (Davis 2011: 315), placing Chute into a queer, extraconsanguinary family tree.

Conclusion

The emphasis in historic houses on the genealogy of the wealthy families that had owned them gives them a strongly heteronormative bias. However, there is a paradox at play, for in addition to being sites of heteronormativity, many were also sites of queer intimacy and lend themselves to exploring these intimacies in a way that objects held in museum collections seldom do. One of the criticisms levelled at historic houses – the elite nature of their owners – here benefits those visitors whose sexualities do not neatly fit within heterosexuality.

Historic examples of lesbian and gay life have often had their 'origins in the elite or the creative upper-middle class' (Oram 2011: 193), partially since economic independence allowed for lives to be lived outside the bounds of social norms, so while identification will need to be 'mobilised across class lines' (Oram 2011: 193), the sites can provide historic precedents for contemporary LGBT visitors.

A pilot study of LGBT visitors to cultural institutions in North America by Heimlich and Koke – from art museums and the opera through to zoos and parks – found that for LGBT interviewees to experience a sense of truly belonging they would like to see:

> Inclusions of GLBT [*sic*] individuals, couples and groups within the imagery and narrative associated with exhibits [which would] … truly model its institutional acceptance to all patrons [and address the fact that] GLBT history is so hidden that often times GLBT artists and performers are presented as asexual or heterosexual, or their gender non-conformity is not mentioned. (2008: 100)

The historic house, which provides us with collections of objects and environments developed by individuals in order to reflect their interests and desires, therefore has the potential to provide us with rich, and as yet under-mined, seams of knowledge about queer pasts. In addition, if we start to re-view the historic house as a site of queer family romances rather than merely one of heteronormative family trees, we have the potential to connect with queer affect in meaningful and unique ways.

In their own ways, each of the interventions commissioned for Nymans House and The Vyne operates in a manner that Hein equates with feminist practice: 'The reversal of foreground and background, which draws attention to the overlooked and suppressed, and, having exposed it, asks why it has been neglected' (Hein 2010: 57). Curatorial silence does not always erase queer histories. Attuned visitors can sometimes intuitively read that something queer may be going on within historic houses. If these queer histories are not being discussed by the institution, it suggests to the aware visitor that queer lives (and possibly visitors) may be unwelcome, or at least should be silent or silenced.

The representation of 'the other' in these sites should not be seen as an intellectual exercise but as a step towards a more accurate representation of the past. As curators at these properties become more comfortable with negotiating and telling their queer histories, they may come closer to achieving their aim of 'being relevant to everyone' (Davies n.d.).

References

Beaton, C., C. Fry, P. Glenville, S. Hall, R. Myerscough-Walker, R. Pinkham, S. Rosenfeld, C. Toms and R. Vercoe (1983). 'Oliver Messel and the theatre'. In *Oliver Messel, An Exhibition Held at the Theatre Museum, Victoria and Albert*

Museum 22 June – 30 October 1983, edited by R. Pinkham, 17–35. London: Victoria and Albert Museum.

Bentley, R. (1840). *The Letters of Horace Walpole, Earl of Orford: Including Numerous Letters now First Published from the Original Manuscripts Vol 3, 1753–1759.* London.

Bentman, R. (1997). 'Horace Walpole's forbidden passion'. In *Queer Representations: Reading Lives, Reading Cultures*, edited by M. Duberman, 276–89. New York: New York University Press.

Britton, A. (2011). 'Old stuff – new life – still life: The lure of junk'. In *Ting Tang Trash: Upcycling in Contemporary Ceramics*, edited by J. Veitberg, 28–37. Bergen: Bergen National Academy of the Arts and Arts Museums Bergen.

Brown, K. (2007). *The Nymans' Story: The Messel Family.* Swindon: The National Trust.

Butt, G. (n.d.). 'How I died for Kiki and Herb'. In *The Art of Queering in Art*, edited by H. Roger, 85–94. Birmingham: Article Press.

Camille, M. (2001). 'Editor's introduction'. In *Other Objects of Desire, Collectors and Collecting Queerly*, edited by M. Camille and A. Rifkin, 1–6. Oxford: Blackwell.

Castle, C. (1986). *Oliver Messel.* London: Thames and Hudson.

Cook, M. (2003). *London and the Culture of Homosexuality, 1885–1914.* Cambridge, UK: Cambridge University Press.

Cook, M. (2014). *Queer Domesticities: Homosexuality and Home Life in Twentieth-Century London.* Basingstoke: Palgrave Macmillan.

Crimp, D. (n.d.). 'Coming together to stay apart'. In *The Art of Queering in Art*, edited by H. Rogers, 43–54. Birmingham: Article Press.

Davies, L. (n.d.). 'Proud to be National Trust'. *National Trust*, 17 September. Available online: http://www.nationaltrustjobs.org.uk/articles/proud-to-be-national-trust (accessed 30 May 2013).

Davis, W. (2011). 'Queer family romance in collecting visual culture'. *GLQ: A Journal of Lesbian and Gay Studies* 17, no. 23: 309–29.

Haggerty, G. (2011). *Horace Walpole's Letters: Masculinity and Friendship in the Eighteenth Century.* Lanham: Bucknell University Press.

Heimlich, J. E. and J. Koke (2008). 'Gay and lesbian visitors and cultural institutions. Do they come? Do they care? A pilot study'. *Museums & Social Issues: A Journal of Reflective Discourse, Where Is Queer?* 3, no. 1: 93–104.

Hein, H. (2010). 'Looking at museums from a feminist perspective'. In *Gender, Sexuality, and Museums*, edited by A. Levin, 53–64. London: Routledge.

Howard, M. (2010). *The Vyne.* Swindon: The National Trust.

Jennings, L. (2010). 'Sergei Diaghilev: First Lord of the dance'. *The Observer*, 12 September 2010. Available online: http://www.theguardian.com/stage/2010/sep/12/sergei-diaghilev-and-the-ballets-russes (accessed 24 May 2013).

Jobling, P. (2012). 'A twitch on the thread: Oliver Messel between past and present'. In *Unravelling Nymans*, edited by M. J. Smith and P. Harknett, 48–55. Sussex: Unravelled Arts.

Lord, B. (2006). 'Foucault's museum: Difference, representation, and genealogy'. *Museum and Society* 4, no. 1: 1–14.

Mathieu, P. (2003). *Sexpots: Eroticism in Ceramics.* London: A&C Black.

Messel, T. (2011). *Oliver Messel: In the Theatre of Design.* New York: Rizzoli.

The National Trust (1997). *Nymans Visitor Guide.* Swindon: The National Trust.

Oram, A. (2011). 'Going on an outing: The historic house and queer public history'. *Rethinking History* 15, no. 2: 189–207.

Oram, A. (2012). 'Sexuality in heterotopias: Time, space and love between women in the historic house'. *Women's History Review* 21, no. 4: 533–51.

Pinkham, R. (1983). 'Biographical outline'. In *Oliver Messel: An Exhibition Held at the Theatre Museum, Victoria and Albert Museum 22 June – 30 October 1983*, edited by R. Pinkham, 15–16. London: Victoria and Albert Museum.

Rault, J. (2010). 'Designing sapphic modernity: Fashioning spaces and subjects'. In *Fashion, Interior Design and the Contours of Modern Identity*, edited by A. Myzelev and J. Potvin, 185–204. Farnham: Ashgate.

Sontag, S. (1999 [1964]). 'Notes on camp'. In *Camp, Queer Aesthetics and the Performing Subject: A Reader*, edited by F. Cleto, 53–65. Edinburgh: Edinburgh University Press.

Steorn, P. (2010). 'Queer in the museum: Methodological reflections on doing queer in museum collections'. *Lambda Nordica, Queer Methodology* 3–4, no. 15: 119–44.

Taylor, A. (1997). 'A queer geography'. In *Lesbian and Gay Studies: A Critical Introduction*, edited by A. Medhurst and S. Munt, 3–19. London: Cassell.

Tucker, M. (1996). *A Labor of Love.* New York: The New Museum of Contemporary Art.

Victoria and Albert museum collections database. Victoria and Albert Museum. London. Available online: http://collections.vam.ac.uk/item/O133534/theatre-costume-messel-oliver-hilary/ (accessed 24 May 2013).

Walpole, H. (2011[1776]). 'Letter dated 27 May 1776'. Quoted in *Horace Walpole's Letters: Masculinity and Friendship in the Eighteenth Century*, edited by G. Haggerty, 14. Lanham: Bucknell University Press.

7

A bend in the river:
Queer home and heritage
in a house in Hammersmith[1]

Matt Cook

There is a bend in the river Thames at Hammersmith, West London, where the suspension bridge connects Hammersmith to Barnes. On the south side is the Putney towpath – once famous for cruising; on the north bank is Lower Mall, a 500-metre footpath linking the bridge to Hammersmith Creek. It is a busy stretch, accommodating a sailing club, longstanding mooring for houseboats, the Blue Anchor (an eighteenth-century pub) and a row of houses and cottages dating from roughly the same period. One of these houses – number 9 – commands views of the river, towpath, bridge and footpath from a first-floor balcony and also from the banks of windows installed as the house was expanded upwards in the early part of the twentieth century (Fig. 7.1).

The playwright Donald Howarth (b.1931) has lived in this house with a shifting cast of characters since 1960. A queer story of his time here through the extensions, adaptations and partial make-overs; through the pictures on the walls and the photos and postcards layered on mantelpieces; and through the anecdotes and stories that link these things. A mutual friend has traced the queer resonance of the house back to the late nineteenth century and to the early homophile movement.[2] Altogether, this place has a richer and much queerer history than the one suggested on its façade by the blue heritage plaque announcing that George Devine, founder with Tony Richardson and George

FIGURE 7.1 *A view of Hammersmith Bridge from the balcony of 9 Lower Mall. Photograph © Matt Cook.*

Goetschius of the English Stage Company (ESC) in 1955 and artistic director of the Royal Court Theatre from 1956 to 1965, lived in this house (Fig. 7.2).

This chapter sketches out some of the queer dimensions of 9 Lower Mall and the ways in which they touch particular strands of identity and relationality across the twentieth century. It is about how queer heritage is rendered tangible through domestic space and about Howarth's desire to sustain particular non-heterosexual forms of domestic affiliation and community associated with the house. The piece emerges out of an interview and house tour Howarth generously gave me in June 2015, out of my separate research into queer London and domesticity in the twentieth century (Cook 2014) and out of a friendship that helped me to link the two.[3] The first half, 'Histories', recounts three phases in the house's queer past and sketches out the historical trajectory of the house and household. The second, 'Heritage', relates those histories to queer dimensions of heritage, their tangibility or otherwise and how they speak to ideas about identity, community and their temporal and spatial underpinnings (Oram 2011, 2012). I use 'queer' as a convenient umbrella here – referring to love, sex and relationships (including intense friendships and romances) between men that may have been organized and understood in association with particular identities (with the differently conceived figures of the 'invert', 'homosexual' or 'gay man', for example). Howarth himself prefers 'non-heterosexual' as a similar and open catch-all. 'I'm not going to say gay or queer,' he said. 'I don't approve of those words – I just think they're labels, heterosexual labels for "those people"' (Howarth 2015). Like queer, 'non-heterosexual' suggests multiple ways of being (rather than a single identity), though for me it carries an oppositionality

FIGURE 7.2 *Donald Howarth on the balcony of 9 Lower Mall, with the blue plaque commemorating George Devine to the right. Photograph © Matt Cook.*

that frequently founders, given the heterosocial lives and heterosexual liaisons of many 'queer' men. I have nevertheless used it here in relation to Howarth's words and ideas. It perhaps signals his sense of life in the house (and 'non-heterosexual life' in general) being lived in opposition to heterosexual norms, values and expectations – a mode of living he is seeking to promote, even as the house's history also suggests something of the complex intersection of 'queer' and 'normal' (Weigman and Wilson 2015; Boellstorff 2007).

Histories

I

In 1899, London solicitor, poet and editor Charles Kains-Jackson (1857–1933) moved the few hundred metres from his parents' Georgian riverfront house on Upper Mall (the now grade II-listed Woodroffe House) to 9 Lower Mall (Fig. 7.3). Kains-Jackson's younger cousin, Cecil Egbert Jackson, moved in too – or was at least living there in 1901 just prior to his marriage in nearby Fulham. The pair had lived together before as companions and possibly lovers, and in marrying, Cecil was doing nothing particularly unusual for men who also had (or had had) intimate physical and emotional relationships with other men at this time (Cook 2014, ch.1). As with Kains-Jackson's previous homes – including his rooms in Chelsea in the late 1880s at 109 Cheyne Walk near Oscar and Constance Wilde's home – Lower Mall was quickly tied into a network of men linked by their desires for other men and a drive to build around those desires a cultured and artistic identity and identification, often underpinned by an

FIGURE 7.3 *9 Lower Mall from the Bridge (in the middle). Photograph © Matt Cook.*

imagined ancient Greek past (Cook 2003, ch.5). Weaving through this nascent queer subculture was a commitment to male–male comradeship and mutual support. Kains-Jackson had described this ethos in his high-flown prose piece 'The New Chivalry', which appeared in the homophile *Artist and Journal of Home Culture* in 1894 (Brake 2001: 142; Cook 2003: 127–9; Kains-Jackson 1970). This commitment was embodied subsequently by the Order of the Chaeronea – a secretive group founded by Kains-Jackson's friend George Ives in the mid-1890s and named after the last battle of the ancient homophile Theban Bands of 338 BCE (Cook 2006). Kains-Jackson was a committed member of this 'brotherhood' and friendship was in this way elevated for him, as it was for other members of his circle (Carpenter 1902). In this spirit, Kains-Jackson conducted an extensive and committed correspondence from 9 Lower Mall with like-minded men based on affection but also on a belief in an intrinsic bond determined by the direction of their desires and an associated sense of 'duty' (see, for example, James 2015; Kains-Jackson 1970).

The Order of the Chaeronea met at Lower Mall as well as at Ives' homes in Albany, Piccadilly and then Primrose Hill. Kains-Jackson held regular Thursday 'at homes' for his queer clique and attended those held by the artist couple Charles Shannon and Charles Ricketts in Chelsea (Cook 2014, chap.1). They are likely to have returned visits, and 9 Lower Mall quickly became one site in an elite homophile domestic circuit that sustained queer friendship groups and provided a valuable space for their exchange of views, ideas and gossip. Such spaces were largely out of reach of lower class or less moneyed men whose queer circuits, though they might overlap with those of a homosocial elite, were also generally riskier (as arrest and prosecution figures indicate – Cocks

2003; Houlbrook 2005). The house and its watery setting (complete with swimmers and rowers)[4] was a source of inspiration for Kains-Jackson's friends – including photographer Fred Holland Day and the painter Henry Scott Tuke. Earlier, Tuke had been rather taken with cousin Cecil and painted him in 'The Bathers' (1888).[5]

Kains-Jackson moved from Lower Mall in 1909 and the house passed to photographer Alvin Langdon Coburn (1882–1966), Day's younger cousin. Day's queer artistic connections had allowed Coburn to find a home with space to develop a studio (out of the second attic floor) and a printing press in a new rear extension. This made him self-sufficient in the production process, rather in the spirit of William Morris who had run his own Kelmscott Press nearby in the first half of the 1890s. Coburn developed his own homosocial network, including artist Roger Fry (formerly a protégé of Shannon and Ricketts), playwright George Bernard Shaw (who had earlier supported Wilde) and painter Max Weber, with whom Coburn kept up a regular and intimate transatlantic correspondence for over fifty years, including an exchange of resonant images of Brooklyn and Hammersmith Bridges. The point here is not to suggest that Coburn was queer in a sexual sense; he was married and there is no evidence to suggest he was drawn erotically to men. He nevertheless enjoyed intense male friendships and a network that certainly crossed over with that of queerer men (for example, with his cousin Day, Charles Shannon, Charles Ricketts and Edward Carpenter – each of whom he photographed). The divisions of sexuality were then less stark than they have become; the class and bohemian connections more pressing. It is also possible to trace the homoeroticism of Day's photographs in some photographic portraits Coburn took at Lower Mall (Langdon Coburn 1913). Desire, art, home, friends and family often blurred supposedly defined lines between queer and normal (Cook 2014: 7–10).

II

On the second floor of the house, Coburn created a light-filled studio, a photographic dark room and two further rooms at the back. This formed a relatively self-contained space (especially once the darkroom became a galley kitchen and one of the rear rooms a bathroom in a 1970s refit). When Coburn and his wife moved permanently to north Wales in 1928 (despondent after the Thames flood of that year), the new occupant – Michael A. E. Franklin – commissioned a further storey from architect Maxwell Fry. Fry's design – complete with large horizontal windows, functional bathroom and roof terrace – is probably the earliest domestic modernist scheme by an English architect. Modernism, in the interwar years, spoke of a departure from the past and of framing the world and relations within it in new ways (Darling 2006, chap.

5). The modernist hallmarks of light and space are present, and it is tempting to see the extension as a materialization of Lower Mall's avant-garde associations.

Certainly adaptations commissioned by Coburn and Franklin facilitated ensuing queer configurations in the house once director, actor and theatre manager George Devine (1910–66) moved in in 1953. Devine lived there with his wife, Sophie, and daughter, Harriet. He gathered an artistic, theatrical and decidedly queer crowd around him. He had made friends with John Gielgud in the 1930s (Ackerley 2006: 239) and later with young bisexual actor and director, Tony Richardson (1928–91), who moved into that 'cool white modernist flat' at the top of 9 Lower Mall and constructed a conservatory on the roof terrace, which he populated with caged birds (Heilpern 2007: 154). Richardson picked up the American sociologist George Goetschuis at Speaker's Corner, Hyde Park, and by 1954 they were living together at Lower Mall as – in Howarth's word – each other's 'other half, or quarter or three quarters' (Howarth 2015). In this formulation Howarth neatly signals the difficulty of capturing or quantifying relationships beyond convention.

Richardson and Devine's plans for the ESC evolved (with input from Goetschuis [Devine 2006]) at Lower Mall, and in 1956 the pair became the new theatre's first joint artistic directors. The house now became a hub for playwrights and directors, including John Osborne, then living in a nearby houseboat with his friend and probable lover Anthony Creighton (Sinfield 1999: 260). There was 'a thriving little theatrical community' at Lower Mall, sustained in part by the regular Sunday lunches and 'Sophie [Devine's] ritual teas' (Heilpern 2007: 254). This 'family' (as playwright Barney Norris described it) was key to the success of the Royal Court Theatre (Norris 2014). The queer dimensions of that 'family' may not have been explicit, yet there was a strong echo of the homophile and artistic milieu from Kains-Jackson's time in the house – especially given the queer-themed output for the ESC of some of those involved (including Howarth's first play *Sugar in the Morning* [1959], Tennessee Williams' *Orpheus Descending* [1959] and Osborne's *A Patriot for Me* [1965]).

This queer domestic pulse continued to evolve after Harriet Devine invited her friend, Peter Gill, a fellow assistant stage manager at the nearby Lyric Hammersmith theatre, to lodge in a room on the ground floor of Lower Mall. Gill subsequently became assistant and then associate director at the Royal Court between 1964 and 1976, and from then until 1980, the first artistic director of Hammersmith's Riverside Studios. Gill, by now 'out' as a gay man, developed the studio's reputation for cutting-edge performance – inspired perhaps by Devine and Richardson's vision for the Royal Court. The Lower Mall household again served as something of a motor for artistic work, challenging convention by forging a space for outsider and queer voices.

Gill was already living at Lower Mall by the time Howarth arrived. Howarth had become Goetschuis' lover and moved into the house shortly after

Richardson left in 1959 to marry Vanessa Redgrave. Howarth had a prior connection with Devine's network. He had known Richardson when taking acting classes in Bradford in the 1940s and was inspired to write *Sugar in the Morning* by Osborne's *Look Back in Anger* (the ESC's third production). Howarth shared Peggy Ramsay as an agent with other court writers (as well as with Joe Orton, a friend of Gill's and sometime Lower Mall visitor). We do not know what George Devine himself understood or thought of the changing configuration of lovers on the upper floors of his house. As in other accounts of this period (Murray 2010), Howarth spoke of the tacit knowledge associated with 'non-heterosexual' life – even in this bohemian, artistic context. Howarth describes a group of non-heterosexual writers and actors sitting around at Lower Mall, and Devine 'famously' speaking as if they were all 'straight'. 'We don't want any of those Binky Beaumonts in the new theatre,' Devine had said (Howarth 2015). Hugh (Binkie) Beaumont was a West End theatre manager and producer associated with 'that effete kind of theatre ... and these "anyone for tennis" kind of plays' (Howarth 2015). Beaumont was at the centre of a queer, theatrical clique involving John Gielgud, Noel Coward and Terrence Rattigan, and Devine may have been signalling his distaste for such men. He may also or instead have been signalling his distaste (shared by Osborne and Orton) for that particular articulation of queerness, linked to the establishment, convention and what a *Daily Express* columnist referred to in 1959 as an 'unpleasant free-masonry' (Sinfield 1999: 7; Osborne 1959).[6] Devine may in this way have been speaking to a sense of alterity he had in mind for the Royal Court – and which was to an extent being lived out by the occupants at Lower Mall. George Goetschius told George Devine that he and Donald were lovers; Goetschius also told Donald that George Devine had once seen him and Tony Richardson having sex through a window. None of this was ever discussed, however, even though Donald, the two Georges and George Devine's new partner, stage designer Jocelyn Herbert, were close. Queerness – even among friends and co-residents – was most often couched in this kind of unspoken and tacit knowledge in this period.

Devine died in 1966, but this unconventional and expansive pulse continued at the Royal Court and at Lower Mall, and in ways resonant with wider counterculture. In the latter half of the 1960s, Gill moved up to Coburn's former studio rooms to the second floor, Howarth and Goetschius to the modernist rooms at the top, and Harriet Devine (who now owned the house) 'on the first two floors with a lot of hippies', including a boyfriend 'who said the house was bourgeois and that they should sell and live in the country and be flower people' (Howarth 2015). The dimensions of what was meant by 'bourgeois' are unclear, but with Gill, Howarth and Goetschius upstairs (the former two in theatre, the latter an academic) it is possible that he was brushing up against the term's queer associations (Hennessy 1994). Harriet Devine did indeed sell up – and Howarth's growing success meant he and Goetschius were able to buy the house from her. They took possession in 1970; Gill, refusing to leave, moved from the second to the top floor.

III

Howarth and Goetschius' relationship was 'hitting the skids by the late 1960s' (Howarth 2015) but they decided to buy the house nevertheless – signalling what Alan Sinfield and Kath Weston see as a particularly queer openness to and accommodation of shifting relationship dynamics (Sinfield 1992; Weston 1991). Howarth observed that 'the house was big enough for us both to live in it and for us both to be friends. It was the best thing I ever did because we were life long friends' (Howarth 2015). That onus on friendship, supportive networks and community endured. It resonated with – and was perhaps in part nurtured by – Goetschius' own influential academic work, which focused on community formation (Goetschius 1967, 1969), his interest in Edward Carpenter (who was photographed by Coburn and was linked to Lower Mall's earlier twentieth-century milieu) and his Quakerism. Goetschuis attended the local Quaker – or Friends' – meeting house and initiated 'the gay Quakers of Hammersmith', who sometimes gathered for tea at Lower Mall. From Kains-Jackson through to Goetschius and Howarth, there was a community of ideas associated with this house that pivoted on a heightened appreciation of (queer) friendship.

In the early 1970s, Goetschius picked up a man on the towpath opposite (a cruising spot 'stately homo' Quentin Crisp and editor and writer J. R. Ackerley had also enjoyed in their time). This man, Jonathan Hudson, 'came and lived [in the first-floor balcony room] and cooked George's food' during one of Goetschius' bouts of severe anxiety and while Howarth was working in South Africa. Soon after, Hudson 'stopped cooking, became an interior designer and moved up here [to Coburn's former second-floor studio]'. The result was a 1970s makeover that has survived, complete with flamboyant wallpaper, built-in seating and fitted bathroom that exhibits a touch of the then new queer taste in art deco (Gardiner 1997: 130). Meanwhile, down on the ground floor, a young gay couple, South African playwrights Nick Wright and David Lan, had moved in. Wright had been a visitor at Lower Mall after he began work at the Royal Court, shortly before Devine's death. Though they only lived at Lower Mall for a short period, they too were part of the queer artistic network associated with the house and indeed with the Royal Court (Wright became joint artistic director in 1975–77; Lan was writer-in-residence there in the mid-90s). They went on to work (respectively) as associate director at the National Theatre and artistic director of the Young Vic theatre in Waterloo.

If burgeoning rhetoric in the fifties and sixties touted a narrower form of nuclear domesticity, Lower Mall suggested other possibilities. Throughout that period and into the seventies and eighties, the house accommodated family, friends and lovers in a variety of configurations. There was a sense of continuity in this (apparent) chaos for Howarth. He describes his formative years at one remove from 'conventional' family life and in a series of different homes:

> My parents separated when I was two and I didn't meet my mother until I was 18 when I came to London from Bradford. It was very good. I did very well without [parents]. [I was looked after by] Mrs Palmer in Feltham [West London] who had a daughter called Violet and a dog called Spot. Then my aunt Mabel in Leeds. Then in Bradford, which was a slum. Florence Greenwood looked after us [Howarth and his older brother] there … I called everyone mummy and daddy if they were old and gave us food. (Howarth 2015)

In the late 1940s, Howarth traced his mother to a flat in Earls Court where she was working as a dressmaker. He stayed there with her intermittently and they reconnected. Her artwork now hangs downstairs at Lower Mall, a testament of his attachment to her. This was nevertheless a bond – like others in Howarth's life – that was made rather than automatic or given.

Howarth's account of his London domestic life in adulthood – in a boarding house in Notting Hill with his first lover, Felix (who had arrived from Jamaica on the Empire Windrush in 1948), with his mother in Earls Court and then at Lower Mall[7] – extends the fluid sense of home from his childhood. His play *Sugar in the Morning* explores the dynamics of desire and belonging in a boarding house in Manchester, and a 'home' and 'family' in various ways flouting contemporary convention (Howarth 1999). Howarth makes sense of his childhood in part through the non-heterosexual kinship and domesticity of his adult years. His childhood, meanwhile, opened up domestic and relational possibilities in adulthood and perhaps inculcated a sense of the importance of care beyond kin. This is especially tangible in the caring role he took with Goetschius and with his lover Jimmy in New York who died of an AIDS-related illness in the late 1980s. Howarth and Goetschius became civil partners in 2006, and when Goetschius died a few months later, Howarth and some friends took the body to their house in Wales in an estate car. They buried him there in the garden in a funeral ceremony created by Howarth. Across their years together and apart – in the way they made home and domestic life, in the way they organized their relationships and friendships, and even in the rituals of death – there is a sense of improvisation, of self-determination, of making things up at odds with or eccentric to society's expectation.

Queer heritage

The house at Lower Mall testifies to all this. It is a tangible archive, vivid in its resonance with the past forty years during which Howarth has lived there; tantalizing but more muted in what it reveals of earlier queer networks. When Gill, Hudson, Goetschius and Howarth were living on their respective floors in the 1970s, the house touched a series of loose ideas about queer domesticity and style. There was the 'cool modernism' at the top, the fashionable 70s (sub) art deco of the second floor, the 'gentile drawing room' on the first, and the 'unholy chaos' (of the undomesticated queer) on Howarth's ground floor.[8] The differences between these floors have softened since, and there is now a connection to yet another strand of queer domesticity – an accumulation of 'stuff' that is perhaps not intrinsically valuable but is invested with meaning and worth through association with queer networks and genealogies (Cook 2014: 78–86). Ephemera, paintings, photographs and books provide traces of those who have lived here or passed through as lovers or friends, and of other people and places linked in to Howarth and Goetschius' lives and networks. These form an affective history of queer love and affiliation across the decades.

Such accumulations of things are not only queer, of course. But they perhaps hold particular value in contexts where family has been reformed and rethought beyond blood and convention. During the tour Howarth gave me, photos, paintings, objects, windows, views and even wallpaper each prompted stories and anecdotes – of things known and half-known (Fig. 7.4). Such stories have been the backbone of queer identification, especially in the context of illegality and social disapprobation (Butt 2005) and of what Howarth describes as a necessary 'non-heterosexual hypocrisy', which leaves much unsaid or shared

FIGURE: 7.4 *A mantelpiece of memories in a room on the ground floor of 9 Lower Mall. Photograph © Matt Cook.*

only selectively (even between the residents of Lower Mall). The material culture that evokes such tacit knowledge, such nebulous connections and networks beyond kin, is part of a capacious yet distinct queer heritage and inheritance. And 9 Lower Mall is part of that: 'Heterosexuals reproduce themselves and have families and they leave homes to their families,' Howarth observed, adding:

> If you're a true non-hetero you don't believe in reproducing yourself because you have quite enough on with your chosen partners. ... So the houses that you live in and the way you live in them are your children or is your child. The house is a community, its part of the community.

This differential significance of house and home Howarth claims for 'true non heteros' is something he plans to sustain at Lower Mall (though who qualifies as a 'true' non-hetero remains opaque). The house is ripe for redevelopment and refurbishment at a very tidy profit; other houses in the row have been revamped and are valued in their millions. But the materiality of that house and what it captures for Howarth is too significant to be absorbed into the London property market. The house is now protected by a newly founded trust – comfortably and casually named G & D Sofas (George and Donald's Society of Friends' Awards). The aspiration for Howarth and the trustees is that the house rumbles on, a place for artists and writers to stay for periods without living expenses. While at Lower Mall, they would work and form those creative queer networks that Howarth has benefitted from in his time there. What marks the operation of the trust is its informality. Howarth wants there to be no website or formal process of application, but rather the kind of random, ad hoc, word-of-mouth connections that have formed and sustained the artistic networks in the house to date and that were a feature especially of Kains-Jackson and Devine's respective circles. 'It won't be sold and it will just go on as if we're still living in it,' he said. 'The ghosts will still be here. There will be other alternative non-heterosexuals carrying on'. In this way 9 Lower Mall's heritage is potentially captured not only in its material presence and the stuff it contains but in the plans for its future modus operandi. The stuff will remain, providing layers of inspiration to a coming generation of artists who will doubtless add to it, creating something akin to what Alison Oram found in the historic houses she examined, that is 'a kaleidoscope of simultaneous historic periods and diverse means of interpreting them' (Oram 2011: 192; Plummer 2010). This, she and Howarth both suggest, can provide uneven ballast and inspiration for a queer present and future.

There is in Howarth's legacy an attempt to nurture some sense or semblance of another way of doing things – and at one remove from online media and insulated from London's voracious property market, which have each in different ways changed the way (queer) individuals relate and create. The Sofa

Trust signals a nostalgia for older non-heterosexual formations (of friendships, relationships, and notions of community) that substantially shifted with gay liberation, AIDS and then the arrival of the Internet (Grube 1990; Weeks 2007; Mowlabocus 2010).

Howarth's experiences of collaboration, congeniality and creativity at Lower Mall will fade from the memories of those people he has described them to. They will be passed on misremembered, reshaped, recontextualized as stories about – rather than from – him. That perhaps is part of a process that he seeks to fuel and foster through the Sofa Trust – preserving not a fixed history and heritage, not an authorized version of his and the house's past, but the scope for such chains of association and for storytelling and reformed meanings and significance. There is a randomness and diffuseness in this. Even the name G & D Sofas is unrevealing. There is a story behind it that needs explaining and passing on. This is the kind of occlusion that Howarth associates with the way non-heterosexuals have had to function – including at Lower Mall. And it is one way of thinking about queer heritage – as beset with doubleness and twists in meaning, often barely apparent, and unreadable at first.

The house and its situation were not simply backdrops for these queer interactions and creativity; they also shaped and facilitated them. The area has a rich dissenting and bohemian past. Locals I have mentioned include William Morris, Ackerley, Osborne and the theatrical Redgraves; physique magazine entrepreneur and pornographer John Barrington lived just across the river. The arrival of what would later be known as the Piccadilly Line in 1906 connected Lower Mall more easily to other parts of the queer city – to Earls Court, Hyde Park (where Richardson picked up Goetschuis) and Piccadilly Circus. The bridge linked the house to the towpath. The balcony and the 'new' bank of windows on the upper floors brought new perspectives on the scene beyond, inspiring the various artists, photographers, designers and writers who worked from these rooms and encouraging a certain voyeurism and reverse flânerie (there is a proximity to the passers-by on the path and river below and the scope to look and eavesdrop unobserved from above). Inside, the additions to the back of the house and upwards formed extra spaces to live and work, allowing for differently configured intimate lives (of hippies, non-heterosexual couples and queer singles, for example) to be lived in parallel with crossings on stairs and in corridors.

There was an intimate relationship between the shape, situation and contents of 9 Lower Mall and the ways in which the lives lived there unfolded. Tracking that relationship is tricky – full of hearsay and conjecture, anecdote and guesswork, but, as Oram has argued, this is perhaps also a feature of queer history and heritage. While Historic England and the National Trust make historic houses and the things they contain readable in particular ways, she suggests that the queerness of those houses and their pasts is frequently spectral, taking the form of tacit knowledge and suggestion and involving (for queer visitors) a nebulous sense of connection or identification with lives which were yet lived in radically different ways (Oram 2011: 203). Acknowledging and marking such oblique traces suggests a richer, queerer past than heritage house guidebooks and, at Lower Mall, that blue plaque, are ever able to capture. There is in this a kink in the cultural fabric; a bend in the river.

Notes

1 This piece is for Malcolm Williams; true friend and homemaker extraordinaire.
2 I am extremely grateful to Chris Majeika for first telling me about the house and sharing his research on its history from the late nineteenth century onwards.
3 See note 2.
4 The Oxford and Cambridge boat race has been a regular annual event since 1856.
5 Tuke also contributed a 'Sonnet to Youth' to *The Artist*; Kains-Jackson's 'Sonnet on a Picture by Tuke' appeared later, celebrating the young naked bathers characterizing his friend's paintings.
6 I am grateful to Justin Bengry for this reference – and for his comments on the piece more broadly.
7 These West London areas were linked by their strong queer associations.
8 Citations are from Heilpern's descriptions of the house in Heilpern 2007: 154; for discussion of these 'styles', see Cook 2014: pt.1.

References

Ackerley, J. R. (2006). *My Father and Myself.* New York: NYRB Classics.
Boellstorff, T. (2007). *A Coincidence of Desires: Anthropology, Queer Studies, Indonesia.* Durham and London: Duke University Press.
Brake, L. (2001). *Print in Transition, 1850–1910: Studies in Media and Book History.* Basingstoke: Palgrave MacMillan.
Butt, G. (2005). *Between You and Me: Queer Disclosures in the New York Art World, 1948–1963.* Durham: Duke University Press.
Carpenter, E. (ed.) (1902). *Ioläus. An Anthology of Friendship.* London: Swan Sonnenschein.
Cocks, H. (2003). *Nameless Offences: Homosexual Desire in the Nineteenth Century.* London: I. B. Taurus.
Cook, M. (2003). *London and the Culture of Homosexuality, 1885–1914.* Cambridge: Cambridge University Press.
Cook, M. (2006). 'Sex lives and diary writing: The journals of George Ives'. In *Life Writing and Victorian Culture*, edited by D. Amigoni, 195–214. Farnham: Ashgate.

Cook, M. (2014). *Queer Domesticities: Homosexuality and Home Life in Twentieth Century London*. Basingstoke: Palgrave MacMillan.

Darling, E. (2006). *Re-forming Britain: Narratives of Modernity before Reconstruction*. London: Routledge.

Devine, H. (2006). 'Obituary: George Goetschius'. In *The Guardian* (6 November).

Gardiner, J. (1997). *Who's a Pretty Boy, then? One Hundred & Fifty Years of Gay Life in Pictures*. London: Serpent's Tail.

Goetschius, G. (1967). *Working with Unattached Youth*. London: Routledge.

Goetschius, G. (1969). *Working with Community Groups*. London: Routledge.

Grube, J. (1990). '"Native and settlers": An ethnographic note on early interaction of older homosexual men with younger gay liberationists'. *Journal of Homosexuality* 20, no. 3: 119–36.

Heilpern, J. (2007). *John Osborne: A Patriot for Me*. London: Vintage.

Hennessy, R. (1994). 'Queer visibility in commodity culture'. *Cultural Critique* 29 (Winter): 31–76.

Houlbrook, M. (2005). *Queer London: Perils and Pleasures of the Queer Metropolis, 1918–1957*. Chicago: Chicago University Press.

Howarth, D. (1999). *Four Plays*. London: Oberon.

Howarth, D. (2015). Interview with Matt Cook.

James, C. (ed.) (2015). *My Dear KJ: The Letters of Frederick Rolfe to Charles Kains-Jackson*. Portsmouth: Callum James Books.

Kains-Jackson, C. K. (1970). 'The new chivalry'. In *Sexual Heretics: Male Homosexuality in English Literature from 1850–1900*, edited by B. Reade, 313–19. London: Routledge.

Langdon Coburn, A. (1913). *Men of Mark*. London: Duckworth.

Mowlabocus, S. (2010). *Gaydar Culture: Gay Men, Technology and Embodiment in the Digital Age*. Farnham: Ashgate.

Murray, H. (2010). *Not in this Family: Gays and the Meaning of Kinship in Postwar North America*. Philadelphia: University of Pennsylvania Press.

Norris, B. (2014). *To Bodies Gone: The Theatre of Peter Gill*. Bridgend, UK: Seren.

Oram, A. (2011). 'Going on an outing: The historic house and queer public history'. *Rethinking History* 15, no. 2: 189–207.

Oram, A. (2012). 'Sexuality in heterotopia: Time, space and love between women in the historic house'. *Women's History Review* 21, no. 4: 533–51.

Osborne, J. (1959). 'John Deane Potter's charges: A reply by John Osborne'. *Daily Express* (10 April).

Plummer, K. (2010). 'Generational sexualities, subterranean traditions, and the hauntings of the sexual world: Some preliminary remarks'. *Symbolic Interaction* 33, no. 2: 163–90.

Sinfield, A. (1992). 'Thom Gunn and the largest gathering of the decade'. *London Review of Books* 14, no. 3 (13 February): 16–17.

Sinfield, A. (1999). *Out on Stage: Lesbian and Gay Theatre in the Twentieth Century*. New Haven: Yale University Press.

Weeks, J. (2007). *The World We Have Won: The Remaking of Erotic and Intimate Life*. London: Routledge.

Weigman, R. and E. Wilson (2015). 'Antinormativity's queer conventions'. *Differences* 26, no. 1: 1–25.

Weston, K. (1991). *Families We Choose: Lesbians, Gays, Kinship*. New York: Columbia University Press.

8

The living room and sexuality: Lesbian homes as political places

Rachael M. Scicluna

Introduction: Home, sexuality and anthropology

Anthropologists have argued that no society can be adequately understood without giving home life a weight equal to the more acclaimed spheres of economy, politics and religion (Carsten and Hugh-Jones 1995). The notion of home, and the house more generally, is a relatively recent subject for British social anthropology as more attention has been paid to the domestic customs of 'exotic' communities. During the 1960s and 1970s, structural anthropologists cast their attention to the domestic sphere as a meaningful context for understanding the social organization of traditional societies, and produced a deep analysis of forms of dwelling and their cultural significance (e.g. Humphrey 1974; Bourdieu 2003 [1971]).

Despite the recent interest in contemporary Euro-American families, it is right to state that the anthropology of British domestic settings is relatively under-researched and under-theorized, with a few exceptions (Attfield 1997, 1999; Miller 1988, 2001, 2009; Parrott 2010; Buchli 2013). Moreover, it can be claimed that lesbian domestic lives, their activities, categories and values and how they cope with problems, constitute an under-researched subject in the anthropology of home in Britain and elsewhere. Equally, despite there being a growing interest in queer domesticities from other disciplines such as social history (Cook 2014), sociology (Gabb 2005), architectural history (Friedman 2015; Pilkey 2015) and cultural geography (Gorman-Murray 2007, 2008a,b, 2012), more research on alternative homes and family formations, including lesbian homes, is needed.[1]

As Carsten and Hugh-Jones suggest in their edited volume, *About the House: Lévi-Strauss and Beyond*, it is important to move towards a 'holistic anthropology of architecture' by 'seeing houses "in the round"' and drawing links between the body, architecture, social and symbolic significance (1995: 2). For Carsten and Hugh-Jones (ibid), the interrelationship between bodies and buildings is difficult to meaningfully disassemble. The anthropologist Victor Buchli (2013), in his book *The Anthropology of Architecture,* explores the latter argument further by emphasizing the importance of the materiality of architectural forms while simultaneously stressing the significance of how architectonic forms *relate* differently to other registers such as 'image, metaphor, performance, ruin, diagnostic or symbol and how the specific material conditions of these registers – their materiality – enables human relations' (2). By following this theoretical framework, this chapter explores the interrelationship between the home and sexuality, where certain domestic settings such as the living room and the kitchen are seen as an enabling form that enhances social relations. In this chapter, sexuality, home and friendship networks are combined in order to provide an intimate understanding of the lives of a group of older lesbians living in the 'gay' capital of Brighton and Hove, south-east England.

Anthropological practice in Brighton and Hove

I conducted this research over an eight-month period with a group of older lesbians, where I explored their daily life experiences in Brighton and Hove, and the vicinity (Scicluna 2010).[2] The older lesbians in this study formed part of an informal local social network, known as the 'Link', but were also part of other networks and groups. The methods and techniques adopted to conduct this fieldwork were based on anthropological practice (Okely 2012), mainly through a combination of long-term participant observation, informal conversations and biographical interviews. I attended their organized activities such as discos, lunches and dinners at local restaurants, as well as special religious rituals and other social activities at the participants' homes. In total, twelve self-identified lesbians, aged between fifty-three and seventy-six years, were interviewed. All of the individuals that feature in this research are white and of British and American nationalities. Five out of the twelve are divorced (from a previous heterosexual marriage), of whom four have children.[3] All moved to Brighton in their mid-twenties and early thirties for reasons such as following a husband's employment, to be with a partner, and above all due to the liberal ideology that Brighton projects as a leading 'gay capital' in England. Despite Brighton's reputation as an ideal place to live as a lesbian, they all agreed that it can be simultaneously liberal and hostile to diversity.

The social network I was part of – the 'Link' – is made up of an independent group of lesbians. The members are mainly older. The core group of the Link, which is made up of four members, is responsible for the smooth running of the network such as decision-making, fundraising and the organization of activities and special events such as a celebration of the Gateways nightclub, a famous lesbian club that ran from 1935 to 1958 in London. Further, doing research in a 'gay capital' like Brighton and Hove was enlightening, yet challenging. I was struck by a *double Brighton,* as one participant continuously iterated. I observed two coexisting planes: a liberal Brighton based on an all-inclusive, anti-homophobic political discourse; and a conservative Brighton based on a heteronormative ideology, especially prevalent outside central Brighton. This observation has been a major influence in this research and central to my overall argument in relation to how this contradiction between the real (lived experience) and the imagined (liberal ideology) created a social gap that impinged heavily on the lesbian self and the relationship between sexual identity and daily life (see also Rooke 2007; Tunåker 2015).

Having the possibility to move beyond the domestic realm gave me the possibility to experience the way older lesbians dealt with subtle hostility both at home and outside. As an anthropologist, I was also able to understand what Geertz (1974) refers to as an 'experience-near' concept. His concept of experience-near offers an insightful analytical framework that helps the researcher gain a deeper meaning in experiencing what the locals experience in their daily lives. According to Geertz, the trick is 'to figure out what the devil they think they are up to' (1974: 29). Hence, intimate conversations and encounters at home offered me the chance to understand better the world view of this group of older lesbians. Generally, the intimate and safe setting of the home emerged as a significant place for the birth and continuation of social networks based on the politics of sexuality.

Home as a political spatial landscape

Many of the older lesbians I spent time with met at each other's homes to socialize and even to celebrate Christian rituals, such as Easter and Christmas. They often used each other's living rooms as meeting places to discuss matters related to the informal social networks or lesbian – feminist discussion groups they were part of.[4] This section will look at how the home serves as a bridge that connects the more subversive acts of activism, such as the birth of the Link and the politics of friendship. Some years ago, the British anthropologist Eric Hirsch (1995), in the introduction to the edited book *The Anthropology of Landscape*, argued that anthropology had a tendency to treat space and place as the passive backdrop upon which social and cultural life is lived. In a similar way, I would support this and would further argue that relatively little work has been done on the way in which wider social inequalities can be redrawn and contested through arranging or rearranging domestic place, or through everyday use and occupation. Thus, in this section, I seek to bring the home to the forefront of my theoretical discussion by illustrating how the domestic spatial landscape is active and dynamic and not just a framing device. As I highlighted at the outset, the home as (architectural) form is what enabled the sustenance of social relations (Buchli 2013).

In this chapter, the meaning of home as a political, lively setting needs to be understood against the specific historical context of the 1970s and 1980s. According to the British anthropologist Sarah Green (1997), during this period some women, in order to abide by their feminist belief that 'the personal is political', chose to live and work within women-only workplaces and households. As I argue elsewhere (Scicluna 2013, 2015, 2017), living communally and squatting was a significant reality for some radical feminist lesbians. This offered lesbians a safe place in times when there was a housing shortage where many women had difficulties finding accommodation in the metropolis (Egerton 1990). Subsequently, communal living can be understood as an act of resistance, through a combination of comradeship and ideology where women could feel safe for a time from the hostility of the outside world. The impermanence brought about by moving houses was common and was further exacerbated by living as a lesbian feminist (Green 1997). Also, lesbian – feminist politics had a huge impact on the domestic sphere since they represented a major site of woman's oppression, that is, 'of women being both restricted to it, and of the sexual and emotional abuses they experienced within it' (Green 1997: 94).

The above socio-historical context is important as it sheds light on the complexity of sexual lives and how they intertwine and are influenced by larger social forces such as gender inequality, housing and feminism. Sexuality was, in a way, used as a tool to challenge institutionalized heteronormativity. This shows how *sexuality* is complex, culturally and politically loaded and, as the sociologist Ken Plummer argues, it 'is always locatable in social worlds' and must be 'characterised as having both a generational and subterranean character' (2010: 196). According to Plummer (ibid), the wide spectrum of human sexuality across time demonstrates how sexuality is not fixed but rather dynamic and always in flux, hence there are no fixed norms but constantly emergent ones. Giving attention to how 'different generations at any moment come to live and talk about their sexualities' gives more depth to why certain relationships, such as friendship networks, are more powerful than others (Plummer 2010: 170).

This context of the 1970s and 1980s is important as it indicates why tightlyknit networks have emerged from behind closed doors and how homes served as a safe place where political activism based on sexuality could be practised.[5] For instance, one of my key participants, Natasha, recalled how the Link started from her own living room. She recalled how at first they used to meet in the basement of a friend's house. However, as the number of women increased, Natasha decided to use her own flat's living room as it was large enough to accommodate all. She reminisced,

> It was a mixture of women who had all sorts of interests. There were women who went on the walking groups; there were women who belonged to a singing group and all sorts of things. So between us we had a lot of knowledge of what was happening and that worked for a while as a Kenric group[6] ... there were about eighteen of us who used to meet and it seemed a great pity that we were going to lose this because the reps had stopped working. So some of us suggested that it would be good to meet again and perhaps start a new group, which we did. I think we had two planning meetings and, erm, so we started the Link. So we used to meet in my flat, we had plenty of meetings there for some time.

The birth of this network illustrates the way home settings can provide the right conditions to offer safety in a hostile society while simultaneously enabling human relationships to flourish, as I argued at the outset. Over the years, the Link expanded and now has over 200 members, although, as Caroline explained, not all attend the organized events. Often I heard the core members complain about the lack of attendance at social events, especially the evening meals that Mary, a longstanding Link member whom I visited often for tea, ran for eight years. When I asked Mary why she thought the lunches were not as popular and well attended, she said that this was due to the nature of such social activities, which in her experience are always time bound. Moreover, she related the lack of attendance to the general low pensions that women received. Due to the expansion of the Link's membership, many of the monthly social activities, such as afternoon lunches and drinks, are carried out in local cafes and restaurants. However, the home still features as a core place where certain social activities happen, as I will illustrate below.

From the above ethnographic illustrations, social activities and friendship networks emerge as webs of meaningful relationships that need to be seen in their historical and social specificity (Weston 1991; Blackwood 2005). As Weeks et al. state, friendship has a powerful meaning for non-heterosexuals in a world of 'institutionalised rejection' (2001: 7). Here, the home transforms into an 'in between' political space: it is that place between civil society and institutions that offers the right material conditions to forge significant relationships. In what follows, I will illustrate how the intimate setting of the home can become ideal for the researcher to understand group dynamics.

Home as an ideal social and moral place to understand group dynamics

Older lesbians have been largely good at creating informal social networks, which are important for sociability, emotional support and company (Weston 1991; Weeks et al. 2001). According to the American anthropologist Kath Weston, the establishment of 'nonerotic ties among homosexuals constituted a key historical development that paved the way for the emergence of lesbian and gay "community" that later appear as alternative "family" formations or "families we choose"' (1991: 118). Friendship networks tend to offer a sense of homeliness and belonging, which often provides the specific knowledge that helps individuals negotiate the hazards of everyday life. Weston further argues that the historical development of friendship ties based on sexual identity 'turned out to be merely an introductory episode in a more lengthy tale of community formation' (ibid: 122). As I outlined above, these informal networks need to be understood as being of their time in a specific socio-historical context. Many lesbian networks go back half a century, where some even survived for up to two decades while others are still active (e.g. Kenric). In this section, the focus will be on the meaningful link created through networks and groups and not on the network itself (Green 2002). It is the effort of these older lesbians' attempts to make sociability possible that is of importance, and not the more ephemeral conditions that networks are often associated with. Having the possibility to participate in domestic daily activities, rituals and to be engaged in mundane talk, including gossip and disagreements, was significant as it also shed light on the way this friendship network functioned.

Groups are never without their tensions, despite their good intentions. Some disagreements were related to the Link's decision-making on finances. The hosting of the Link meetings was rotated between the core member's homes. During one quarterly meeting, which was held in Caroline's living room, there was a dispute on a small donation made towards the maintenance of a local lesbian cafe. Decision-making rules were based on the consensus of at least two other core members. Kate had followed these rules before donating the money. The accountant had disagreed with this decision and wanted to enquire with the funding body whether the Link was allowed to give donations like these. According to Kate, this was a power game. During this conversation, Kate expressed that she might have to leave the network. Cornelia explained that the accountant was going through a very rough time with her mum being ill. Kate did not accept that as a good excuse and said that she was not part of the core group. To which Cornelia replied, 'Oh I never really understood how that worked and the reason behind it.' Kate quickly explained the rules again: 'If I and, for example, Sarah agreed on something it meant that we could proceed, always by including a third person. This means that the core group had agreed on the donation.' Kate was mainly upset because the accountant should not be calling the funding body behind her back.

In a way, the above scenario asks the question whether there is stability or a high turnover in friendship circles, but it also alludes to moral values. The Norwegian anthropologist Marianne Gullestad, in her ethnography *The Kitchen-Table Society* (1985), for instance, pointed out how women's talk when they are together may be seen as a kind of moral discourse about what is right and wrong in relation to child-rearing practices and the division of labour among couples. It was also very clear from Gullestad's ethnography on working-class women that one may quickly get on intimate terms, if conditions are favourable, but friendships can equally be brittle and break due to conflicts. The above scenario brings out the ordinariness and flow of daily conversations and the tensions that are so common of group dynamics. Similar to other anthropologists (Gluckman 1963; Gullestad 1985), I argue that everyday talk is imbued with moral values that are significant to both the solidarity and conflicts of this group. Despite the disagreement on financial decisions, as soon as the meeting was over we all settled down to watch a short film and enjoyed some pear wine that Caroline had purposely prepared for this occasion. Here, the social aspect emerges as a core part of the maintenance of this friendship group.

The plumber as the epitome of heteronormativity in daily practice at home

This imaginative, discursive and experiential place, which we call home, is not always ideal and happiness is not always guaranteed (Douglas 1991). Home can also be a place of abuse, work and exploitation (Cieraad 1999; Das et al.

2008; Gorman-Murray 2012), as I will illustrate here through seemingly trivial daily practices. From previous research on gay and lesbian homemaking in (sub) urban Australia, cultural geographer Andrew Gorman-Murray (2007) illustrates how 'some gay men and lesbians queer the ideal Australian home, generating domestic spaces which affirm sexual difference', and can be a positive experience. The process of queering home is achieved through certain *uses* from social activities and gatherings held within the home to queer domestic practices that change the materiality of the home. However, experiences of home are multiple and complex, and as Gorman-Murray (2012) argues, for many non-heterosexuals 'home is not a matter of belonging *or* alienation, resistance *or* conformity, but a negotiation between these different engagements'. In what follows, I shall highlight this type of negotiation that older lesbians engage in with tradespeople and neighbours (see Pilkey, this book).

Sarah, aged fifty-five, narrated how she was overcome with shame when she had to arrange an appointment for a plumber from a local agency to come and fix her boiler. She was concerned that the plumber would realize that she was in a lesbian relationship, as she had photographs of her and her partner as a couple dotted around the living room and the kitchen. This encounter created anxiety because it was connected to thoughts of Sarah exposing her lesbian self within the safety of their home. Another participant, Clare (seventy-three years old), told me of a similar incident with a plumber:

> He [the plumber] was fixing my central heating and he kept putting his arm around me and he was telling me that he lived with an older woman and that he loved older women and it was obviously believed as offering me … you know … and I just said, 'Look I am a lesbian' and he carried on with his arms around me saying that 'we both love women then', but he did not put his arm around me again. I complained to the manager, the owner of the electric company in Lewes about him but *unfortunately* the bloke came back again, and I had asked not to send him anymore when he finished the central heating. When I had a problem for someone to come back to adjust something he turned up again and he said, 'Why did you ask them not to send me? Why did you say you had a problem with me?' And I phoned the owner and said, 'He's arrived again.' And he [the owner] said, 'He insisted on coming.'

This narrative illustrates the implicit and unconscious power embodied in gestures ('his arm around me') and behaviour that lives in the mundane. Here, the home transforms into a place where hostility and abuse can be performed behind closed doors, away from the public gaze. The plumber felt he had the right to behave that way, used Clare's disclosure of her sexual orientation as a lesbian to his own advantage and oppressed her through heterosexism – 'we both love women'. It did not occur to him that his behaviour may have been abusive. He simply took the fact that she desired him for granted. The plumber epitomizes the visible social world and the rigidity of its social norms – that is, the taken-for-granted world. This type of social interaction illustrates how heterosexism is at its apex in the practice of the everyday.

The neighbours, home and sexuality

Cornelia generally came across as a rather contained and diplomatic person. She told me that, overall, she has been lucky in how her family and friends behaved towards her when she came out to them. The storyline changed as soon as I asked how she got on with her neighbours. Cornelia's initial reaction was, 'Very well, but again I don't think they know that I am gay, but they might do, because mainly I have women coming to visit me.' She said how on her birthday she received a card from one of her neighbours who described her as a 'generous, helpful neighbour'. For Cornelia, that was a sign that her sexuality did not matter to this neighbour. However, she was quick to mention a specific incident with a neighbour, which makes her keep her lesbianism private:

> There is a gentleman that lives above me. He is a Glaswegian and very, very, very anti-gay and unfortunately there was a chap that I was quite friendly with called Tim, and he was gay. He was obviously gay and evidently Ben [the Glaswegian gentleman] once knocked on his door and Ben said that if you were in Glasgow we'd shoot through your knee caps or something really nasty, you know. And I just felt I didn't really need to come out because if it got to him I think life would be a *bit* difficult. He's not the easiest person anyway. He can be very nasty. I think its best, there's no need. He's early seventies and maybe that makes a difference.

Another key participant, Elisabeth narrated how she has never come up against any overt or covert discrimination, and thinks she has been rather lucky since she 'knows an awful lot of people who have' and continued saying, 'I haven't had any people writing rude words on my door, or sprayed my car or anything like that'. She feels that living in Seaford, a coastal town east of Brighton, is a safe area and once again reiterated that she thinks she is quite fortunate about that. Elisabeth, who is originally from Northampton, said, 'I couldn't think of anything worse than com[ing] out there, where everybody minds everybody's business. That would have been horrendous.' This narrative highlights how the proximity of her home to Brighton is geographically strategic. The area has an ongoing engagement with Brighton's lesbian social networks and with its liberal ideology as a gay capital. She explained,

> Living where I live close to Brighton, I think is brilliant. My neighbours are great. When I was in a relationship I had had some neighbours over and they asked me, 'What is your relationship with Helen', and I said, 'she is my partner' and it went dead quiet for a minute and then you could feel everybody [pause]; the noise went up again and everybody just continued, but obviously you could have heard a pin drop for a second but then everybody suddenly realised what had happened and we started chatting again. And nobody mentioned it again. I am a good neighbour to them. This is it. This is what comes first.

The proximity of one's home to Brighton came up regularly. All of the participants moved to their present house because it was close enough to Brighton and Hove. Some were not particularly satisfied with living in the outskirts, but had to due to their financial situation. Also, only certain localities met their requirements for the type of house they were searching for. Karen said how being a lesbian affected her neighbours and was an issue for them, especially her next-door neighbours,

> I had a few comments by my neighbours about my sexuality but they tend to be uptight persons really … I shouldn't be saying this, really, but they do tend to be tradespeople like taxi drivers and electricians. I have even sat in one neighbour's house and she had one of the other neighbours over and they were discussing who has lived in my next door neighbour's house and she said, 'Oh, do you remember those lezzies that lived there' [bursts out laughing] so obviously there has been a pair of lesbians that have lived in the bungalow next door to me but they have moved [laughs]. So I think that there are areas of Brighton, even though there seems to be a few lesbians living in this area, it is not that well accepted. So as you were saying even in Brighton there is prejudice.

The above narratives bring out many overlapping themes, mainly those of sexuality, class, economy and neighbourhood proximity to Brighton. Overall, these narratives illustrate a dialogue between the two binary oppositions of heterosexism and homophobia. There is a flow of power moving in participants' narratives, for example, in the way they articulate: their existence in relation to their neighbours, their economic background in relation to their chosen locality, class issues and their sexual orientation.

Concluding reflections

The dimensions of sexuality, the 'ordinary' acts of the neighbour or the plumber (among others) and informal networks and friendship groups are here treated as flows of power that bring the spatial landscape of the home to the forefront when considering lesbian daily lives. But the spatial setting of the home is not static; rather, it emerges as a changing social and political process across time. The historical and political context in which these generation-specific social practices and narratives emerge is of utmost importance in order to understand the uniqueness of such networks, which originated pre-Internet in Britain. Some of the meanings of these connections, and the tensions of group dynamics that often create the opportunity for the group to transform into something else (or to disperse), as I demonstrated, are best understood as creative and powerful forms of social relations.[7] Additionally, I sought to bring out through ethnographic examples the way in which this social practice creates a sense of stability and belonging in a world that is still often hostile to lesbianism, even in a gay capital. Moreover, through this subversive practice of socializing at home, this specific group of older lesbians sought to make meaning, and create constructively an alternative lifestyle, out of such oppression. The creation of informal networks and friendship groups, often springing from behind the closed doors of lesbians' homes, is a direct and meaningful engagement with a hetero-patriarchal society. In the context of this ethnography, the lesbian home as an architectural form has the power to enable and sustain human relations across time.

Notes

1 There is also a shift towards the experiences and practices of managing daily life in a queer home, including the negotiation of domestic labour and child-rearing, lesbian donor conception (Nordqvist 2010, 2011), including LGBT youth homelessness (Tunåker 2015). See also the special issue, *Alternative Domesticities* (Pilkey, Scicluna and Gorman-Murray 2015).

2 Brighton has long been considered the UK's 'gay capital'. Brighton is considered to be unique in its diverse population and cosmopolitan atmosphere where sexualities merge (Visit Brighton).

3 Only two are employed on a full-time basis, five retired early due to chronic fatigue syndrome (CFS), and five are retired (compulsory retirement). Besides being part of the Link, I joined a lesbian – feminist discussion group where most of the people suffered from CFS. Here, I highlight CFS as I believe that there is a correlation between the ongoing process of coming out and the stress it caused in the daily lives of the lesbians in this research. Additionally,

my research explored the doctor – patient dyad, especially experiences of disclosing sexual identity to their doctor (see Scicluna 2010).

4 Those who suffer from CFS explained that they were also part of a virtual network that provided much-needed support, especially when they were home bound due to their illness.

5 The hosting of the lesbian – feminist discussion group was rotated between different members' living rooms. Generally, the meetings were held at Natasha's home as she had a very big living room and could easily accommodate fifteen members.

6 Kenric was established in 1965 and is a network run by lesbians for lesbians across the UK. For more information, see Kenric.

7 In fact, towards the end of my research, the Link was being legally transformed into a film club.

References

Attfield, J. (1997). 'Design as a practice of modernity: A case for the study of the coffee table in the mid-century domestic interior'. *Journal of Material Culture* 2, no. 3: 267–89.

Attfield, J. (1999). 'Bringing modernity home: Open plan in the British domestic interior'. In *At Home: An Anthropology of Domestic Space*, edited by I. Cieraad, 73–82. New York: Syracuse University Press.

Blackwood, E. (2005). 'Wedding bell blues: Marriage, missing men, and matrifocal follies'. *American Ethnologist* 32, no. 1: 3–19.

Bourdieu, P. (2003[1971]). 'The Berber house of the world reversed'. In *The Anthropology of Space and Place: Locating Culture*, edited by S. M. Low and D. Lawrence-Zuniga, 131–41. Oxford: Blackwell Publishing.

Buchli, V. (2013). *An Anthropology of Architecture*. London: Bloomsbury.

Carsten, J. and S. Hugh-Jones (1995). *About the House: Levi-Strauss and Beyond*. Cambridge: Cambridge University Press.

Cieraad, I. (1999). 'Introduction: Anthropology at home'. In *At Home: An Anthropology of Domestic Space*, edited by I. Cieraad, 1–12. New York: Syracuse University Press.

Cook, M. (2014). *Queer Domesticities: Homosexuality and Home Life in Twentieth-Century London*. Basingstoke: Palgrave Macmillan.

Das, V., J. Ellen and L. Leonard (2008). 'On the modalities of the domestic'. *Home Cultures* 5, no. 3: 348–372.

Douglas, M. (1991). 'The idea of a home: A kind of space'. *Social Research* 58, no. 1: 287–307.

Egerton, J. (1990). 'Out but not down: Lesbians' experience of housing'. *Feminist Review* 36: 75–88.

Friedman, A. (2015). 'Hiding in plain sight: Love, life and the queering of domesticity in early 20th-century New England'. *Home Cultures* 12, no. 2: 139–67.

Gabb, J. (2005). 'Locating lesbian parent families: Everyday negotiations of lesbian motherhood in Britain'. *Gender, Place and Culture* 12, no. 4: 419–32.

Geertz, C. (1974). 'From the native's point of view: On the nature of anthropological understanding'. *Bulletin of the American Academy of Arts and Sciences* 28, no. 1: 26–45.

Gluckman, M. (1963). 'Gossip and scandal'. *Current Anthropology* 4, no. 3: 307–16.

Gorman-Murray, A. (2007). 'Contesting domestic ideal: Queering the Australian home'. *Australian Geographer* 38, no. 2: 195–213.

Gorman-Murray, A. (2008a). 'Masculinity and the home: A critical review and conceptual framework'. *Australian Geographer* 39, no. 3: 367–79.

Gorman-Murray, A. (2008b). 'Reconciling self: Gay men and lesbians using domestic materiality for identity management'. *Cultural Geography* 9, no. 3: 283–301.

Gorman-Murray, A. (2012). 'Que(e)rying homonormativity: The everyday politics of lesbian and gay homemaking'. *Conference Paper given at the Sexuality at Home workshop.* London: University College London.

Green, S. F. (1997). *Urban Amazons: Lesbian Feminism and Beyond in the Gender, Sexuality and Identity Battles of London.* Basingstoke: Palgrave Macmillan.

Green, S. F. (2002). 'Culture in a network: Dykes, webs and women in London'. In *British Subjects: An Anthropology of Britain*, edited by N. Rapport, 181–202. Oxford: Berg.

Gullestad, M. (1985). *Kitchen-table Society: A Case Study of the Family Life and Friendships of Young Working-Class Mothers in Urban Norway.* Oslo: Universitetsforlaget.

Hirsch, E. (1995). 'Introduction: Landscape: Between place and space'. In *The Anthropology of Landscape: Perspectives on Place and Space*, edited by E. Hirsch and M. O'Hanlon, 1–30. Oxford: Clarendon Press.

Humphrey, C. (1974). 'Inside a Mongolian tent'. *New Society* (31 October).

Kenric. Available online: http://www.kenric.org/.

Miller, D. (1988). 'Appropriating the state on the council estate'. *Man* 23, no. 2: 353–72.

Miller, D. (2001). *Home Possessions: Material Culture behind Closed Doors.* Oxford and New York: Berg.

Miller, D. (2009). *The Comfort of Things.* Cambridge: Polity.

Nordqvist, P. (2010). 'Out of sight, out of mind: Family resemblances in lesbian donor conception'. *Sociology* 44, no. 6: 1128–44.

Nordqvist, P. (2011). 'Dealing with sperm: Comparing lesbians' clinical and non-clinical donor conception processes'. *Sociology of Health and Illness* 33, no. 1: 114–29.

Okely, J. (2012). *Anthropological Practice.* Oxford: Berg.

Parrott, F. (2010). 'Bringing home the dead: Photographic objects, family imaginaries and moral remains'. In *An Anthropology of Absence: Materialisations of Transcendence and Loss*, edited by M. Billie, F. Hastrup and T. F. Sorensen, 131–46. New York: Springer Press.

Pilkey, B. (2015). 'Reading the queer domestic aesthetic discourse: Tensions between celebrated stereotypes and lived realities'. *Home Cultures* 12, no. 2: 213–39.

Pilkey, B., R. M. Scicluna and A. Gorman-Murray. (2015). 'Alternative domesticities: A cross-disciplinary approach to home and sexuality'. *Home Cultures* 12, no. 2: 127–38.

Plummer, K. (2010). 'Generational sexualities, subterranean traditions, and the hauntings of the sexual world: Some preliminary remarks'. *Symbolic Interaction* 33, no. 2: 163–90.

Rooke, A. (2007). 'Navigating embodied lesbian cultural space: Toward a lesbian habitus'. *Space and Culture* 10: 231–52.

Scicluna, R. M. (2010). *A Study of Older Lesbians in Southern England.* Masters Diss., University of Sussex, UK.

Scicluna, R. M. (2013). *The 'Other' Side of the Kitchen: An Anthropological Approach to the Domestic Kitchen and Older Lesbians.* Ph.D. Diss., Open University, UK.

Scicluna, R. M. (2015). 'Thinking through Domestic Pluralities'. *Home Cultures* 12, no. 2: 169–91.

Scicluna, R. M. (2017). *Home and Sexuality: The 'other' Side of the Domestic Kitchen.* Basingstoke: Palgrave Macmillan.

Tunåker, C. (2015). 'No place like home? Locating homeless LGBT youth'. *Home Cultures* 12, no. 2: 241–59.

Visit Brighton. Available online: http://www.visitbrighton.com/site/your-brighton/gay.

Weeks, J., B. Heaphy and C. Donovan (2001). *Same Sex Intimacies. Families of Choice and other Life Experiments.* London: Routledge.

Weston K. (1991). *Families We Choose: Lesbians, Gays, Kinship.* New York: Columbia University Press.

9

Que(e)rying homonormativity: The everyday politics of lesbian and gay homemaking

Andrew Gorman-Murray

(Up)setting the (domestic) scene

The tone of radical queer critiques of lesbian and gay homes and domestic lives has tended to disparage domesticity as 'homonormative', arguably framing investment in the home as part of homosexual assimilation with the conservative, middle-class social mainstream.[1] In this logic, it is claimed that lesbian and gay affiliation to domesticity induces a privatized, demobilized and depoliticized constituency. This chapter critically contests that assumption. Drawing on insights from a range of my own projects on lesbian and gay domesticity in Australia,[2] and a critical reading of extant scholarship in geography and commensurate disciplines, I argue for a less monolithic application of homonormativity and an appreciation of the nuances of homemaking. As ordinary, very much 'lived-in' spaces, lesbian and gay homes are key sites of political and social change, manifested in everyday homemaking practices (Luzia 2010; Scicluna 2015). The lesbian and gay domestic sphere is not necessarily a zone of assimilation (though it can be) but also a space of resistance and transformation (Gorman-Murray 2012; Pilkey 2014). We should be wary of romanticizing traditional notions of home life, but we should also be cognizant of the political leverage of domesticity. To be clear, it is not my goal to reverse the critical discourse: domestic spaces and cultures *can* be assimilative and conservative, even dangerous (see Johnston and Valentine 1995; Valentine and Skelton 2003; Asquith and Fox 2016). Rather, I aim to think through the multiplicities, fractures and possibilities in/of the domestic to suggest *alternative* performative readings of homemaking for lesbians and gay men.

The careful empirical and conceptual consideration of lesbian and gay homes and practices of homemaking in Australia has been one of the fundamental themes of my research. My concern with domestic environments has been mutually political and scholarly: I have sought to examine and understand how lesbians and gay men negotiate their everyday lives, identities and relationships in and through 'ordinary spaces' (Brown 2008) rather than the 'exceptional sites' of the commercial scene (with its pubs, clubs and other venues), the 'hyper-political environment' of lesbian and gay rights activism, or the 'hidden world' of beats (in the case of gay men and other men-who-have-sex-with-men). Greater scholarly interest has been placed hitherto on these overt and exciting spaces, such as 'the scene', ghettos, gatherings, marches, festivals, cruising grounds, etc., rather than the emplacement and experience of lesbians and gay men within the quotidian domestic sphere (Brown 2009). It is, of course, imperative to look at all of these spaces to understand the contemporary experiences of lesbians and gay men. In this context, I have argued for the need to comprehend the nuanced links between the space of the home, identity work (either its affirmation or its suppression) and embodied and emotional well-being for lesbians and gay men, and the role these connections can and do play in sustaining lesbian and gay individuals and their significant relationships, including same-sex families and social networks (Gorman-Murray 2007).

Yet, at times, I have found it difficult to make my perspective heard convincingly. Or at least, I've felt that way. Not always, but sometimes. Through occasional anonymous peer-reviews of journal submissions, audience questions at conferences and even published critiques, I get the impression that sometimes colleagues have read my work as 'celebratory narratives' of lesbian and gay resistance or, paradoxically, have seen my focus on home as complicit in the normative mainstreaming of lesbian and gay lives. Let me take this opportunity to be clear: my intention has never been to 'romanticize' home, resistance or normativity, and I am well aware that homes can be stifling and exclusionary for sexual dissidents (and others besides). Instead, I have been concerned with how lesbian and gay individuals and families 'live' and 'get by' in the ordinary environments of their daily lives and how they must necessarily work out different ways of tacking between resisting and assuming normative socio-sexual expectations (cf. Browne and Bakshi 2013). For many, their lived experience of home is not a matter of belonging *or* alienation, resistance *or* conformity, but a negotiation between these different engagements (cf. Cook

2014). In this context, my intention has been to draw attention to, in different combinations, the role of the politics of domesticity in social change, the subversive possibilities of the home and the continued significance of a home-space for self-worth and well-being. These themes are underpinned by an interest in identity politics and social transformation. In this, I follow work by feminists bell hooks (1990) and Iris Marion Young (2005) on the transgressive and democratic potential of the home and work by Eve Sedgwick (2003) and geographer Gavin Brown (2009, 2012) on reparative modes of critical thinking, which seek to address problematic social disparities rather than perpetuating paranoia about insurmountable exclusions and alienations.

The problem with homonormativity

I think a particular difficulty has recently emerged and inflected academic attitudes towards the appreciation of lesbian and gay home life. Despite certain advances, suggested above, on the contributions of mundane domestic spaces to social understanding and change, it seems to me that suspicion persists about the value of the home and domestic life in lesbian and gay politics (and queer activism), reflecting the notion of home as conventional, normative, withdrawn and assimilative. I suspect this wariness is linked with Lisa Duggan's (2002) chapter on 'the new homonormativity' as the sexual politics of neoliberalism, linked to right-wing lesbian and gay rights movement organizations in the United States. Since Duggan introduced this concept – homonormativity – it has become widely popular in social and geographical scholarship on lesbian and gay lives. While good radical scholarship should critique normalizing tendencies in minority social movements as much as wider external processes of discipline and incorporation,[3] I have reservations about how homonormativity has been deployed in recent geographical scholarship. This, in my assessment, has done a great disservice to our understanding of both the ongoing value of home to lesbians and gay men – David Eng (1997) warns us not to underestimate their enduring affiliations to home – and the role of residential environments and domestic activities in social transformations around sexual identities and lesbian and gay lives.

My apprehension parallels Gavin Brown's (2009: 1496; cf. Brown 2008, 2012) concern about how recent writing in urban, economic and sexual geographies 'presents "homonormativity" as an all-encompassing structure that becomes politically unassailable', offering universal interpretations of lesbian and gay spatialities – which, I contend, certainly includes lesbian and gay domesticities. Brown (2012: 1066–7) argues that 'such theorizations tend to overlook the many other practices that exist that foster alternative ways of relating' and 'fail to adequately identify where change might happen' because they 'produce a representation of the world that appears as if change is too difficult to enact'. These theorizations are often applied in a uniform and sweeping way in located, empirical discussions, without adequate attention to the differences, divergences and nuances generated by geographical setting or quotidian social relationships. In doing so, 'sexualities researchers risk … losing any sense of the specific geographies of the social, political, and economic relations that shape [lesbian and] gay lives, and overlooking how the processes and practices are experienced unevenly and in very different ways depending on their spatial context' (Brown 2012: 1069).

I surmise, then, that these indiscriminate applications and generalizations result from scholars deploying Duggan's (2002) definition of homonormativity without due consideration of the geographical context of *her* argument. The definitive quote typically given is this:

> *The new homonormativity* … is a politics that does not contest dominant heteronormative assumptions and institutions, but upholds and sustains them, while promising the possibility of a demobilized gay constituency and a privatized, depoliticized gay culture anchored in domesticity and consumption. (Duggan 2002: 179, original italics)

In this simple formulation, homonormativity is not simply read as the neoliberal and assimilative dimension of lesbian and gay rights claims but is an apolitical outcome firmly situated – 'anchored', as Duggan puts it – in the domestic sphere. I actually have few qualms with Duggan's original argument because, in her chapter, this definition is established within a very close discussion of the specific geographical, historical and institutional context of turn-of-the-twenty-first-century, right-leaning, neoliberal politics in the United States.

The thrust of her chapter is a careful and pointed critique of the US Independent Gay Forum (IGF), in particular, and like movements that attempt to push a 'third way' for lesbian and gay rights that tracks between anti-gay conservatism (i.e. belief that lesbian and gay lives threaten existing social morality and political order) and queer radicalism (i.e. belief in need for radical social change to accommodate difference). IGF politics is libertarian as opposed to radical, and argues for lesbian and gay assimilation to the normative mainstream, expanded to include same-sex families. This is the crux of homonormativity, and the IGF is also the focus of the famously quoted definition, which is rarely put in its context, as follows:

> The new neoliberal politics of the IGF might be termed *the new homonormativity* – it is a politics that does not contest dominant heteronormative assumptions and institutions, but upholds and sustains

them, while promising the possibility of a demobilized gay constituency and a privatized, depoliticized gay culture anchored in domesticity and consumption. IGF writers produce this politics through a double-voiced address to an imagined gay public, on the one hand, and to the national mainstream constructed by neoliberalism on the other. This address works to bring the desired public into political salience as a perceived mainstream, primarily through a rhetorical remapping of public/private boundaries designed to shrink gay public spheres, and redefine gay equality against the 'civil rights agenda' and 'liberationalism', as access to the institutions of domestic privacy, the 'free' market, and patriotism. (Duggan 2002:179, original italics)

I suggest, then, that there has been a problem with the way Duggan's concept of homonormativity has been deployed by other scholars – and this is a fault that casts unfair suspicion over the home as a site of politics and social transformation. Duggan's argument is unambiguously located in a particular time, place and institutional setting, with historical and geographical sensitivity. This context is the neoliberal politics of the contemporary United States, with its emphatic strategy being 'privatization, the term that describes the transfer of wealth and decision making from public, more-or-less accountable decision-making bodies to individual or corporate, unaccountable hands' (Duggan 2002: 178), where free-market economics and small governments are valorized. Without this understanding, the quote about 'privatized gay culture' 'anchored in domesticity' is wrenched from its temporal and spatial context. The privacy Duggan is referring to is not the spatial privacy of the home, but 'libertarian privacy' revived in the neoliberal discourse of individual material profit and consumption. To be sure, Duggan later indicates that the IGF is indeed pushing a model of privatized domestic life for lesbians and gay men, one which is overtly heteronormative, as monogamous, lifelong coupling. She cites one of the star IGF commentators, Andrew Sullivan, who says he tried to construct a 'mirror image of the happy heterosexuality I imagined around me', which, as Duggan points out, is aspiring to an ideal, not reflecting the reality of heterosexual unions.

I consequently argue that the domestic privacy referred to by the IGF, and so by Duggan, is a specific type that mimics American heteronormative domestic imaginaries and moralized landscapes. It is therefore a particular ideal model of domesticity, and its wider geographical application to questions of home and domesticity by other scholars elides the diversity of domesticities currently practised. Geographically speaking, why should this 'Northern', US theory apply to Australia? Recently, there has been considerable and persuasive discussion about the problems of applying universal neoliberal theories to Australia and calls to instead analyse the differences, nuances and 'mutations' of peripheral geographical contexts (Gibson 2013; Wray et al. 2013; Weller and O'Neill 2014). Given its conceptual lineage in neoliberalism, homonormativity is open to the same critique. Thus, following Brown (2009: 1497–8), I also argue that 'if geographers of sexualities continue to think of homonormativity as uniform and all-encompassing' and '(un)critically apply it to all mainstream expressions of lesbian and gay culture', we will lose appreciation of 'the geographic specificity' of the processes, experiences and meanings that pervade lesbian and gay lives in different spatial – including regional and national – contexts. Equally disturbingly, this also overlooks the vast range of feminist and postcolonial literature on home as a site of politics, resistance and transformation, where the purchase of domesticity reaches far beyond the private sphere and exerts power in the public sphere to affect social changes (hooks 1990; Legg 2003; Tolia-Kelly 2004; Young 2005; Blunt 2005; Blunt and Dowling 2006; Johnston and Longhurst 2010); nor does it account for queer versions of domesticity that try to counter heteronormative imaginaries and enact new social formations (Gorman-Murray 2006, 2008; Luzia 2010, 2013; Vider 2013; Waitt and Johnston 2013; Cook 2014). This decontextualized use of homonormativity, I suggest, has diminished our understanding of, and interest in, the critical value of lesbian and gay home life and homemaking – understood as a broad set of domestic environments and practices – as a key everyday activity space of/for identity work, social dialogue, political agitation and cultural change.

Transformative domesticities and quiet politics

My interest in lesbian and gay homes in Australia has instead been fuelled by a conviction – spurred by feminist work from hooks (1990), Young (2005), and, for Australia specifically, Louise Johnson (2000) and Lesley Johnson and Justine Lloyd (2004) – that the domestic sphere is a key site for fomenting social transformation, and particularly for understanding and fostering changes in power relations around gender and sexuality. On the one hand, across feminist traditions, particularly the liberal, socialist and radical positions, there has been a strong strand of social critique aiming to ameliorate the uneven gender power in the home life of heterosexual couples and families. This is seen in the liberal and socialist feminist traditions through determined calls for equalizing domestic labour, household power and management and financial control between men and women; it is seen in the radical feminist position through direct challenges to male power invested in control over the female body, contesting repugnant domestic violence and patriarchal claims to sexual rights (Johnson 2000). This domestic focus parallels calls for equal participation and opportunities in work and public life – particularly by liberal feminist scholarship – and so understands home/work and public/private as interconnected spheres of action and transformation (Mitchell et al. 2004). I recognize there are significant foundational differences in these diverse feminist philosophies, but my aim is to point to their common deconstruction of the public/private binary and thus to the importance of home as a political site with public reach (cf. Strauss and Meehan 2015; Pilkey 2015). Many feminists of different stripes have argued that home, as much as work, is a key battleground of change, with some emphasizing its role as 'a site of resistance' (hooks 1990).

On the other hand, moving from heterosexual gender relations to lesbians, gay men and same-sex couples, arguably many foundational lesbian and gay rights claims foreground the domestic sphere (e.g. partnership, parenting and property rights). Certainly, for some, this entails a desire for lives that (at least appear to) parallel 'ideal' heterosexual couples, with monogamy, marriage, family planning, 'standard' life courses and community integration. The homonormative formula suggests that 'normalizing' these lesbians and gay men and their lifestyles is tied to neoliberal political economic impulses, where rights-based acceptance connotes the privatization of lesbian and gay cultural aspirations – via partnership rights – and shifting the burden of social welfare to the domestic sphere (Duggan 2002; Richardson 2005). Homonormativity, then, denotes privatizing and domesticating lesbian and gay lives, removing them from the potential to generate public disruption and linking them (and privileging them) with affluent consumption patterns. I acknowledge that this correlative process is problematic, largely privileging economically powerful fractions of lesbian and gay populations with legal and political rights.[4] But I argue that we should also be wary and critical of univocally linking domestication and privacy to normalcy. Irrespective of the assimilative framing of domestic imaginaries made by queer activists and scholars, the desire to simply 'live' unexceptional everyday lives might be significant for some lesbians, gay men and same-sex couples (Browne and Bakshi 2013). Quite simply, some lesbians and gay men desire privacy and domestic 'comfort', not to be 'normal' but just to be 'content'. For them, domestic and associated rights claims have little to do with the neoliberal impulses of political economic privilege. Moreover, many remain outside the normative bounds of neoliberalism, being non-professional, undereducated and reliant on social welfare. Relatedly, there has been little scholarly consideration of the meaning of home for working-class lesbians and gay men.[5] Rather than 'desiring sameness' (Richardson 2005), domestic privacy can be about desiring 'peace and calm'.

Take, for example, Joe, who participated in *Men on the Home Front* in 2009–10. Joe is (or was then) a 57-year-old gay man, a Christian, a working-class 'white' Australian, retired and on a disability pension. His life is not happy, with regular counselling appointments and disagreements with clergy in the multiple churches he attends for support. His depression is compounded by his home life: he lives in a single room in a boarding house in Newtown, a suburb in Sydney's inner west that is known as a 'gay-friendly' neighbourhood.[6] Despite this residential location, Joe 'hates' his home. He feels constricted in the accommodation and spends as much time away from home as possible. But when I asked about his aspirations, he recuperated an affirmative sense of home, domestic life and belonging. His goal is to be living in a detached home with a same-sex partner in a welcoming community. Superficially, this could be interpreted as a homonormative version of the 'Great Australian Dream' – a longing for domestic comfort, privacy and community attachment. But scratch the surface of this 'homonormative longing', as Brown (2009) urges, and we find that Joe's hopes have little to do with aspirational consumption or neoliberal rights claims. His domestic desires are fuelled by emotional, social and economic difficulties underpinning unsatisfactory living conditions. His homely longing is not primarily concerned with 'being normal' but with 'being at peace'. While 'normalcy', 'peace' and 'happiness' are not mutually exclusive goals, a universalizing homonormative frame can give excessive explanatory power to 'desiring sameness' rather than voicing the complex circumstances informing the life courses and housing ladders of individual lesbians and gay men.

Simultaneously, my work on queer homemaking in Australia suggests that the domestic rights claims of lesbians, gay men and same-sex families can contest both heteronormativity *and* assimilative homonormativity and seek to reinvent domestic life in transformative ways. Such domestic imaginaries and practices might include polyamory and open relationships, families-of-choice and communal households, and resistance to marriage (Gorman-Murray 2015a). Some lesbian and gay individuals and families choose to not live in 'hetero-suburbia', but in separatist rural communities (Ion 1997) or the inner city, and some of my respondents reflected on the implications:

> My ideal home is situated close to city life. I wonder if my reaction to suburbia is an expression of my sexuality. I don't think it is an exclusively gay thing – there are lots of straight people who hate the 'burbs. But part of me says, 'You – meaning conservative suburban Australia – won't fully accept me because of my sexuality, you won't let me get married, make it easy for me to have children, give me equal legal rights. So stuff you, you can comatose in your lifeless burbs. We'll have a fabulously interesting time in the inner-city and celebrate its diversity.' (Stephen, 33rs, lives in Melbourne; Gorman-Murray 2007: 242)

Others, meanwhile, choose to live in suburbia but challenge the normative dominance of the heteronuclear family home by using rainbow flags and similar material symbols to assert their presence (Waitt and Gorman-Murray

2007; Gorman-Murray 2012). Such examples demonstrate that the experience and impact of lesbian and gay home life extends beyond the physical borders of the house and embeds in the wider spaces of neighbourhoods and suburbs. The ostensibly 'private' becomes 'public', and there are a variety of tactical choices to be made about whether to 'fit in' or to contest (hetero/homo) normativity that aligns with personal needs, goals and politics.

Indeed, there are other features that underpin all elements of everyday domestic life and which need to be considered and negotiated by almost everyone – whether heteronuclear families, gender-equal heterosexual couples, assimilative same-sex couples or non-normative lesbian and gay families. These are the routine practices of residential life: domestic chores, such as cooking, cleaning, washing, shopping; gardening and yard work; buying furniture, arranging it; organizing the domestic interior – painting, wallpaper, carpet, ornaments, pictures, etc.; decisions about where to live; decisions about home financing (ownership or rental); how to interact with neighbours (or not); and how to negotiate the neighbourhood, get to work and to the shops. The point I want to make here is that there are complex networks of commonalities as well as differences across domestic routines and lives, irrespective of gender and sexuality, and how normative or non-normative a household is or wants to be. The critical upshot of this is that it is difficult to pin down households that actually match the privatized, depoliticized heteronuclear ideal that informs homonormative homemaking. This is not to say that the ideal domestic imaginary is not important: it suffuses our residential dreamscapes and tells us what we should aspire to, whether we want to or not, whether we try to do so or actively resist. Rather, my political and scholarly point is that between the networks of commonality and difference, there are almost always fractures in domestic life that don't match the ideal and through which transformative effects may filter (Cameron 1998; Cook 2014). Even in those heterosexual homes that appear to meet a normative ideal, there are invariably some divergences: the wife who does handy work, the husband who cooks and decorates, the couple who refuse to marry or have kids because of their social and political beliefs, or the making-do with imperfections in domestic style due to green or anti-consumerist principles (Cox 2016; Gorman-Murray 2011, 2015b).

All of these little cuts, swipes and refusals of the 'ideal', while each apparently insignificant in itself, congeal in complex ways to demonstrate that the home is not always mired in convention or unreflective routines, but that it is a critical site where new social behaviours, activities and relationships take place, quietly, almost unnoticed (Reid et al. 2010; Organo et al. 2012; Pilkey 2015). Scholars can be enamoured with the idea that home is a reactive and conservative site sealed off from the public world where 'real change' takes place in vociferous and pointed political agitation and resistance. But how many 'quiet revolutions' might be advanced in domestic relations, through shifting routines, reworked spaces, generational changes, debates between partners (both opposite-sex and same-sex), disagreements between parents and teenagers and cordial or cool relations with neighbours?

Democratizing homemaking

'Quiet politics' underpins my interest and thinking about lesbian and gay homemaking in Australia: I see homes as vital sites for interpreting social change around sexuality precisely because they are critical forums for understated social action and transformation. The home is a space that palpably situates politics and social change in people's everyday lives – where they can grasp, see and experience politics in action. The home brings together the personal and political, the individual and societal, by materializing social transformations in the mundane space and fabric of everyday life. If spatiality is society materialized (Soja 1989), then arguably the home is where society is most clearly manifested and regularly encountered by individuals in the course of their everyday lives. My concern with lesbian and gay homes in Australia is thus underpinned by the role of the politics of domesticity in identity politics and social change.

While the politics of homemaking are not fully realized by everyone, nevertheless I want to emphasize their potential for lesbian and gay Australians' (and also others') spatialized identity work. Young (2005) argues, like hooks (1990), that one's control over domestic space and the material possessions therein should be considered a universal value of home. To be clear, it is 'autonomy and control' (Young 2005: 152) of access to one's own living space and meaningful things that is key to this universal value of home: this facilitates the security that enables a sense of privacy for intrapersonal identity work (cf. Gorman-Murray 2007). Romanticizing traditional notions of home is problematic, privileging domestic values linked to asymmetrical nuclear families and gender relations, but 'there are also dangers in turning our backs on home' (Young 2005: 154). For those, like Joe, who cannot access and control a space to call home, Young (2005: 149) argues that 'the proper response is not to reject home, but to extend its positive values to everyone':

> I argue that while politics should not succumb to a longing for comfort and unity, the material values of home can nevertheless provide leverage for radical social critique. Following bell hooks, I ... suggest that 'home' can have a political meaning as a site of dignity and resistance. To the extent that having a home is currently a privilege, I argue, the values of home should be democratized rather than rejected. (Young 2005: 146)

Homemaking is not always normative or romantic, and some lesbians and gay men use the 'minimal freedom' (Young 2005: 150) of their homes to recover from and mount resistance to social and political marginalization. When access to a place called home is enabled, it becomes a place where sexuality can be materially reconciled with other facets of self, like familial and ethnic-cultural connections, and is thus an important site for affirming lesbian and gay identities and relationships.

Notes

1 Others have recently noted the broadly negative stance of queer critiques towards lesbian and gay domesticity – see Halperin (2012), Vider (2013) and Cook (2014). Personal political ethics inhibit me from naming specific authors who assert a negative stance, but I argue that citing work that questions this position demonstrates the emerging discontent with extant radical queer critique.

2 This chapter is not a standard empirical piece. Rather, I am drawing on insights from my various projects on sexuality, gender and domesticity in Australia. These include my PhD, *Geographies of Sexuality and Home in Australia*, which used interviews, archives and media analysis to examine the politics and practices of lesbian and gay homemaking; *Men on the Home Front*, an ARC project (DP0986666) on gender, sexuality, domesticity and work/life balance; *Home and Away*, a project with Gordon Waitt on lesbian and gay belonging and homemaking in Townsville, in regional Queensland; and *Queering Disasters in the Antipodes*, an ARC project (DP130102658) with Dale Dominey-Howes and Scott McKinnon that examines LGBT experiences of disasters, in which issues of home and displacement loom large.

3 For example, the way 'queer' often continues to foreground gay male concerns and elides lesbian, bisexual and trans subjects (Gurevich et al. 2009; Nash 2010; Browne and Ferreira 2015). I use this example in part because I am mindful of the scope of my chapter. The two empirical illustrations I use later in this largely non-empirical chapter are of gay men. Yet one of these (Joe) is not typical of the gay men usually represented in popular culture. In this way, I follow the notion of queer as *anti-normative*, which includes highlighting anti-normative examples of gay masculinity.

4 But it is also important to note that the 'affluent gay' stereotype is problematic. Recent research in Australia and elsewhere has found *pay gaps* between gay and heterosexual men (La Nauze 2015; Sabia and Wooden 2015). In Australia, gay men's incomes are 20 per cent less, on average, than heterosexual men's incomes.

5 For more on classed intersections in lesbian and gay lives, see Gary Dowsett (1996) on Australian working-class gay men and Yvette Taylor (2007) on British working-class lesbians.

6 For more detail on 'gay'/'gay-friendly' neighbourhoods in Sydney, including trajectories and transformations, see Gorman-Murray and Nash (2015), Nash and Gorman-Murray (2015a, b).

References

Asquith, N. and C. Fox (2016). '"No place like home": Intrafamilial hate crime against gay men and lesbians'. In *Queering Criminology*, edited by A. Dwyer, M. Ball and T. Crofts, 163–82. Basingstoke: Palgrave Macmillan.

Blunt, A. (2005). *Domicile and Diaspora: Anglo-Indian Women and the Spatial Politics of Home*. Malden: Blackwell.

Blunt, A. and R. Dowling (2006). *Home*. London: Routledge.

Brown, G. (2008). 'Urban (homo)sexualities: Ordinary cities, ordinary sexualities'. *Geography Compass* 2, no. 4: 1215–31.

Brown, G. (2009). 'Thinking beyond homonormativity: Performative explorations of diverse gay economies'. *Environment and Planning A* 41, no. 6: 1496–1510.

Brown, G. (2012). 'Homonormativity: A metropolitan concept that denigrates ordinary gay lives'. *Journal of Homosexuality* 59, no. 7: 1065–72.

Browne, K. and L. Bakshi (2013). *Ordinary in Brighton? LGBT, Activisms and the City*. Farnham: Ashgate.

Browne, K. and E. Ferreira (2015). 'Introduction to Lesbian Geographies'. In *Lesbian Geographies: Gender, Place and Power*, edited by K. Browne and E. Ferreira, 1–28. Farnham: Ashgate.

Cameron, J. (1998). 'The practice of politics: Transforming subjectivities in the domestic domain and the public sphere'. *Australian Geographer* 29, no. 3: 293–307.

Cook, M. (2014). *Queer Domesticities: Homosexuality and Home Life in Twentieth-Century London*. London: Palgrave.

Cox, R. (2016). 'Materials, skills and gender identities: Men, women and home improvement practices in New Zealand'. *Gender, Place and Culture* 23, no. 4: 572–88.

Dowsett, G. (1996). *Practicing Desire: Homosexual Sex in the Era of AIDS*. Stanford: Stanford University Press.

Duggan, L. (2002). 'The new homonormativity: The sexual politics of neoliberalism'. In *Materializing Democracy: Toward a Revitalized cultural Politics*, edited by R. Castronovo and D. Nelson, 175–94. Durham: Duke University Press.

Eng, D. (1997). 'Out here and over there: Queerness and diaspora in Asian American studies'. *Social Text* 15, nos. 3–4: 31–52.

Gibson, C. (2013). '"Muting" neoliberalism? Class and colonial legacies in Australia'. *Human Geography* 6, no. 2: 54–68.

Gorman-Murray, A. (2006). 'Homeboys: Uses of home by gay Australian men'. *Social and Cultural Geography* 7, no. 1: 53–69.

Gorman-Murray, A. (2007). 'Reconfiguring domestic values: Meanings of home for gay men and lesbians'. *Housing, Theory and Society* 24, no. 3: 229–46.

Gorman-Murray, A. (2008). 'Reconciling self: Gay men and lesbians using domestic materiality for identity management'. *Social and Cultural Geography* 9, no. 3: 283–301.

Gorman-Murray, A. (2011). 'Economic crises and emotional fallout: Work, home and men's senses of belonging in post-GFC Sydney'. *Emotion, Space and Society* 4, no. 4: 211–20.

Gorman-Murray, A. (2012). 'Queer politics at home: Gay men's management of the public/private boundary'. *New Zealand Geographer* 68, no. 2: 111–20.

Gorman-Murray, A. (2015a). 'Twentysomethings and twentagers: Subjectivities, spaces, and young men at home'. *Gender, Place and Culture* 22, no. 3: 422–39.

Gorman-Murray, A. (2015b). 'Men at life's work: Structural transformation, inertial heteronormativity, and crisis'. In *Precarious Worlds: Contested Geographies of Social Reproduction*, edited by K. Strauss and K. Meehan, 65–81. Atlanta: University of Georgia Press.

Gorman-Murray, A. and C. J. Nash (2014). 'Mobile places, relational spaces: Conceptualizing change in Sydney's LGBTQ neighborhoods'. *Environment and Planning D* 32, no. 4: 622–41.

Gurevich, M., H. Bailey and J. Bower (2009). 'Querying theory and politics: The epistemic (dis)location of bisexuality within queer theory'. *Journal of Bisexuality* 9, nos. 3–4: 235–57.

Halperin, D. (2012). *How to Be Gay*. Cambridge, MA: Harvard University Press.

hooks, b. (ed.) (1990). 'Homeplace: A site of resistance'. In *Yearning: Race, Gender and Cultural Politics*, 41–9. Boston: South End Press.

Ion, J. (1997). 'Degrees of separation: Lesbian separatist communities in Northern New South Wales, 1974–95'. In *Sex in Public: Australian Sexual Cultures*, edited by J. J. Matthews, 97–113. St. Leonards: Allen and Unwin.

Johnson, L. (2000). *Placebound: Australian Feminist Geographies*. Oxford: Oxford University Press.

Johnson, L. and J. Lloyd (2004). *Sentenced to Everyday Life: Feminism and the Housewife*. Oxford: Berg.

Johnston, L. and R. Longhurst (2010). *Space, Place, and Sex: Geographies of Sexualities*. Lanham: Rowman and Littlefield.

Johnston, L. and G. Valentine (1995). '"Wherever I lay my girlfriend, that's my home": The performance and surveillance of lesbian identities in domestic environments'. In *Mapping Desire: Geographies of Sexualities*, edited by D. Bell and G. Valentine, 99–113. London: Routledge.

La Nauze, A. (2015). 'Sexual orientation-based wage gaps in Australia: The potential role of discrimination and personality'. *The Economic and Labour Relations Review* 26, no. 1: 60–81.

Legg, S. (2003). 'Gendered politics and nationalised homes: Women and the anti-colonial struggle in Delhi, 1930–1947'. *Gender, Place and Culture* 10, no. 1: 7–27.

Luzia, K. (2010). 'Travelling in your backyard: The unfamiliar places of parenting'. *Social and Cultural Geography* 11, no. 4: 359–75.

Luzia, K. (2013). '"Beautiful but tough terrain": The uneasy geographies of same-sex parenting'. *Children's Geographies* 11, no. 2: 243–55.

Mitchell, K., S. Marston and C. Katz (2004). *Life's Work: Geographies of Social Reproduction*. Malden: Blackwell.

Nash, C. J. (2010). 'Trans geographies, embodiment and experience'. *Gender, Place and Culture* 17, no. 5: 579–95.

Nash, C. J. and A. Gorman-Murray (2015a). 'Lesbians in the city: Mobilities and relational geographies'. *Journal of Lesbian Studies* 19, no. 2: 173–91.

Nash, C. J. and A. Gorman-Murray (2015b). 'Recovering the gay village: A comparative historical geography of urban change and planning in Toronto and Sydney'. *Historical Geography* 43: 84–105.

Organo, V., L. Head and G. Waitt (2012). 'Who does the work in sustainable households? A time and gender analysis in New South Wales, Australia'. *Gender, Place and Culture* 20, no. 5: 559–77.

Pilkey, B. (2014). 'Queering heteronormativity at home: Older gay Londoners and the negotiation of domestic materiality'. *Gender, Place and Culture* 21, no. 9: 1142–57.

Pilkey, B. (2015). 'Reimagining home and family: The power of ordinary politics'. *Harvard Design Magazine* 41: 64.

Reid, L., P. Sutton and C. Hunter (2010). 'Theorizing the meso level: The household as a crucible of pro-environmental behaviour'. *Progress in Human Geography* 34, no. 3: 309–27.

Richardson, D. (2005). 'Desiring sameness? The rise of a neoliberal politics of normalisation'. *Antipode* 37, no. 3: 515–35.

Sabia, J. and M. Wooden (2015). *Sexual Identity, Earnings, and Labour Market Dynamics: New Evidence from Longitudinal Data in Australia*. Melbourne Institute Working Paper No. 8/15, The University of Melbourne.

Scicluna, R. (2015). 'Thinking through domestic pluralities: Kitchen stories from the lives of older lesbians in London'. *Home Cultures* 12, no. 2: 169–91.

Sedgwick, E. (2003). *Touching Feeling: Affect, Pedagogy, Performativity*. Durham: Duke University Press.

Soja, E. (1989). *Postmodern Geographies: The Reassertion of Space in Critical Social Theory*. New York: Verso.

Strauss, K. and K. Meehan (eds.) (2015). *Precarious Worlds: Contested Geographies of Social Reproduction*. Atlanta: University of Georgia Press.

Taylor, Y. (2007). *Working Class Lesbian Life: Classed Outsiders*. Basingstoke: Palgrave Macmillan.

Tolia-Kelly, D. (2004). 'Materializing post-colonial geographies: Examining the textural landscapes of migration in the South Asian home'. *Geoforum* 35, no. 6: 675–88.

Valentine, G. and T. Skelton (2003). 'Coming out and outcomes: Negotiating lesbian and gay identities with, and in, the family'. *Environment and Planning D: Society and Space* 21, no. 4: 479–99.

Vider, S. (2013). *No Place Like Home: A Cultural History of Gay Domesticity 1948–1982*. PhD diss., Harvard University, Cambridge.

Waitt, G. and A. Gorman-Murray (2007). 'Homemaking and mature-age gay men "down under": Paradox, intimacy, subjectivities, spatialities, and scale'. *Gender, Place and Culture* 14, no. 5: 569–84.

Waitt, G. and L. Johnston (2013). '"It doesn't even feel like it's being processed by your head": Lesbian affective home journeys to and within Townsville, Queensland, Australia'. In *Sexuality, Rurality, and Geography*, edited by A. Gorman-Murray, B. Pini and L. Bryant, 143–58. Lanham: Lexington.

Weller, S. and P. O'Neill (2014). 'An argument with neoliberalism: Australia's place in a global imaginary'. *Dialogues in Human Geography* 4, no. 2: 105–30.

Wray, F., R. Dufty-Jones, C. Gibson, W. Larner, A. Beer, R. Le Heron and P. O'Neill (2013). 'Neither here nor there or always here and there? Antipodean reflections on economic geography'. *Dialogues in Human Geography* 3, no. 2: 179–99.

Young, I. M. (ed.) (2005). 'House and home: Feminist variations on a theme'. In *On Female Body Experience: 'Throwing Like a Girl' and other Essays*, 123–54. New York: Oxford University Press.

PART THREE

Beyond home

Introduction: Beyond home

Ben Campkin and Barbara Penner

As chapters in previous sections have established, neither homes nor sexualities are self-contained, static, securely bounded or autonomous entities. Instead, their shifting boundaries are continuously shaped by external influences. Even so, clear divisions of 'inside' and 'outside' are often desired or represented, and these often illusory lines are vigorously patrolled and enforced, whether by mechanisms of state or psyche. Although fixed gender identities may be desired, and institutionalized categories may attempt to secure them, gender is also characterized by fluidity, mutability and rich diversity. Hence feminist, queer and trans scholars and activists have worked to destabilize normative assumptions of sexuality and gender by focusing on how they are constructed performatively and spatially (Ahmed 2006; Butler 1990; Rendell, Penner and Borden 2000; Scott 1986, 2010).

In this section of the book, authors from architectural history, geography, anthropology, performance studies, sociology and urban studies continue this agenda through addressing the interplay between the insides of sexualities, gender and homes and the outsides of the institutions through which they are formed. But these authors all explicitly reject an inside/outside division as being too simplistic and describe complex situations where the external is internalized or vice versa and relations are dynamic and dialogic. In all cases, the chapters pay attention to the nuances of connections of the wider social and cultural infrastructures in which homes are enmeshed, to the production of normative values, practices, identities and spaces, and to the possibilities for groups and individuals to subvert or remake them through their own agency. In different times and places – from Britain to Guyana to Israel – they examine layers of relations and linkages between homes, sexualities and genders, looking beyond in order to better understand the ways that they intersect and are mutually constituted or contested.

The contributors to this section also work from the premise that relations between home and sexualities have to be understood through intersections with other identity constructs. In their studies, we encounter discussions not only of gender but also of age, class, ethnicity, race and religion. In chapter 10, Brent Pilkey reviews aspects of an ethnographic project in which he interviewed LGBTQ Londoners about their home environments and sought to understand how sexualities are expressed through and shaped by domestic material culture. Here, Pilkey discusses the phenomena of LGBTQ-marketed tradespeople – computer repair engineers, handy-people, plumbers and movers. The chapter thus draws attention to the home as a site invested with economic activity. Commercial transactions with these tradespeople are shown to work in parallel with transactions in the politics of identity and visibility. The evidence that interviews with these workers provides about the performance of identities and sexualities through interiors and material culture operates as a counterbalance to the testimonies of LGBTQ homemakers themselves. This work reveals how the interior decor of those with nonconforming gender and sexual identities are read – or equally often misread – through stereotypes. It also highlights how, for many, the home is not always a 'safe space', given that clients choose businesses marketed to LGBTQ people because of previous experiences of homophobia or transphobia.

The double nature of home – as castle and cell at once – emerges as a theme in Laura Marshall's chapter, which considers the domestic experiences of three men with trans identities and histories in the UK. Marshall observes that the personal freedom implied in the old adage 'an Englishman's home is his castle' is not equally shared and, in fact, has often been denied – as her interviewees confirm. Rather than having the liberty to exclude unwanted outside forces or express themselves openly, these individuals have been scrutinized and misidentified by suspicious neighbours, harassed and attacked. These incidents show how normative gender regimes continue to operate under the guise of the domestic. Indeed, home can be a site of violence, and can itself incite that violence – as when neighbours justify the harassment of gender-variant people on the grounds that they are defending their homes. Normative regimes require careful and constant negotiation, but Marshall, following bell hooks, argues that, in part, it is through these negotiations and through embodied practices of homemaking that affirmative 'havens' for trans people can be created.

While Pilkey and Marshall remind us that homes consist of multiple thresholds through which the external world may enter, invited or not, Narmala Halstead's chapter instead considers how the domestic can extend outwards and interrelate to other geographical boundaries, such as the street. In her ethnographic study of a Guyanese village with Indian inhabitants, Halstead demonstrates how domestic arrangements are spread out across a series of spaces, including houses, yards and inner roads. The use of these spaces is dictated by gendered rituals and boundaries that work to uphold 'proper' behaviour, especially sexual behaviour, and render the domestic 'chaste'. By focusing on activities and rituals, both everyday (such as the male practice of 'liming') and exceptional (such as weddings), Halstead provides a valuable exploration of the fluidity of domestic boundaries and the role gender, sexuality and chastity play in making them.

The idea of unstable homes, or of destabilizing notions of home, is another theme that runs throughout this section. Precarious homes appear again in another account of an interface between domesticity and markets in Dana Kaplan's chapter about the 'home-like' spaces of the sex industry in Tel Aviv. This is a further case where the rigid binary of home/not home fails to account for the ways in which domesticity can also be informed by – and informs in turn – contexts beyond the home (Penner 2005; Preciado 2014). Kaplan develops her analysis in reference to recent scholarship on atmospheres. She considers how sex in commercialized forms infiltrates the fabric of the middle-class city by focusing on brothels and asks whether middle-class domestic aesthetics in turn permeate those spaces. She concludes that these spaces rather feature aesthetic textures of poverty, and that this contributes to their taboo status – a necessary part of the attraction to clients. The rooms in which sex takes place exhibit an 'unrespectable quasi-domesticity', an atmosphere which Kaplan argues is also commodified within the city's branding, as a mark of a creative and authentic city.

In the final chapter, Ben Campkin and R. Justin Hunt, working in the context of urban studies and performance studies, respectively, respond to an artistic intervention at London's Hayward Gallery as part of a series of works and events that explored diverse practices of LGBTQ homemaking. The artwork, a performance by Benjamin Sebastian, provokes discussions of how the home might be thought (or rethought), written or actioned through queer methods (see Haver 1997; Browne 2010; Muñoz 2009), and of the elusive qualities of the home and sexualities as objects of research. Hunt contemplates and deploys queer methods and epistemologies through a performative writing mode. Taking his cue from the dress-like and tent-like paper structure Sebastian made and inhabited, he plays with the notion of the fold as a concept that brings together ideas and images of home, sexuality and gender. The text itself enfolds practices and temporalities of writing and reading, inviting the reader to make an intimate home for themselves. For Campkin, Sebastian's artwork is a pathway into contemporary debates about queer heritage in London and other cities. He investigates three categories and processes that strongly feature in discussions of housing in urban studies and that are also central to recent considerations of sexualities in queer theories on relationality, domesticity and futurity: failure, heritage and dispossession. The intersection of sexual orientation, gender and domesticity centres here on the question of how those with minority identities make themselves at home within hegemonic patriarchal and heteronormative structures, including a heritage industry which prioritizes the reproduction of certain values, identities and practices while excluding others.

These reflections, as with the other contributions to this section and the book as a whole, point to the interplay between dominant and oppressive domestic rhetoric and practices – which are themselves dynamic and layered – and the possibilities for individual and collective agency to remake, adapt, oppose or subvert them. Specifically, these chapters ask us to look beyond in order to consider how homes are constructed in public and semi-public as well as private and psychic spaces, and to reflect in a fundamental way on how knowledge about the home, sexuality, gender or the intersections between them is constructed, and the kinds of understanding that are privileged. In so doing, they connect with emerging discussions about home as wider 'infrastructures of care and intimacy' such as those that explore the notion of a 'queer commons' or sexual commons (Browne 2015). They also point to the inevitable absences that elude conventional epistemologies and methodologies in understanding the multiplicity of contemporary domestic relationships and home-space configurations, and to the unknowable aspects of sexualities, gender and homes. In this, the chapters conclude the book with a provocation towards future work that exceeds the comfort zones of established spatial disciplines.

References

Ahmed, S. (2006). 'Orientations: Toward a queer phenomenology'. *GLQ: a Journal of Lesbian and Gay Studies* 12, no. 4: 517–42.

Brown, G. (2015). 'Marriage and the spare bedroom: Exploring the sexual politics of austerity'. *ACME: An International E-Journal for Critical Geographies* 14, no. 4: 975–88.

Browne, K. (ed.). (2010). *Queer Methods and Methodologies: Intersecting Queer Theories and Social Science Research*. London: Routledge.

Butler, J. (1990). *Gender Trouble: Feminism and the Subversion of Identity*. London: Routledge.

Haver, W. (1997). 'Queer research; Or, how to practice invention to the brink of intelligibility'. In *The Eight Technologies of Otherness*, edited by S. Golding, 277–92. London: Routledge.

Muñoz, J. E. (2009). *Cruising Utopia: The then and there of Queer Futurity*. New York: New York University Press.

Penner, B. (2005). 'Rehearsing domesticity: Postwar Pocono honeymoon resorts'. In *Negotiating Domesticity: Spatial Productions of Gender in Modern Architecture*, edited by H. Heynen and G. Baydar, 103–20. Abingdon: Routledge.

Preciado, P. (2014). *Pornotopia: An Essay on Playboy's Architecture and Biopolitics*. Cambridge, MA: The MIT Press.

Rendell, J., B. Penner and I. Borden (2000). *Gender Space Architecture: An Interdisciplinary Introduction*. London: Routledge.

Scott, J. W. (1986). 'Gender: A useful category of analysis'. *The American Historical Review* 91, no. 5: 1053–75.

Scott, J. W. (2010). 'Gender: Still a useful category of analysis?' *Diogenes* 57, no.1: 7–14.

10

Crossing the domestic threshold: LGBTQ-marketed tradespeople working in London's homes

Brent Pilkey

Introduction

At the back of London free press magazines *Boyz, g3* and *QX*, one can find a variety of advertisements, including postings for jobs and domestic services such as computer repair engineers, handy-people, plumbers and movers.[1] If the service one is looking for cannot be found in the free press or in other magazines, the business directory gaytoz.co.uk includes hundreds of entries for tradespeople located largely in London, but also across the UK. This chapter takes this trade phenomenon as its focus in an effort to read the intersection of sexuality with home.

The archetypal English home is a secluded space, where its architecture, including walls, fences, gates and even thick hedges, adds privacy to the domestic performance (Gregson 2007: 6). Upon embarking on a large project investigating LGBTQ domesticity in London, UK (Pilkey 2013), it seemed imperative to find creative ways to gain an insider's view of home – to cross the threshold of the front door and gain a deeper understanding of private domestic space. I assumed it would be important and possible to view unstaged representations. The goal was to access what sociologist Erving Goffman referred to as the back stage, the place where 'the performance of a routine is prepared', beyond simply the 'front region ... where the performance is presented' (Goffman 1990 [1959]: 231). However, learning from this research, this essay makes the case that there is no straightforward link between access to domestic spaces and the revelation of true identity. As the chapter goes on to show, while methodological creativity can be enlightening, it is limiting to take an approach that believes identity at home can be observed in any systematic way. Following the seminal work of gender theorist Judith Butler (1990), identity is rather seen as a complicated entanglement of performativity that does not play out rationally in space.

The large research project, completed in 2013, employed primarily qualitative interviews with forty-eight residents across London, ranging in age from twenty-two to seventy-eight; forty interviews were conducted in total, undertaken both in the home and in a public setting. A further eleven participants – ranging in age from twenty-seven to fifty-eight – working as tradespeople in homes belonging to mainly gay men and lesbian women in the capital were consulted; this was undertaken in ten short semi-structured interviews, which were all conducted in a public setting.[2] The interviews with tradespeople did not specifically focus on the homes belonging to the larger pool of interviewees. On the surface, it could seem that these interviewees are exposed to spaces that a researcher may never get to see. Cory, a gay painter and decorator, elaborates.[3] When asked if there are any visible identifiers in the homes he visits that might signify a patron's sexuality, he replied: 'Yeah, pictures and things; statues. And in the bedroom I've seen leather gear and stuff. I do wardrobes and things, so I'll have to get the leather gear out.' This short quote from the interview data with LGBTQ-marketed plumbers, painters, contractors and movers is somewhat illustrative of the views that tradespeople in this research hold, which can parallel those found in cultural and media representations – for instance, the view that sees gay men as highly sexual beings (Manuel 2009), while other quotes suggest gay men are arbiters of domestic style and sensibility (Pilkey 2015). The majority of the quotes from tradespeople do not acknowledge the varied and complicated ways identity plays out at home. Framed against the qualitative data with LGBTQ interviewees from the larger research project, it is clear that the spaces that these tradespeople offer a glimpse into are not representative of the diversity extant in the wider non-heterosexual community.[4] The wider LGBTQ community is heterogeneous, like any other group, shaped by intersections of wealth, class, ethnicity and age, inter alia.

Working with two collections of qualitative data, the following chapter is broken down into two main sections. First, this largely metropolitan-based service industry is contextualized, including with reference to data from both the larger project with home occupiers in London and the subset of interviews with domestic tradespeople. In the second half of the chapter, the focus switches to look specifically at the distinct representations of home offered by tradespeople. But in doing so, towards the end of the section, some contradictions are drawn out in the seemingly monolithic data in order to highlight the specificity of the research material and the complicated relationship between identity and home.

Contextualizing the LGBTQ-marketed domestic trade network

The fact that many of the LGBTQ-marketed domestic services are located in and aimed at Londoners is not insignificant. The connection between the city and sexual minorities has been the focus of scholarly work (e.g. Aldrich 2004; Abraham 2008). Economist Alan Collins suggests that the existence of services like this can be understood in terms of a critical mass of sexual minorities in a large urban area:

> With the growth of new urban sub-centres and with a constant or increasing percentage of lesbian/gay male households, there must exist a critical mass ... at a particular population/city size that is sufficient to foster and sustain higher-order gay amenities such as gay nightclubs, gay hotels, gay gyms and gay sauna/health clubs. This causes 'secondary explosions' as businesses form or move to the location (gay plumbers, gay carpenters, gay cleaners, gay accountants, gay law practices, etc.). (Collins 2004: 1792)

Collins's study remains one of the only scholarly sources to discuss this domestic trade network – albeit briefly. This is surprising, in that considerable research on the 'pink' or LGBTQ-driven economy does exist (Hennessy 2000; Badgett 2001; Brown 2009). Much of this literature agrees that in fact the pink economy, as a concept, is flawed. Geographers David Bell and Jon Binnie (2000: 144) have argued 'that the utopian promise of the pink economy is a myth which hides economic inequality.' Others have shown that media coverage of pink spending tends to 'stereotyp[e] gay men as affluent middle class consumers ... as exceptional and somehow operating outside of normal economic cycles' (Andersson 2008: 92). And literary critic Martin Dines (2006: 136) shows that this discourse is taken up by the homophobic right to argue that the gay community is actually a privileged, affluent group and therefore further legal reform is unnecessary. This body of work, which admittedly focuses almost exclusively on gay men and to a lesser extent gay women, clearly attempts to overturn the notion of a stereotyped, affluent gay community, and as such chimes with this chapter's aim to show the complicated nature of non-heterosexual identity and domesticity. When framing these domestic service businesses, it is important to recall the specificity of their clientele – mainly gay men and some lesbian women, that fits with wider representations of identity in media and popular culture; in other words, a specific stratum of a diverse and varied community.

Sexuality remains a lacuna in an expanding body of literature on domestic labour; however, gender has been a well-established theme of enquiry. Geographer Rosie Cox looks at gender by focusing on the handyman franchise, 'Hire a Hubby', in New Zealand (Cox 2010). She argues gender issues are at play through the construction of female domestic work as unskilled and worthy of low pay, while for male handymen their training is gained in a similar 'learn by doing' way yet these jobs are viewed as more skilled and deserving of a higher wage (Cox 2010 and Cox 2013). Others argue that research on domestic labour usually treats it as exclusively women's work, while men are also taking part in labour in this domain (Kilkey and Perrons 2010). Interdisciplinary anthropologist Sarah Pink's ethnographic sensory study of home finds that, through their housework practices, 'men and women may in fact perform genders that refer to, resist or challenge hegemonic discourses ... or normative housewifely gender identities' (2004: 43, 23). In other words, Pink makes the case that these interactions with space and people are partial performances which allow us to rethink and challenge the gendering of housework as *a priori* female.

While the frameworks of gender, as well as class, ethnicity and race (Gregson and Lowe 1994; Anderson 2000; and Treas and Drobnic 2010) have been key foci in the work produced on home and domestic work, we know little about LGBTQ-marketed domestic labourers who advertise *to* and are recruited to work *in* the homes belonging to those with non-normative gender and sexual identities. Focusing on sexuality would not only address an elision in this research; it would also provide a new lens to look at the role of paid domestic work in communities. In other words, the literature on gender, class and race in paid domestic work draws distinctions between communities – especially class and race-based differences – in that the workers often do not belong to the same community as their employers, and in many cases the latter group's employment of them highlights class and race distinctions between the two groups. However, for LGBTQ-marketed domestic labourers, their work, in part, does the contrary: it helps create a community rather than divide groups of people. Community building offers a likely reason to support LGBTQ-marketed domestic tradespeople.

Returning to Collins's study, he found that there are two reasons that residents will support these domestic trades, and both relate to community: 'It may be gay community camaraderie', supporting one's own community, but it could also have to do with 'more functional possible reasons relating to deliberately minimising the likelihood of encountering homophob[ia]' (Collins 2004: 1792). These reasons for supporting the trade network were cited by both residents and tradespeople. Research participant Sharon would hire an LGBTQ-marketed tradesperson for the same reason she took time out of her schedule to meet with me: to help out the community to which she belongs (a similar finding was discovered in Scicluna 2013). Handyman Carl felt that 'keeping it in the family' was one of the main reasons that there is a market for his services. Carpenter Julie suggests that a client recently said, 'We really want to make sure that we're supporting our community.' And when asked about the advantages of working as a carpenter in non-heterosexual homes, Julie's partner, Carina, also present at the interview, observed that shared life experiences work to make both parties more relaxed and sociable.

The media hysteria around the AIDS crisis in the 1980s and the 1988 law that prohibited the 'promotion' and education of gay lifestyles, known as Section 28, helped solidify homophobia into the public discourse in the UK, which bolstered a greater determination among LGBTQ people to create community ties. Journalist Hugh David argues that the fact that one can find LGBTQ-marketed tradespersons and 'the flourishing [of] gay businesses ... [is] an indirect result of the emergence in the mid-Eighties of a new homosexual solidarity' (David 1992). Remembering what it was like setting up England's first all-gay construction company, founding partner Dwayne notes that one of the reasons he decided to work in the business was because gay men felt unsafe in their homes. Lesbian carpenter Julie put herself in the position of her clients by commenting 'If I was employing somebody to come into my house ... it's quite nice to know that they're similar minded and that you're not going to get any shit.' And as Brenda notes: 'Inviting somebody into your home is quite a personal thing really, you don't want anyone in there who might be making judgments and going off.' Given that home is a site in which one can feel safe and comfortable, the ability to display personal objects that relate to one's sexuality or gender is, for some respondents, important. Despite the progress of human rights in some parts of the world, including the UK, homophobia and transphobia still exist and the fact remains that many people still fear retaliation in their domestic space – particularly older people who may be more vulnerable, and who may have begun to identify with their non-normative gender or sexuality in an earlier, less accepting era (Stonewall 2011). Although many interviewees from the larger study with residents in London noted that they would use these services, others expressed reasons for avoiding this trade niche altogether and this is equally valuable to understand in this contextualization.

The two main themes that emerged from the interview data with residents in London that explain why one would avoid using LGBTQ-marketed tradespeople within the home are respectability, the disassociation from casual sex, and the perceived expense. Regarding the former, Jerry offers a succinct view: '*Really?* A gay plumber? That's actually how porn starts.' Ritchie and Alison both shared the view that unless one 'intend[s] to sleep with the plumber', it's not really needed. And Parker feels 'there's [*sic.*] the people that think "if I have a gay plumber come in then maybe I'll get something out of it" … I don't like that; I think it's cheap.' Those who have the expectation that sex is foregrounded in this service industry may not be far from the truth, which resonates with the cultural trope of promiscuity in representations of gay men, as depicted in TV shows like *Queer as Folk* (Gallagher 2004). Although it is clear that the tradespeople interviewed were not offering sexual services, in seven out of the ten interviews it was noted that being propositioned by customers was not unusual. A few interviewees remarked that they would receive sexual enquiries in advance, whereas others recalled the men who go for a shower and then walk around scantily clad with a tradesperson in the house. Randy believes there's a 'fantasy of the electrician coming into their home and satisfying their needs.' And finally, Dwayne notes he occasionally receives phone calls: 'Where people will call up and ask a silly question. I usually redirect them to a suitable website and tell them "You'd have much more fun looking there rather than talking to me."'

Regarding the second theme of money or expense, prevalent in the interview material, both Hugo and Darrell assumed the LGBTQ-marketed tradesperson might want to charge more than the straight competition. Margaret proposes that, rather than actively seek out these tradespeople, she would 'go for the cheapest [because she is] tight with money.' Dale similarly 'assume[s] you'd pay more for that.' And like a few others, Mario commented that he 'would want the best and the cheapest: my plumber doesn't have to be gay.' Despite this, the expectation that an LGBTQ-marketed tradesperson charges more is unfounded. In nine out of the ten interviews with domestic tradespeople, it was noted that pricing was competitive. Gay cleaner Jackson, who no longer works in the business, was one of the few tradespeople that noted he charged a premium over similar services found in the straight community, but at the time of the interview admitted that he probably could not charge more now given the economic hardship currently faced by many households. This contextualization has begun to reveal that the people who might employ LGBTQ-marketed tradespeople are a slice of a much larger, diverse community and as such their homes may be distinct rather than representative.

A distinct view into London's living spaces

Looking closely at the interviews with tradespeople, this section builds on a theme briefly touched on in the first part: the politics of visibility at home.

Drawing from this small pool of transcripts, the following analysis presents what can be understood, at least on the surface, as a relatively homogenous view of non-heterosexual London homes. Specifically, spaces that fit with a stereotypical version of (mostly) gay male identity linked to domestic aesthetics. It is clear that these views exclude alternative expressions of embodied and diverse everyday non-heterosexual domesticity. The tradespeople's views suggest there are a few telling interior design choices that can visibly identify a client's minority sexuality, including artworks, whether paintings, statues or framed photographs; literature; visual culture from the gay community; objects pertaining to sexual acts; and for some, stylistic flair.

The first theme discussed by almost all tradespeople is that of sexual materiality, which was noted as something often found in the homes in which they worked. Marshal is one such interviewee who recalls seeing erotic artwork: 'For some bizarre reason', he comments, 'sometimes there's a big decorated dildo in the living room! ... You can often see pornography in the toilet and calendars in the kitchen.' Julie and Carina also recall seeing erotic art: 'The gay guy that I used to work for had a big David statue; lots of paintings of cocks all over the place; lots of nude males all over the place.' Other domestic tradespeople noted seeing adult media in the homes they visited. Brenda observed: 'Porn collections are a dead giveaway!' At one client's home, Jackson was confronted with sexual accoutrements on more than one occasion, often as a result of 'wild nights beforehand.' He felt his unaffected approach was one of the reasons gay clients employed him: with a gay cleaner, he notes, 'if you happen to leave a porn DVD out it's fine ... no one is going to judge you.'

Randy also believes the non-judgemental approach to the display of objects that reference sex is one of the reasons his clients employ LGBTQ-marketed domestic tradespeople. He draws a relevant distinction between these types of objects in the gay homes he works in and those hidden away in straight households he visits:

> Gay people aren't shy and they wouldn't put that stuff away. ... [There may be] a fishbowl of condoms on the bedside table. ... I know if I'm in a straight home because sexuality is hidden, put away into the cupboard (with the exception of the calendar in the kitchen of the home belonging to two straight lads). There are no signs of any sexual life at all in most straight homes. I'm sure if I looked under the mattress or in the top drawer I'd find something. I think straight people think it's distasteful, whereas gay people aren't about to hide anything, we like to shock.

Gay cleaner Marshal expands on this by suggesting the wish to avoid hiding one's sexualized material possessions is a reason his clients patronize him: 'There may be X-rated material that people don't want to put away.' Of course, the desire to not have to hide other objects like photographs of a partner and living arrangements also works as a reason to patronize an LGBTQ-marketed domestic tradesperson.

Sexualized material culture, objects of display and signifiers associated with non-heterosexual identities were also emphasized in interviews with tradespeople.[5] Both Tommy and Jackson recalled seeing rainbow flags in the homes they work in. Dwayne notes two objects that might declare an occupant's sexuality: 'Magazines or photographs of their partners', he observes, 'are all pretty "normal".' Randy also feels it is not uncommon to see literature, free press magazines or books in the home. For Marshal, a divide exists between younger and older generations of the Londoners he visits with respect to gay press magazines in the home, where the latter 'tend to have them hidden away.' While Marshal suggests a generational divide exists in the homes visited as part of the larger research project investigating LGBTQ domesticity in London, such a split was not so straightforward. Gay press periodicals could be found in older households as well as younger ones; equally, there were homes from both age categories that did not have any of these items on display.

A quote from handyman Carl captures the way pictures and artwork can identify one's home: 'Pictures is the big one. ... Generally its pictures which show them [sic] and a partner or a gay art work.' Carl was not the only tradesperson to mention pictures with partners as being a key identifier of minority sexuality. Julie and Carina note: 'A lot of the homes we go into will have family pictures of their same-sex partner or their children that they have together.' Even though most items are packed up by the time Sean is hired to move his clients, he noted seeing larger objects like 'pictures of Marilyn Monroe or Madonna, things like that.' Sean's quote touches on those objects that are stereotypically linked to gay-male identity (i.e. Marilyn Monroe and Madonna, among other gay icons in show business) and that have, for some gay men, been idols for their embodiment of the diva persona and strong independent nature (Halperin's 2012 study on gay culture touches on this). Cleaner Tommy also remarked along similar lines: 'Generally pictures speak to a client's sexuality, as well as other artwork.' Sharing his experience of the home he had just cleaned prior to our interview, Tommy recalls:

> The guy today, you could pretty much tell. If you walked into his house you would have thought he's either a teenage girl or a young gay guy – in a cliché kind of way, because there's [sic] lots of male torsos, and a Glee poster which is quite gay.

Of course, the issue of visibility is not always as simple as finding readily identifiable material objects, whether sexualized or otherwise. Shifting away from materiality to interior design and domesticity more generally, one begins to see a more complicated reading of the politics of visibility, shaped by multiple intersections of identity. It is worth continuing Randy's earlier-mentioned approach by looking to comparisons between homes occupied by heterosexuals and (mainly) gay male-occupied homes – something that was beyond the scope of the larger research project. Marshal was confident that there are clear distinctions between the two. He used the adjective 'fussy' to describe the style of homes belonging to gay men: 'I find a lot of gay homes tend to be very fussy on style … you open the doors and there's loads of cutlery and towels that all match.' As a result of this attribute, Marshal feels that 'it's tough cleaning for a gay individual because they'll want specific things' done in a certain way, which can be difficult. Mover Sean offers a similar view: 'You see stuff putting it on the van [and] you think "that wouldn't be at everyone's house", like pictures … nice things, nice ornaments; you wouldn't see those in a straight guy's house.' Tommy agrees: 'They [gay men] generally have fairly good taste in furnishings … it's quite tidy with good taste.' In other words, 'There's decor that I can tell is gay just because it's particular, like if it's really stylish: an eye for detail; I can just tell.' And Randy contends that there are clear distinctions:

> I can always tell as soon as I go in if it's a straight home or a gay home. The stereotypes are true: the straight boy home has stacks of CDs on the floor and clothes around; the gay home has style. … These [straight] women and gay males tend to have a higher disposable income and they have a desire to care for their home. A straight man living alone would just run an extension cord across the floor rather than hire an electrician to put in a socket.

While many of the above excerpts fit with media representations of gay homes based on stereotypes of style and an aesthetic sensibility (Pilkey 2015), with this quote, Randy hints at larger factors beyond sexuality that play into the visibility of identity at home, which is an important factor when looking at domesticity. Here, Randy is implicitly referring to wealth, class and family living arrangements. In an effort to acknowledge the diverse ways domesticity can be experienced, it is worth briefly looking to other identity factors that intersect with sexuality in the process of making a home. Regarding wealth, Cory observed that 'normally if someone can afford to pay someone to decorate, they're in a slightly higher income bracket otherwise they would do it themselves, or not bother.' Family arrangements and the presence of children add another layer of complexity to the politics of visibility. Not only do children necessitate practical homemaking approaches, but they can also demand one's disposable income, which could be otherwise used on renovating the home; most of the homes the LGBTQ-marketed tradespeople visited were owned by singles or couples without children. Brenda suggests that some of the homes she visits might be different, but since 'they do not have kids they can be a bit more expensive with what they spend their money on … but that would be the same for straight people who don't have kids.' And finally, Julie was confident that there are discernible traits – namely better taste – in the gay and lesbian-occupied homes she visits, but after thinking this through she begins to acknowledge the specificity and that it's a bit more complicated – that other factors are at work beyond sexuality:

> Maybe it's the class as well. Most people that I work for do have a disposable income, so they keep up to date, they get rid of stuff, they renew and replace. Most people I work for don't have kids.

Although, for the most part, a rather monolithic representation of domesticity emerges from the interview data, distinctions do appear. These final few quotes begin to show the way in which some of the interviewed LGBTQ-marketed tradespeople articulated the specificity of the homes they visit.

Conclusion

After contextualizing the under-researched LGBTQ-marketed domestic trade network, this chapter has critically analysed two sets of qualitative data, gathered for a larger project. The primary research consisted of semi-structured interviews with both tradespeople and non-heterosexual residents in London. Revisiting this material, especially the smaller pool of interviews with tradespeople, has been a valuable exercise. Despite setting out to access a group of people who were originally thought to see a private back-stage view of domesticity – an effort in research triangulation – the process has both challenged the original intent and, in doing so, highlighted the complications of identity in space. The process revealed that it is problematic to think of identity playing out at home in a structural binary, which falsely imagines an authentic back stage that a researcher is challenged to access. Clearly, there is no straightforward link between access to domestic space and the revelation of identity.

The chapter has presented a range of material from tradespeople. On the one hand, these interviews showcased a relatively homogeneous view into exclusive domestic spaces, which align with known representations and stereotypes. In other words, spaces that belong to non-heterosexual Londoners who likely have a desire to visibly display their minority identity in the homemaking process, who wish to foreground sexuality in the process of hiring a tradesperson, and who are at a specific moment in life allowing for the renovation or upkeep of the proprietary home. On the other hand, the data have also revealed that, even within the small pool of interviews, it is difficult to draw generalizations about domestic spaces. As Cory conceded at the end of our interview:

> Some places I go to are beautiful, very stylish, but some of them are absolutely minging. And I'm shocked that gay men have such terrible taste. I think they're as good or as bad as anyone else. So it's very mixed.

Keeping in mind the diversity of humanity generally, and the LGBTQ community specifically, as well as that not all non-heterosexual households would patronize this trade niche, it is difficult to draw generalizations of the homes these tradespeople visit. Undoubtedly, monolithic views of domesticity are limiting. Rather, it is productive to imagine every home as a unique performance of diverse intersections of subjectivity, including sexuality, class, wealth, socio-economic background and lifestyle choices. Through crossing the domestic threshold, employing a qualitative approach and engaging reflexively in this process and the data it uncovered, this chapter adds to a body of literature that makes the case that sexuality at home is experienced in an endless multiplicity of ways.

Notes

1 In recent years, for reasons unknown but possibly related to economics, the number of advertisements for these services has dwindled in the free press.
2 All but one of the interviewed tradespeople identified as lesbian, gay, bisexual or queer (the outlier suggested 'it's complicated').
3 To protect anonymity, pseudonyms are used throughout this chapter.
4 While it is possible that these participants may be drawing on wider stereotypes in the performance of the interview and/or sharing representations of home that they feel make for more interesting research, quotes are taken at face value.
5 By no means is this meant to deny the importance of material engagement in the process of homemaking for those whose homes include these more visible objects – rather it is important to recognize that embodied experiences of domesticity are varied and complicated. Underscoring the interconnected relationship between material objects and domesticity has been a valuable focus in homemaking literature (Morrison 2013: 415). As anthropologist Daniel Miller argues, domestic possessions underwrite subjectivity through their realization of identity in concrete rather than abstract form (2008: 152). Domestic materiality can be especially important for sexual and gender minorities 'whose sense of self includes subjectivities which are marginalized, and thus not affirmed or easily performed in the public sphere' (Gorman-Murray 2008: 284).

References

Abraham, J. (2008). *Metropolitan Lovers: The Homosexuality of Cities*. Minneapolis: University of Minnesota Press.

Aldrich, R. (2004). 'Homosexuality and the city: An historical overview.' *Urban Studies* 41, no. 9 (August): 1713–37.

Anderson, B. (2000). *Doing the Dirty Work? The Global Politics of Domestic Labour*. London: Zed Books.

Andersson, J. (2008). *Consuming Visibility: London's New Spaces of Gay Nightlife*. Ph.D. diss. London: University College London.

Badgett, L. (2001). *Money, Myths, and Change: The Economic Lives of Lesbians and Gay Men*. Chicago: University of Chicago Press.

Bell, D. and J. Binnie (2000). *The Sexual Citizen: Queer Politics and Beyond*. Malden: Polity Press.

Brown, G. (2009). 'Thinking beyond homonormativity: Performative explorations of diverse gay economies.' *Environment and Planning A* 41: 1496–1510.

Butler, J. (1990). *Gender Trouble: Feminism and the Subversion of Identity*. London: Routledge.

Collins, A. (2004). 'Sexual dissidence, enterprise and assimilation: Bedfellows in urban regeneration.' *Urban Studies* 41, no. 9 (August): 1789–1806.

Cox, R. (2010). 'Hired hubbies and mobile mums: Gendered skills in domestic service.' *Renewal* 18, no. 1–2:51–8.

Cox, R. (2013). 'The complications of "Hiring a Hubby": Gender relations and the commoditisation of home maintenance in New Zealand.' *Social and Cultural Geography* 14, no. 5: 575–90.

David, H. (1992). 'In the pink.' *The Times*, Features (13 June).

Dines, M. (2006). *Homecoming Queens: Gay Suburban Narratives in British and American Film and Fiction*. Ph.D. diss. London: Kingston University.

Gallagher, M. (2004). '*Queer Eye* for the heterosexual couple.' *Feminist Media Studies* 4, no. 2: 223–5.

Goffman, E. (1990 [1959]). *The Presentation of Self in Everyday Life*. London: Penguin.

Gorman-Murray, A. (2008). 'Reconciling self: Gay men and lesbians using domestic materiality for identity management.' *Social & Cultural Geography* 9, no. 3: 283–301.

Gregson, N. (2007). *Living With Things: Ridding, Accommodation, Dwelling*. Wantage, UK: Sean Kingston Publishing.

Gregson, N. and M. Lowe (1994). *Servicing the Middle Classes: Class, Gender and Waged Domestic Labour in Contemporary Britain*. London: Routledge.

Halperin, D. M. (2012). *How to be Gay*. Cambridge, MA: Harvard University Press.

Hennessy, R. (2000). *Profit and Pleasure: Sexual Identities in Late Capitalism*. New York: Routledge.

Kilkey, M. and D. Perrons (2010). 'Gendered divisions in domestic work time: The rise of the (migrant) handyman phenomenon.' *Time and Society* 19, no. 2: 239–64.

Manuel, S. L. (2009). 'Becoming the homovoyeur: Consuming homosexual representation in Queer as Folk.' *Social Semiotics* 19, no. 3: 275–91.

Miller, D. (2008). *The Comfort of Things*. Cambridge: Polity Press.

Morrison, C.-A. (2013). 'Homemaking in New Zealand: Thinking through the mutually constitutive relationship between domestic material objects, heterosexuality and home.' *Gender, Place and Culture* 20, no. 4: 413–31.

Pilkey, B. (2013). *Queering Heteronormativity at Home*. Ph.D. Diss. London: University College London.

Pilkey, B. (2015). 'Reading the queer domestic aesthetic discourse: Tensions between celebrated stereotypes and lived realities.' *Home Cultures* (Special Issue 'Alternative domesticities: A cross-disciplinary approach to home and sexuality') 12, no. 2.

Pink, S. (2004). *Home Truths: Gender, Domestic Objects and Everyday Life*. Oxford: Berg.

Scicluna, R. (2013). *The "Other" Side of The Kitchen: An Anthropological Approach to the Domestic Kitchen and Older Lesbians* Ph.D. Diss. Milton Keynes: Open University.

Stonewall (2011). 'Lesbian, gay and bisexual people in later life.' Written by April Guasp. Available at: http://www.stonewall.org.uk/documents/lgb_in_later_life_final.pdf. (accessed 19 December 2011).

Treas, J. and S. Drobnic (2010). *Dividing the Domestic: Men, Women, and Household Work in Cross-national Perspective*. Palo Alto, CA: Stanford University Press.

11

Castle and cell: Exploring intersections between sexuality and gender in the domestic lives of men with trans identities and histories

Laura Marshall

Homes are complex spaces, imbued with contingent and contradictory meanings and shaped by spatially, geographically and historically embedded social, cultural, economic and political interrelations. This chapter explores the domesticities of three men with trans identities and histories living across the UK, with a specific focus on intersections between gender, sexuality and home. Following trans studies scholars (Browne et al. 2010), the experiences of these men are foregrounded throughout, including through positioning participants' voices first within empirical discussions. The men's narratives illustrate how homes can materially, socially and symbolically anchor identities, values, relationships and emotional attachments and how domestic spaces and their inhabitants may offer protection, belonging and safety as well as insecurity, vulnerability and alienation, simultaneously or at different moments. Interwoven with the socio-spatial fabric of one's neighbourhood, homes emerge as sites that may offer escape from, as well as exposure to, disciplinary social norms that structure heteronormative and cisnormative[1] power relations. How such norms permeate public/private boundaries and contour domesticities hinge upon personal, socio-spatial, geographical and historical context-specific circumstances.

While illustrating certain specificities and pluralities regarding relationships between identities and domesticities among men with trans histories, this chapter highlights resonances with wider anglophone, Western literature on home (Scicluna 2015; Choi 2013; Elwood 2000; Varley 2008; Blunt and Varley 2004; Massey 1994; Pratt 1984; Gorman-Murray 2007). Specifically, I highlight the enduring salience of bell hook's (1990) writing on home as a site of resistance and subjecthood, Anthony Giddens' (1984) concept of ontological security and Iris Marion Young's (1997) advocacy of recognizing the value of home, including as an anchor for identity, while critiquing oppressive domestic circumstance.

Gender and sexuality are intersecting facets of identities, situated within geographically, culturally and historically specific – in this case, Western – ways of knowing, being and relating (Valentine 2004; Goel 2016; Blackwood 2005). Following Valentine (2004: 217), I understand identity categories as lenses through which to apprehend experiences rather than actual descriptors of experience. Importantly, gender and sexuality intimately interlace through embodiment, making embodied, lived experiences a vital and valuable lens through which to investigate domesticity (Pilkey 2013; Nash 2010). With notable exceptions (Choi 2013; Doan 2010; Pfeffer 2010; Sanger 2010; Felsenthal 2009), there is a paucity of research regarding trans domesticities. By exploring the embodied, lived experiences of men with trans identities and histories, I work towards addressing this research gap in ways that unsettle cisnormative assumptions underpinning most research on homes, extend existing work on relationships between home, gender and sexuality and gesture towards productive avenues for future work.

In what follows, I first discuss key literature informing this research, give a brief methodological overview and introduce the participants. I then contrast the experiences of two men whose narratives illustrate the porosity of public and private boundaries by demonstrating ways that domesticities are affected by a person's self-defined identity, as well as how one's gender and sexuality are *perceived* and *policed* socially. Following this, I explore the narratives of the three men regarding how identities may (or may not) be accommodated through embodied homemaking practices and domestic relationships.

Something to write home about...

This essay extends a body of literature that analyses relationships between sexuality and domesticities and examines the queering of ideals, experiences, relationships and spaces that naturalize heteronormativity within the family home (Jones 2016; Pilkey et al. 2015; Pilkey 2013; Gorman-Murray 2008a,b; Ahmed 2006; Johnson and Valentine 1995). The significance of this work is particularly evident when contextualized within the history of writing on home, some contours of which I sketch below.

In response to geographers' explorations of homes as sites of emotional attachments, authentic meaning and value during the 1970s (Blunt 2003; Seamon 1979; Relph 1976), feminist scholars highlighted oppressive and unequal power relations embedded within the 'traditional' Western home and their complicity within reproducing patriarchal labour relations (Varley 2008; McDowell 2003; Young 1997; Massey 1994; Oakley 1974). Subsequently, vital interventions by women of colour, lesbians and/or working-class women questioned the white, Western, heterosexual, middle-class subjects who tacitly figured within (and authored) feminist analyses of home (McDowell 2003; Pratt 1999; Young 1997; Price-Chalita 1994; hooks 1990; Pratt 1984). These critiques of certain feminists' tendencies to narrowly cast homes as sites of oppression variously highlight and re-politicize the values, meanings and protection homes may provide, depending on one's subject position (Varley 2008; McDowell 2003; Ahmed 1999; Young 1997; hooks 1990). In short, 'it is easier to criticize home from the position of having a secure one' (Ahmed 1999: 335; Pratt 1999: 157; Varley 2008: 62). Accordingly, I endeavour to explore complexities and intersections between identities and domestic meanings, values and experiences, interrelations between home-related actualities and ideals, and negotiations of heteronormativity and cisnormativity this may require.

By integrating strands of queer and trans studies with thinking on the home, this research sits between the disciplines of geography, queer theory and trans studies. Echoing wider absences within queer studies, the domesticities of trans people have received scant attention (exceptions include Choi 2013; Doan 2010; Pfeffer 2010; Felsenthal 2009). Queer scholarship has tended to position transness as an 'ethereal act of gender deconstruction' (Hines 2006: 50) rendering fluid undesirable, essentialized identity categories including man/woman and heterosexual/homosexual (Garber 1992; Sedgwick 1998; Browne 2006; Butler 1999). Contrastingly, certain radical feminists (Jeffreys 1997; Raymond 1979) and medical/psychoanalytical discourses (see Drescher 2010) have positioned trans people as reinforcing gender dichotomies that reproduce 'traditional', stable and hegemonic male/female binaries. Such perspectives neglect vital complexities and plurality within and between gender-diverse people's identities and experiences across their life courses (See Plummer 2010 on generational sexualities). Due to the absence of trans people's voices within this work, neither approach is sufficiently epistemologically or ontologically situated within specific socio-spatial, cultural, political, economic and geographical contexts in which the lives of trans people are embedded (Nagoshi and Brzuzy 2010; Davis 2009; Hines 2006; Whittle 2006; Serano 2007; Nelson 1999).

In response, trans studies scholars advocate foregrounding the embodied, lived experiences of trans people and reading theory through empiricism in order to advance understandings of trans lives (TSQ 2014; Hines 2010; Browne et al. 2010; Stryker 2004). This ethical and political approach is central to my research practice and informs the format of this chapter; participant's experiences are presented as extended visual and verbal narratives, positioned so as to ensure participants speak first and for themselves – insofar as possible – within empirical sections. This ethos underpinned a methodology involving participant photography, the output of which structured participant-led, in-depth conversational interviews that explored spaces that participants identified as significant.[2] Home emerged as an important but complicated site for each participant, especially in relation to creating affirmative spaces that support their identities and, with varying success, seeking refuge and belonging away from heteronormative and cisnormative disciplinary practices. This research closely explores the narratives of three individuals who, insofar as possible, speak for themselves in what follows. Where I have recounted and interpreted their lived experiences, I am deeply attentive to avoiding any potential for misrepresentation. I make no claims to represent trans people or trans men broadly, though I do gesture towards potentially fruitful avenues for more extensive research exploring intersections where gender, sexuality and domesticity coalesce in relation to trans people of all genders. In doing so, I hope to contribute towards redressing the absence of gender diversity in much of the existing research.

Before moving on, I shall introduce the participants[3]. Alex is in his forties and lives alone with his cat in Bradford, where he works as a gardener, labourer and trans activist. Alex discussed never having identified as female or lesbian and how for years he felt unable to gender himself, though now he describes himself as a man. He did not define his sexuality. Alec is also in his forties and lives alone in London, where he studies counselling. He identifies as a man and trans man. Alec feels no need to define his sexuality. Tanner is in his late teens and is studying at university in Bradford. He grew up in London and St Albans, where his family still live. Tanner identifies his gender as male and trans male and his sexuality as queer.

An Englishman's home is his castle

Alex: *I've lived in this area for 16 years, I've not wanted to live here for the last two years. And that's because people who know what I am have changed their attitude towards me. ... [One] neighbor's letter circulated saying I was unfit to be around children because of my transgender status. They were new to the street and they thought I was a trans woman. I was*

Image description: Alex is standing on the pavement in front of his home, garden and a For Sale sign positioned just inside the front gate. Behind him is a waist height stone wall and the garden, into which you descend from street level to reach the front door, is brimming full of colourful flowers and luscious green leaves.

FIGURE 11.1 *'With my plants in my front garden. There was a time when I couldn't get outside due to all the abuse but the gardening helped me get past it.' With permission from research participant (Alex), 2014.*

FIGURE 11.2 *'My garden is incredibly important to me. It is my little oasis amongst the noise and rush of London. Whenever I am overwhelmed or feeling lost I like to either sit out there or basically just tend it. It isn't a tidy or regimental garden, nor am I a talented gardener, but it suits me, and attracts lots of wildlife from squirrels in the twisted hazel tree to tadpoles in the pond. I love growing flowers and vegetables. Being out there helps me to feel grounded. My cat Hizzy has been my friend for over 10 yrs. He doesn't care what gender I am, he has helped me when I have been lonely, desperate and at rockbottom. I know that the day I brought him home was one of my wisest decisions. This space also allows me to shake off any pressure I might feel in public, to behave a certain way for example. I swim and usually feel okay showing my chest scars, but I feel safe, free and more comfortable removing my shirt in my garden without potential quizzical staring'. With permission from research participant (Alec), 2014.*

assaulted in my garden by a friend of that neighbor and he was saying things like 'have you had your cock chopped off yet?' 'Why bother anyway, who'd want to come inside you?' He then came into my garden, pushed me around the floor. I got in the house and he repeatedly kicked at the door … I've had windows smashed, you can see the marks on the windows. Marks on the floor where the bricks came through.

I've been spat at, been pushed, had broken bones … some people assumed I was a gay woman … so it was homophobic.

[My home] slowly healed me … on every piece of new timber that went up I wrote hope and positivity and peace and good health, I wrote lots of positive affirmations on the walls and stuff and yeah, I'm free.

[My home is] a castle and sometimes it's felt like a cell … I used to stand at the window knowing that I had to get out to do the plants and saying 'you've got to go out' and I couldn't … a bit of that came back when I was assaulted in February this year … When I move house I'll [change my name] … I don't want it to follow me … I never want to be in this position again.

Alec: *When I moved [from Horsham to London] I was very much at the beginning of my transition … [and] still presenting as … quite a butch lesbian … I was getting an awful lot of flak from neighbors and it was very, very uncomfortable, very, very difficult. I was not happy at all. To the point where I basically didn't unpack anything … I started on hormones while I was there and I pretty much isolated myself and I had a lovely garden there as well but I didn't want to go outside. I basically just became a bit of a hermit … I just didn't want anybody to see me.*

I don't think that visibility [as a trans-man] ever really bothered me at all. At home where I live [in London] I prefer that anonymity … I am quite nervous what neighbors might think, I think maybe because of my past experiences.

Underpinning this 'Englishman's' proverb that titles this section are socioeconomic, heteronormative and gendered assumptions and historical, cultural and geographical specificities, a detailed critique of which I lack scope for here. When evoked here as a familiar cultural frame and departure point, Alex and Alec's narratives immediately and importantly complicate the proverb. This juxtaposition illuminates ways that normative sexuality and gender regimes function within historically embedded, dominant (masculine) English imaginaries of home and geographically specific power relations operating through the socio-spatial fabric. While somewhat negotiable (De Certeau 1984; Foucault 1995 [1977]), such disciplinary regimes serve to shape and limit *if* and *how* one's home constitutes this ideal space of personal freedom from which the external world may be excluded.

Existing literature on trans peoples' domesticities includes analyses of collective living among trans women (Felsenthal 2009) living with cis partners (Choi 2013; Pfeffer 2010) and living alone (Doan 2010). The following comparison extends the latter. Through Figures 11.1 and 11.2 and Alex and Alec's narratives, their homes emerged as spaces imbued with complex, evolving and often conflicting meanings that have been mutually constituted by their *self-defined* identities as well as their *perceived* sexuality and gender. Their narratives resonate with research indicating that most trans people have experienced verbal, physical and sexual abuse due to their gender nonconformity and perceived sexuality. In one large-scale UK-based survey, 73 per cent of respondents had experienced public harassment (Whittle et al. 2007). Trans people often feel especially vulnerable during transitions, when non-normative embodiments and identities can be particularly socially visible (TMW 2011: 6; Whittle et al. 2007). For people with non-binary identities and/ or nonconforming gender expression, such vulnerabilities can endure. As Alex and Alec illustrate, although general concern about how knowledge of a person's trans status among neighbours may threaten their safety at home is common (Choi 2013; Whittle et al. 2007), this can be amplified during the beginning of transitions.

Within public and private spaces, actual and perceived transgressions of normative genders and sexualities often spark violence against gender-variant people. From an objectifying gaze to verbal and physical abuse, these forms of gender policing constitute disciplinary practices that punish bodies and identities that exceed and/or seek to extend socially accepted limits of heteronormativity and cisnormativity (Namaste 1996; Browne 2004; Butler 2004). While neither Alec nor Alex specifically self-defined their sexualities, they encountered homophobic abuse during their nascent transitions when their embodiments were misread as signifying female masculinities. Indeed, experiencing such hostility is not uncommon among lesbians, particularly older lesbians (Elwood 2000; Scicluna 2015).

The targeting of each man's perceived sexualities within abuse is striking. During a violent transphobic attack by a neighbour's friend, Alex's attacker sought to punish his 'otherness' and invalidate his (wrongly) assumed feminine gender through a discourse on sex and genitalia, situated in cisnormative and heteronormative assumptions: that trans means trans women ('actually' a cis-man, hence justifying physical violence), who would want/have genital surgery and have penetrative sex with/be fucked by (given the violent language) cis men. Gender policing experienced by trans people frequently targets their genitalia (Lester 2014), which alongside Alex's narrative, illustrates how trans bodies and identities are often understood as exceeding the limits of knowability, legibility and possibility that structure 'acceptable' social norms. This resonates strongly with Butler's contention that heteronormative regulatory regimes define and naturalize 'the parameters of what will and will not appear within the domain of the social' (Butler 2004: 42; Davis 2009).

Alec and Alex now move through the world with normatively masculine gender expression that no longer attracts transphobic and homophobic abuse from those without knowledge of their personal histories. Their narratives reveal how incidences of and anxieties regarding potential abuse have variously left emotional and physical scars that profoundly and enduringly affect their domestic lives, especially in relation to feeling safe. These experiences starkly illuminate how, for trans people living alone, homophobia and transphobia situated outside the home cannot easily be left at the front door or consigned to the past. Thus, as research with lesbians has similarly illustrated (Elwood 2000), boundaries between domestic and public, social and personal, and emotional and material become blurred to varying degrees, and the rational and contingent nature of meanings of home becomes more visible.

Embodiments that are perceived socially as ambiguous or signifying non-normative genders and/or sexualities can limit one's agency to move safely through the social world and feel secure in one's home (Browne 2004; Johnson and Valentine 1995; Namaste 1996; Elwood 2000). Alex and Alec testify to arguments by trans studies scholars, that expressing one's identity as normatively male or female almost always reflects binary transgender peoples' identities but is also safer than presenting ambiguously (Cromwell 1999; Davis 2009: 116). Importantly, Alex and Alec's senses of their own manhood did not shift through homophobic and transphobic encounters. Yet, as Doan's auto-ethnographic description of her experiences as a trans woman articulates, these incidents illustrate how genders are 'mutually constituted by the performer and by the viewer in a particular space' (2010: 645). This mutual constitution does not guarantee congruence between personal identity and social recognition. Alex and Alec powerfully articulate how ways in which embodied aesthetics are socially registered and responded to, especially in close proximity to home, and mediate how domestic spaces are experienced.

Collectively, Alex and Alec's narratives, images and captions (Figures 11.1 and 11.2) illustrate a complex and sometimes contradictory picture of meanings imbued within their homes and how these are shaped by experiences within domestic, neighbourhood and public spaces. Abuse from neighbours and personal struggles with gender dysphoria have, at certain moments, contributed periods of intense social isolation and anxiety that left them feeling unable to leave their homes. Alex and Alec's domestic spaces have also provided belonging, security, catharsis and the privacy to be themselves away from disciplinary heteronormative and cisnormative regimes. Since his new beginning in London, Alec cautiously safeguards his home through non-disclosure of his transness, thereby protecting his valuable sense of belonging and confidence to express himself creatively and freely. Understandably, Alex aims to move, leaving abusive neighbours behind. Like Alec, he feels his personal and domestic safety and privacy are contingent upon future non-disclosure of his gender history to neighbours. Requesting that his image is not used (Figure. 11.1) constitutes part of protecting his present and future home. Gorman-Murray (2012) highlights instances in which gay men in Australia practice a queer politics of 'domestic publicity', disclosing their sexuality to neighbours to create affirmative socio-spatial relations while maintaining their homes as a space for identity affirmations. Yet, Alec and Alex's experiences demonstrate just how high the stakes can be when one's actual and/or perceived non-normativity is neighbourhood knowledge. Whether through active disclosure or embodied gender expression that exceeds normative expectations, this may render a person and their home vulnerable to cisnormative and heteronormative disciplinary practices.

Alex describes his Bradford home as having felt like a 'castle' and 'cell' where belonging and isolation have coexisted. This proverbial cultural reference, positioning *his* home partially as a castle, illustrates a certain sense of protection, pride and control within his home, albeit alongside 'cell', which (not unlike certain meanings around castle) invokes strong carceral and disciplinary connotations (Foucault 1995 [1979]). Similar concerns and experiences regarding disciplinary practices within close proximity to home have been widely expressed by trans people (Whittle et al. 2007; Choi 2013) and feature within some research of lesbians and gay men (Gorman-Murray 2012; Elwood 2000; Scicluna, this book). These shared experiences highlight how, even for trans people living alone, with normative male/female gender expression and identities, achieving and maintaining the sense and actuality of emotional, physical and domestic security can demand successfully navigating heteronormative and cisnormative expectations and relations. Such moments, where the social, personal, public and private collide, overlap and/ or blur in ways that serve to (in)form how wider socio-spatial circumstances and norms are (able to be) negotiated, have significant implications for trans peoples' domesticities.

As Alex and Alec articulate, domestic privacy and safety away from the policing of sexualities and gender at home and in their neighbourhood – which is not always possible (Choi 2013) – may serve as something of a double-edged sword by offering escape *and* heightening social isolation. Nonetheless, this research extends existing literature on trans peoples' domesticities (Choi 2013; Doan 2010), which further supports Iris Marion Young's (1997) feminist argument that the value of privacy and safety at home should be neither underestimated nor overlooked. Alec and Alex's narratives illustrate how the capacity of home to provide refuge from the 'tyranny of gendered spaces'

(Doan 2010) is shaped by real and imagined threats of abuse. This may be manageable through non-disclosure but remains contingent upon embodying one's gender according to heteronormative expectations.

'Ontological security' is defined by the sociologist Anthony Giddens as confidence 'that the natural and social worlds are as they appear to be, including the basic existential parameters of self and social identity' (1984: 375). This concept has featured within literature on home regarding heterosexual (Saunders 1989) and non-heterosexual people (Johnston and Valentine 1995). Alex and Alec illustrate the potential salience of 'ontological security' as a lens regarding interrelations between gender, sexuality and home for trans people. In reality, social worlds are inevitably messy; they can never be clearly and neatly ordered, bounded or fixed. Yet Alec and Alex highlight the precariousness of necessary conditions for *feeling* confidence in experiencing security and belonging in one's self, home, neighbourhood. Thus, achieving a sense of ontological security in one's domesticities may be desirable. Yet, a trans person's ontological security at home can be seriously compromised by incongruences between their self-defined and socially perceived sexualities and gender identity.

When reading Alex and Alec's narratives, I am struck by certain resonances with bell hook's writing on 'homeplace', which powerfully articulates how African American women resisted the hostility, violence and indignity inflicted upon them through racism's structuring of social relations and economic inequalities (1990). Clearly, the contexts differ, not least because for Alec and Alex racial prejudice has not figured within abuse enacted upon them. While emanating from different sociopolitical, spatial, geographical and historical contexts and oppressions, there are similarities concerning how one's embodied identity can consign a person to living within a public world in which prevailing norms and hierarchies can feel (and be) objectifying and hostile to one's existence. In response, creating and maintaining affirmative homes that nurture one's sense of self and restores the dignity and well-being denied within public worlds can be read as resistance (hooks 1990; Young 1997; Certeau 1984). Elements of hook's (1990) thinking may, therefore, prove productive regarding the politics and value of creating and protecting homes as 'havens' (or 'castles') in which one can exert control that resists and aids recovery from emotional and physical wounds inflicted by heteronormativity and cisnormativity.

This discussion has gestured towards significant intersections between identities, social recognition and domesticity, regarding how achieving emotional and physical security at home may hinge upon negotiating disciplinary practices that punish perceived and actual non-normativities and blur public/private boundaries. In the following, I develop this discussion through Alec, Alex and Tanner's narratives around homemaking.

Making yourself at home

Tanner: University was the place where I finally came out ... I have my own space ... the benefit of being a student is that usually you move every year and there's no on-going attachment to a place.

I consider home the place where I feel most comfortable and even at uni, home was my girlfriend's flat and not mine ... I tend to say I'm going back to my parents for the summer, and I don't really consider it my space anymore ... [Their house] is problematic ... partly because of the people who are in it and partly because ... that space hasn't changed and I have.

Gender was never a discussion that happened in our house ... communication has never happened in that house, whereas it's happened a lot at uni.

Alec: I was never interested in [gardening] but just to have that space and realize that it's mine and I can do with it what I want. And I suppose it brings out a little bit of the creative in me ... [Gardening] settles me.

If you went into my home ... I'm trying to think if you would guess what gender I was ... There's a few motorbike photos up ... but then there's other things that would be considered, perhaps more sort of female ... ornaments and things like that ... they're things that I've kept cause I'm certainly not ashamed.

Alex: I had a family member who liked gardening and just thought it'd be different ... also it was a bit of, 'fuck you look at these flowers ... you can smash the windows but you can't stop nature.'

Living in a house that loves you, to paraphrase bell hooks (New School 2014), requires negotiating domestic relationships as well as performing embodied homemaking practices that reflect one's history, taste and identities in ways that nurture *feeling* at home. Meanings and embodied practices relating to home invoke senses of belonging, of being 'in place' and alienation and isolation that entwine with one's sense of self (Blunt and Varley 2004). In the UK, since home is contextually embedded within a web of social norms and disciplinary practices relating to sexuality and gender that can make trans people feel 'out of place', home can play a vital and valuable role in forming and affirming trans identities and histories (Choi 2013; Whittle et al. 2007; Felsenthal 2009). By placing participants' narratives in dialogue with Young's (1997) understanding of normative values of privacy, individuation and preservation, I seek to figure trans people within her thinking around home, thereby somewhat complicating her cisnormative epistemology while echoing her calls to re-politicize and revalue domesticities and while rejecting oppression where it exists.

Young's contention that homemaking provides identities with a material support, with objects of homemaking carrying sedimented meanings and functioning as 'retainers of personal narratives' (1997: 151), variously resonates with Alec, Alex and Tanner's experience. Through his physical and emotional labours, Alex has found catharsis, belonging and affirmation. Making a space for himself at home has served to help heal the wounds inflicted by gender dysphoria, the abusive behaviour of others, and previously feeling unable to conformably place himself within the social world. Gardening is partly about engaging with positive memories of family members as well as articulating a defiant challenge to neighbours who threaten his domestic and physical security. This passion for gardening is shared by Alec (Figure 11.2). Enabled by having his own space, for Alec, gardening enacts senses of calm, unselfconsciousness and self-expression. In London, his ability to make and maintain feelings of belonging and domestic spaces that reflect his history and identity differs markedly from previous experience living in the town of Horsham, where his unhappiness and isolation manifested in all but essential possessions remaining unpacked. Tanner found freedom at the university in Bradford and by moving away from his parent's home, in which his identity had not yet been accommodated. His sense of home seems strongly attached to his relationship with his partner and university friends, while understanding the transience of his material home as beneficially enabling escape from difficult memories.

Tanner, Alec and Alex's narratives variously support Young's (1997: 151) contention that, rather than fixing identity, homes can materially and symbolically anchor identity and enable continuities between past and present. Through presences and absences of homemaking practices and processes, these men speak of complexities around whether they have felt able to accommodate, support and affirm their changing and/or stable senses of self within their *own* spaces. Moments of dislocation between identity and domesticity for Tanner and Alec have informed and motivated geographic relocations to places where a greater degree of agency over their domestic spaces and identity are possible. As Alex demonstrates, making and maintaining domestic spaces that affirm one's identity and feeling socially isolated and experiencing abuse may coexist. Collectively, the men illuminate how domestic and personal circumstances are negotiated is context-specific. Anchoring one's identity may not be desirable regarding people, places and moments where attachments feel more painful and restrictive than comforting. Nevertheless, it is necessary to recognize and politicalize the value of spatially and emotionally being able to access a home and inhabit affirmative domestic spaces where one's identities, histories and experiences can be located and supported.

Along with hooks (1990), Young (1997: 154–9) critically illuminates homes as sources of affirmation, agency and resistance, arguing that homemaking involves creating and maintaining belonging through practices and objects imbued with identity-related meanings. In this discussion of individuation and preservations, Young includes practices of remembrance – 'the affirmation of what brought us here' (ibid) – which she distinguishes from nostalgia – longing for an elsewhere (ibid; see also Pilkey 2013). Alex, Alec and Tanner have each felt liberation and belonging through homemaking practices, including forming relationships (human and feline) through which they have made and maintained affirmative domesticities that accommodate their identities. Respectively, this has depended on negotiating a certain distance from heteronormative and cisnormative confines, expectations, oppressions and experiences elsewhere. Family homes most often constitute an intimate geography in which, through relationships and practices, heteronormativity and cisnormativity are naturalized. For people whose genders and/or sexualities somehow defy heteronormativity and cisnormativity, having the space and privacy to know and be oneself as LGBT often requires moving away from parents and/or finding one's own space (Pilkey 2013; Choi 2013; Johnston and Valentine 1995).

Tanner, Alex and Alec's experiences resonate with and complicate the above. While Alec and Alex had long moved out of their parents' homes when transitioning during their thirties and forties, having their own domestic spaces in which to anchor their identities and memories have certainly formed part of their homemaking processes and practices. Tanner's experience, however, differs in significant ways due to his youth, family relations and the social and temporal contexts in which his experiences are embedded. Preservation through remembrance is markedly absent from Tanner's description of home, which he locates largely in present connections with his partner and friends whom he feels supported and comfortable communicating and sharing space. His narrative positions his present home in opposition to his parents' home, yet rather than disconnected, this opposition is relational. Much of what he values about the home he has made since coming out as trans in Bradford is precisely what he finds lacking within his parents' house. In the latter, Tanner describes an unaccommodating stasis, causing him to feel unable to locate his identity and consequently uncomfortable socially and spatially inhabiting his family home. As such, Tanner highlights the value of domestic spaces and relationships that support one's identity though periods of change and stability.

Family homes tend to be the primary geography in which heteronormativity is 'naturalised' (Ahmed 2006; Pilkey 2013). Despite growing up in a heteronormative family, notably, Tanner did not experience homophobia from his family during his adolescence when, before identifying as male, he identified as bisexual and later gay. This perhaps speaks of how increasing socio-political acceptance of lesbian, gay and bi sexualities in the UK (Pew 2013; NatCen 2013) can affect LGBT people's home and family lives. However, this picture remains complex, as recent regional increases in LGBT youth homelessness suggest (Tunåker 2015). The lack of communication around Tanner's gender within his family may signal limited societal and personal awareness and/or acceptance of transness as well as established non-communicative family dynamics. However, these circumstances are liable to change and such a shift could enable Tanner to feel that his manhood is socially and spatially accommodated at his parent's home.

Collectively, Alec, Alex and Tanner's narratives compliment and complicate Young's advocacy of recognizing the value of domestic privacy and the ability to anchor one's identity at home as a privilege that should be, but is not always, afforded to everyone. While trans folks do not figure within Young's work (1997: 149), there are key resonances in how social, material and spatial domestic relations do not fix sexual orientations and gender identities but variously support them in ways that can productively create continuities between past and present. Crucially, homemaking necessarily involves having space of one's own in which to anchor one's identity through embodied meaning-making, sustaining and changing practices which are always, even when characterized by stability, works in progress. Yet, where identity-related discontinuities and misrecognitions exist (temporally, spatially and geographically) it is vital to recognize that domestically anchoring one's identity may not be possible or preferable.

Conclusion

This chapter has placed the narratives of three men with trans identities and histories in conversation with strands of thinking around gender identity, sexuality and domesticity. While focusing on trans men specifically, their experiences have salient implications for trans and non-binary folks and literature regarding domesticity more generally. By addressing gender diversity within thinking around home and sexuality, I have aimed to highlight the need to address complex intersections between gender and sexuality without conflating them. Participants' narratives were shown to resonate with, complicate and extend established scholarly work from hooks (1990), Giddens (1984) and Young (1997) by speaking back in ways that challenge heteronormative and cisnormative assumptions around home. These scholarly engagements gesture towards further avenues where interrelationships between sexuality, gender diversity and domesticities may be productively explored (Pilkey et al. 2015).

Heteronormative and cisnormative gender policing, as well as incongruences between self-defined and socially perceived identities, have been highlighted as profoundly blurring boundaries between gender and sexuality, the personal and the social, and public and private. This porosity can considerably shape meanings and values imbued within domestic spaces and render trans people's agency in being and feeling secure somewhat contingent upon embodied practices of non-disclosure and making geographical relocations from spaces of abuse within one's neighbourhood. As work with lesbians has similarly shown (Elwood 2000; Scicluna 2013, 2015), it is necessary to consider how particular embodiments may (in)form and affect domestic meanings and experiences. That said, it is notable that embodied aesthetic regimes associated with gay and queer female identities and trans women appear to register as more thinkable within prevailing public consciousness in the UK than trans men and non-binary people. The domesticities of trans people, like other minorities, may require negotiating disciplinary practices with neighbours, strangers, family, partners and friends (Whittle et al. 2007) that target the property, bodies and/or emotional well-being of people whose sexualities and genders challenge normative frames of acceptable difference.

Supporting existing literature (Pilkey 2013; Young 1997; Gorman-Murray 2009) embodied homemaking practices such as gardening, having pets and decorative objects were shown to be crucial in making domestic spaces that affirmed stable and changing facets of identities. Feeling ownership over a domestic space in which identities could be anchored (or not) emerged as a vital condition for a sense of belonging and freedom forged and maintained through homemaking practices and processes.

Experiencing and/or imagining homes as 'castles' or 'havens' is not simply a myth, aspiration, (contingent) reality or privilege worthy of white, Western, heterosexual, able-bodied, cisgender men. Domesticities are refracted through intersectional configurations of gender, sexuality, race, ethnicity, religion, cultural and socio-economic background, age and ability. Thus, future research must engage more extensively and inclusively with these (and other) facets of identities. Affirmative and secure homes that anchor complex intersectional facets of identities and offer refuge from and resistance against disciplinary norms are to be valued and politicized.

Notes

1   Heteronormativity and cisnormativity are distinct but interrelated concepts. Heteronormativity privileges dominant forms of heterosexual kinship, and gendered embodied practices, norms and relations have historically become culturally accepted as constituting the 'natural' social order (Wieringa 2014: 210;

Butler 1990; 2004). Cisnormativity describes assumptions that all individuals' genders match their birth-assigned sex, thereby precluding the possibility of gender-sex diversity beyond cisgender binaries (Bauer et al. 2009: 365).

2   As a queer, cis-woman I have attempted to negotiate my positionality insofar as possible and appropriate. I follow Choi (2013: 122), positioning myself as an 'outside observer ... and active learner' and remained attentive to potential misrepresentations throughout the research process (Hines 2009). Deliberately broad photography guidance, structuring interviews using participant's images and captions and using a 'narrative approach' in interviews (Hollway and Jefferson 2000; Hines 2009: 92) were also integral to the research ethic and design. Though demographic details were not recorded, all participants appeared to be white British, were working or middle class and used masculine pronouns.

3   Informed consent was received from all participants. While given the option of using pseudonyms, each participant chose to use their first names. In order to protect certain aspects of participants' lives, some information around the precise location of their homes has been withheld due to participant's requests and/or my own judgement.

References

Ahmed, S. (1999). 'Home and away: Narratives of migration and estrangement'. *International Journal of Cultural Studies* 2, no. 3: 329–47.

Ahmed, S. (2006). *Queer Phenomenology*. Durham: Duke University Press.

Bauer, G. R., R. Hammond, R. Travers, M. Kaay, K. Hohenadel and M. Boyce (2009). '"I don't think this is theoretical; this is our lives": How erasure impacts health care for transgender people'. *Journal of the Association of Nurses in AIDS Care* 20, no. 5: 348–16, 365.

Blackwood, E. (2005). 'Gender transgression in colonial and postcolonial Indonesia'. *The Journal of Asian Studies* 64, no. 4: 849–79.

Blunt, A. (2003). 'Home and identity'. In *Cultural Geography in Practice*, edited by A. Blunt, P. Gruffudd, J. May, M. Ogborn and D. Pinder, 71–87. London: Edward Arnold.

Blunt, A. and A. Varley (2004). 'Introduction: Geographies of home'. *Cultural Geographies* 11, no. 1: 3–6.

Browne, K. (2004). 'Genderism and the bathroom problem: (Re)materializing sexed sites, (re)creating sexed bodies'. *Gender, Place and Culture: A Journal of Feminist Geography* 11, no. 3: 331–46.

Browne, K. (2006). 'Challenging queer geographies'. *Antipode* 38, no. 5: 885–93.

Browne, K., C. J. Nash and S. Hines (2010). 'Introduction: Towards trans geographies'. *Gender, Place & Culture: A Journal of Feminist Geography* 17, no. 5: 573–7.

Butler, J. (1999). *Gender Trouble: Feminism and the Subversion of Identity*. London: Routledge.

Butler, J. (2004). *Undoing Gender*. London: Routledge.

Certeau, M. de. (1984). *The Practice of Everyday Life*. Berkeley: University of California Press.

Choi, Y. (2013). 'The meaning of home for transgender people'. In *Queer Presences and Absences*, edited by Y. Taylor and M. Addison, 141–158. London: Palgrave Macmillan.

Cromwell, J. (1999). *Transmen & FTMs: Identities, Bodies, Genders and Sexualities*. Chicago: University of Illinois Press.

Davis, C. E. (2009). 'Situating "Fluidity": (Trans)gender identification and the regulation of gender diversity'. *GLQ: A Journal of Lesbian and Gay Studies* 15, no. 1: 97–130.

Doan, P. L. (2010). 'The tyranny of gendered spaces – reflections from beyond the gender dichotomy'. *Gender, Place & Culture: A Journal of Feminist Geography* 17, no. 5: 635–54.

Drescher, J. (2010). 'Queer diagnoses: Parallels and contrasts in the history of homosexuality, gender variance, and the diagnostic and statistical manual'. *Archive Sex Behavior* 39, no. 2 (April): 427–60.

Elwood, S. A. (2000). 'Lesbian living spaces'. *Journal of Lesbian Studies* 4, no. 1: 11–27.

Felsenthal, K. (2009). 'Creating the queendom: A lens on Transy House'. *Home Cultures* 6, no. 3: 243–60.

Foucault, M. (1995 [1979]). *Discipline and Punish: The Birth of the Prison*. New York: Random House.

Garber, M. (1992). *Vested Interests: Cross-Dressing and Cultural Anxiety*. New York: Routledge.

Giddens, A. (1984). *The Constitution of Society*. Oxford: Polity Press.

Goel, I. (2016). 'Hijra communities of Delhi'. *Sexualities*, published online 26 May.

Gorman-Murray, A. (2007). 'Contesting domestic ideals: Queering the Australian Home'. *Australian Geographer* 38, no. 2: 195–213.

Gorman-Murray, A. (2008a). 'Masculinity and the home: A critical review and conceptual framework'. *Australian Geographer* 39, no. 3: 367–79.

Gorman-Murray, A. (2008b). 'Queering the family home: Narratives from gay, lesbian and bisexual youth coming out in supportive family homes in Australia'. *Gender, Place and Culture: A Journal of Feminist Geography* 15, no. 1: 31–44.

Gorman-Murray, A. (2009). 'Queer-friendly neighbourhoods: Interrogating social cohesion across sexual difference in two Australian neighbourhoods'. *Environment and Planning A* 41, no. 12: 2855–73.

Gorman-Murray, A. (2012). 'Queer politics at home: Gay men's management of the public/private boundary'. *New Zealand Geographer* 68, no. 2: 111–20.

Hines, S. (2006). 'What's the difference? Bringing particularity to queer studies of transgender'. *Journal of Gender Studies* 15, no. 1: 49–66.

Hines, S. (2009). 'A pathway to diversity? Human rights, citizenship and the politics of transgender'. *Contemporary Politics* 15, no. 1: 102–987.

Hines, S. (2010). 'Queerly situated? Exploring negotiations of trans queer subjectivities at work and within community spaces in the UK'. *Gender, Place & Culture: A Journal of Feminist Geography* 17, no. 5: 597–613.

Hollway, W. and T. Jefferson (2000). *Doing Qualitative Research Differently: Free Association, Narrative and the Interview Method*. London: Sage.

hooks, b. (1990). 'Homeplace (a site of resistance)'. In *Yearning: Race, Gender and Cultural Politics*, 41–9. Boston: South End Press.

Jeffreys, S. (1997). 'Transgender activism'. *Journal of Lesbian Studies* 1, nos. 3–4: 55–74.

Johnston, L. and G. Valentine (1995). 'Wherever I lay my girlfriend, that's my home'. In *Mapping Desire: Geographies of Sexualities*, edited by D. Bell and G. Valentine, 88–103. London: Routledge.

Jones, R. (2016). 'Sexual identity labels and their implications in later life: The case of bisexuality'. In *Ageing and Sexualities: Interdisciplinary Perspectives*, edited by E. Peel and R. Harding, 97–118. London: Routledge.

Lester, C. (2014). 'Our clothed bodies are not yours to strip bare'. *A Gentleman and a Scholar*, 4 June. Available online: https://cnlester.wordpress. com/2014/06/04/your-right-to-feel-safe-does-not-outweigh-my-right-to-be-safe/.

Massey, D. (1994). 'A place called home?' In *Space, Place and Gender*. Cambridge: Polity Press.

McDowell, L. (2003). 'Place and space'. In *A Concise Companion to Feminist Theory*, edited by M. Eagleton, 11–31. Oxford: Blackwell Publishing.

Nagoshi, J. L. and S. Brzuzy (2010). 'Transgender theory: Embodying research and practice'. *Affilia* 25, no. 4: 431–43.

Namaste, K. (1996). 'Genderbashing: Sexuality, gender, and the regulation of public space'. *Environment and Planning D: Society and Space* 14, no. 2: 221–40.

Nash, C. J. (2010). 'Trans geographies, embodiment and experience'. *Gender, Place & Culture: A Journal of Feminist Geography* 17, no. 5: 579–95.

NatCen (2013). 'Homosexuality'. *British Social Attitudes 30*. London: Nat Cen Social Research. Available online: http://www.bsa.natcen.ac.uk/latest-report/british-social-attitudes-30/personal-relationships/homosexuality.aspx.

Nelson, L. (1999). 'Bodies (and spaces) do matter: The limits of performativity'. *Gender, Place & Culture: A Journal of Feminist Geography* 6, no. 4: 331–53.

New School (2014). *bell hooks and Laverne Cox in a Public Dialogue at The New School*. New York. Available online: https://www.youtube.com/watch?v=9oMmZlJijgY.

Oakley, A. (1974). *The Sociology of Housework*. New York: Pantheon Books.

Pew (2013). 'The global divide of homosexuality: Greater acceptance in more secular and affluent countries'. *Pew Research Center Report*, 4 June. Washington: Pew Research Center.

Pfeffer, C. A. (2010). '"Women's work"? Women partners of transgender men doing housework and emotion work'. *Journal of Marriage and Family* 72, no. 1 (February): 165–83.

Pilkey, B. (2013). 'LGBT homemaking in London, UK: The embodiment of mobile homemaking imaginaries'. *Geographical Research* 51: 159–65.

Pilkey, B., R. M. Scicluna and A. Gorman Murray (2015). 'Alternative domesticities'. *Home Cultures* 12, no. 2: 127–38.

Plummer, K. (2010). 'Generational sexualities, subterranean traditions, and the hauntings of the sexual world: Some preliminary remarks'. *Symbolic Interaction* 33, no. 2: 163–90.

Pratt, G. (1999). 'Geographies of identity and difference: Marking boundaries'. In *Human Geography Today*, edited by D. Massey, J. Allen and P. Sarre, 151–67. Cambridge: Polity Press.

Pratt, M. B. (1984). 'Identity: Skin blood heart'. In *Ours in Struggle: Three Feminist Perspectives on Anti-Semitism and Racism*, edited by E. Bulkin, M. B. Pratt and B. Smith, 11–63. New York: Long Haul Press.

Price-Chalita, P. (1994). 'Spatial metaphor and the politics of empowerment: Mapping a place for feminism and postmodernism in geography?' *Antipode* 26, no. 3: 236–54.

Raymond, J. G. (1979). *The Transsexual Empire: The Making of the She-Male.* Boston, MA: Beacon Press.

Relph, E. (1976). *Place and Placelessness.* London: Pion.

Sanger, T. (2010). *Trans People's Partnerships: Towards an Ethics of Intimacy.* Basingstoke: Palgrave Macmillan.

Saunders, P. (1989). 'The meaning of "home" in contemporary English culture'. *Housing Studies* 4, no. 3: 177–92.

Scicluna, R. M. (2013). *The 'Other' Side of the Domestic Kitchen: An Anthropological Approach to the Domestic Unit and Older Lesbians.* PhD diss. Milton Keynes, UK: The Open University.

Scicluna, R. M. (2015). 'Thinking through Domestic Pluralities'. *Home Cultures* 12, no. 2: 169–91.

Seamon, D. (1979). *A Geography of the Lifeworld: Movement, Rest and Encounter.* London: Croom Helm.

Sedgwick, E. K. (1998). 'What's queer?' In *Gender Inequality: Feminist Theories and Politics*, edited by J. Lorber, 205–9. Los Angeles: Roxbury.

Serano, J. (2007). *Whipping Girl: A Transsexual Woman on Sexism and the Scapegoating of Femininity.* Emeryville, CA: Seal Press.

Stryker, S. (2004). 'Transgender studies: Queer theory's evil twin'. *GLQ: A Journal of Lesbian and Gay Studies* 10, no. 2: 212–15.

Trans Media Watch (TMW) (2011). 'The British press and the transgender community'. *Submission to the Leveson Inquiry into the Culture, Practice and Ethics of the Press.* December. London: Trans Media Watch.

TSQ, (2014). *Transgender Studies Quarterly* 1, no. 1–2: 1–302.

Tunåker, C. (2015). 'No place like home?' *Home Cultures* 12, no. 2: 241–59.

Valentine, D. (2004). 'The categories themselves'. *GLQ: A Journal of Lesbian and Gay Studies* 10, no. 2: 215–20.

Varley, A. (2008). 'A place like this? Stories of dementia, home, and the self'. *Environment and Planning D: Society and Space* 26, no 1: 47–67.

Whittle, S. (2006). 'Foreword'. In *The Transgender Studies Reader*, edited by S Stryker and S Whittle, xi–xvi. London: Routledge.

Whittle, S., L. Turner and M. Al-Alami (2007). *Engendered Penalties: Transgender and Transsexual People's Experiences of Inequality and Discrimination.* Manchester: Press For Change.

Wieringa, S. E. (2014). 'Symbolic subversion'. *TSQ: Transgender Studies Quarterly* 1, nos. 1–2: 210–12.

Young, I. M. (1997). 'House and home: Feminist variations of a theme'. In *Intersecting Voices: Dilemmas of Gender, Political Philosophy, and Policy.* Princeton, NJ: Princeton University Press.

12

Relational persons of the home: Intimacy, transgressions and boundary-making

Narmala Halstead

Introduction

As dusk falls on a Guyanese village, a few men gather in small groups outside their homes. They sit on a short concrete barrier at the side of the road, which marks a canal from the road, or alternatively sit on small 'drinks'[1] boxes. The road has no street light. The sky is darkening. The men are on a *lime*[2] (hanging out), chatting casually (see Eriksen 1990; Miller 1994). It is a usual pastime activity for these men. One of the men is sitting on the road directly in front of his house. The others are neighbours in this group who have left their nearby homes for the lime.

These houses are usually on pillars with a space underneath, which can be described as a part or full-bottom house – an unenclosed space that is seen as part of the domestic setting. The women in his household are his wife, his mother and his teenage daughter. His mother is lying in a hammock in the bottom house. His wife's sister, who is a migrant, is visiting and sitting in another hammock. His wife is sitting on a bench next to the other two women. I sit on another bench nearby. They are mainly conversing with me and telling me stories about their lives. The daughter is upstairs, inside the house, but comes down the outside stairs at different times, ostensibly not to speak to us. A young son is somewhere in the house, tasked with doing school homework. The men, liming on the road in front of the house, are silhouetted in the dark and visible in this manner to us. The women would never join with the men in this night-time liming activity or any other liming activity on these roads (see Sidnell 2003). However, they advise me that it is permissible for me to go and speak to the men on this lime and take their photographs as an acceptable researcher's activity. I go out with my camera and the men facilitate my presence, briefly, to take still photographs. The women greet me with some satisfaction on my return, as having been helpful in facilitating the photographs of the men. The women's avoidance of such activities and separation from the men liming on what is a side road in the village signal the arranging of a set of domestic relations through understandings of boundaries, place and gendered roles (cf. Abu-Lughod 1990; Alvi 2013; Busby 1997).

The villagers are mainly of East Indian[3] descent and would also self-describe themselves as Indians. This category is discussed here as self-ascribed, part of everyday usage and considered in terms of fluid identities. Some of the villagers can behave as 'strangers' to each other by 'minding own business'; however, everyone is known to each other. The accounts relate to established practices of managing intimacy amid knowledge of contradictory behaviour, vis-à-vis particular ideals. These practices implicate both men and women in *performed* absence of displays of sexual behaviour, that is, avoidance reflects particular roles meant to render invisible the roles of sexual intimacy between husbands and wives, where the family relations of everyday living are arranged through this absence. This relies on ostensible boundaries upheld through understandings of respect. The chapter considers that the domestic emerges through particular understandings and activities that encompass roads near houses: these roads are described here as inner roads and are distinguished from roads away from houses. The latter are public 'express' roads. On this basis, the extended domestic setting includes inner roads as part of an intimate space; the public (non-domestic) road marks off this space to show what is impersonal (i.e. not part of the domestic) and thus ostensibly beyond or outside persons in their immediate settings.

The domestic setting as one that includes the houses, yards and inner roads allows for boundary-making as spaces for constructing rules and managing intimacy at home. The chapter considers this landscape as allowing for social processes *in the making* through meanings and understandings by relational actors where people and place are socially presenced (cf. Hirsch 1995). It looks at everyday and expressed rituals to consider gendered appearances of the person with regard to houses and the land: notions of non-sexuality and sexuality co-reside in these constructions. It considers that persons become visible in particular forms and in terms of larger endeavours that carry and/or transform their presences in minute domestic forms of belonging. Their relations in arrangements and activities demonstrate the landscape, as marked by different forms of visibility of the person, dwellings and roads. These are spaces and places of ritualized routines. In these processual spaces, opposed ideas of boundaries are collapsed or transformed to extend the ways people realize the capacities of being at home.

Houses, roads and liming

The village, known during these years as a squatting area, is seen to be away from a public 'express road'. This public road connects other villages and leads to other coastland districts. It has an *impersonal visibility* (not of persons and houses), in general, to villagers. This is as distinct from the inner roads, which are drawn into people's lives and have meanings as part of the extended spaces of the home. In the village, the houses are arranged along a couple of inner main roads. Other houses have been built behind the houses close to these two roads. A couple of side roads connect the two roads and/ or lead to other houses behind. Here and there, mud pathways have been formed behind houses in varying unstructured ways and relate to the form of settlement where people turned up and built houses of all descriptions and sizes as squatters on the land – occupants without any legal land titles.

As noted, the men who lime on roads in front of houses in the village are visible in a gendered domestic space that also signals the conduct of women through their physical absence from these types of gatherings. The activity and demarcation of this road lime as exclusive to men render rules of the household and the interactions between genders as ideal forms of behaviour: women are explicitly visible in this ideal, where as mothers and daughters, they uphold 'culture'. The appearance of men on the road in front of houses in relation to this ideal suggests that the men are excluded from this upholder role and can behave outside of cultural norms. However, their behaviour supports the ideal: any role beyond an ascribed non-sexual one (mother, daughter, father, son) is made hidden by the boundary that marks what men and women *may do* as part of the norm. Thus, the domestic space is rendered 'chaste' to accommodate the intimacy of everyday living where both men and women 'appear' in non-sexual roles in order to maintain sexual boundaries. Men will behave with an ostensible lack of comfort in certain shared spaces that emerge as a tacit denial of sexuality in these communal settings. Respect is upheld, variously, in different ways in the socialized, embedded practices that are then deemed cultural and can be essentialized. As an ideal, it is also subject to pressures, evident for instance through *chutney* music[4] where initially men began to sing of 'culture-wild' women, too easily flouting conventions and revealing their sexuality. The *chutney* songs, as laudatory songs, are in contradiction of these types of gendered boundary-making. The nightfall liming brings out particular forms of gendered boundary-making through proximity to the domestic space. This is where this type of boundary-making supports rather than upsets the gendered relations in the home (cf. Eriksen 1990: 27). This is so alongside the more general practice of liming, widely, across groups in Guyana and the Caribbean.

The lime – general and situated

The lime has historically been seen to be practised by men and discussed by scholars in relation to the Victorian respectability–reputation paradigm (see Eriksen 1990) that marked colonial settings into which Africans,[5] Indians and other groups were transplanted. Historically, Africans who were liming on street corners did so away from their homes: the reputation was not about helping to uphold the respectability of women within the home but about their sexual exploits and conquests, hence the need to be away from the eyes of those 'at home'. Daniel Miller points to this overt reputational behaviour in Trinidad in the practice of men having *deputies* – one or more lovers, along with their wives (1994: 92). This relates to the historical context of sexual conquests where 'macho men' have lovers, along with their wives and as reputational markers. The lime has visibly shifted from this male reputational space and, at the same time, delinquent behaviour in relation to the respectability ethos to become an acceptable form of hanging out in wider settings of partying and socializing in the Caribbean. Eriksen notes how liming depends on 'its own negation', embedded in representing core Trinidadian values and 'anti-structure' (1990: 40).

Given the larger understandings of liming as discussed above and particular understandings of its origins, men liming at nightfall might be seen as an incorporation/crossover into another ethnic group's more general liming activity. However, the at-dusk/nightfall lime by men on inner roads near their homes presents extended domestic spaces in everyday relations: this returns to boundary-making that occurs as a contributory process to the in-group relations. Changes relate to ideas of non-ethnic relations rather than to a crossover from the ethnic group.[6] The gendered interactions rely on the performing[7] of an explicit boundary for the benefit of in-group relations. The configuring of domestic spaces in relation to the lime among Indians in this Guyanese village suggests the ethnic space of distinctive identity, overtly cultural. Of significance, is both the configuring of domestic spaces in relation to the lime among Indians in this Guyanese village and the understanding of behaviour while, in one instance, overtly cultural is also about everyday forms of living that include the non-ethnic. Thus, this is not about engaging with an outsider ethnic group, but rather about demonstrating an identity that challenges the ethnic prescribed identity – a social field of relations in the contemporary (cf. Bourdieu 1977). Men and women also show themselves as not fixed in a cultural setting as a form of belonging occurring through critical scrutiny and distance, that is, a non-ethnic space (see Halstead 2012 for extended discussions on this non-ethnicity). The villagers in these accounts do not represent the unified norms of any one particular religion, but rather an ethnic identity that, while conceived as different to other ethnic groups, is more than ethnic or religious-bound outside of context-specific settings.

Regional scholarship on Guyana and the Caribbean has brought out a polarization of ethnic groups (see Premdas 1996, for instance) and ascription of Indians into a closed space, culture-bound and devoid of creativity (see Munasinghe 2008, for instance, for a critique of this position and wider discussion on the issue). Note, however, Lee Drummond's (1980) work where he discusses Indians in Guyana in a cultural continuum as a fluid space beyond the ascribed closed identity. Hindus and Muslims, as well as Christians, can and do belong to one household; however, in this village, Hindu practices are dominant, such as weddings and ceremonies of worship, which take place within homes and extended spaces of the home. For instance, a Muslim wife who is married to a Hindu notes that she 'keeps up' (carries out) Jandhi ceremonies (Hindu ceremonies of worship for/with her Hindu husband). They would hold a Jandhi at least once yearly where many villagers and others would accept invitations to attend this ceremony in their home (see Jayawardena 1980). At an everyday level, there are more spaces for cultural contradictions that can insufficiently *show* a fluid identity. This fluidity occurs in a setting where implicit relations also rely on fixed ideas that resurface as gendered boundaries. These forms of gendered boundary-making emerge in the constructions of the inner roads as part of the house.

Women, 'talk name' and liming

While the inner roads *belong* to the houses and are thus part of the domestic spaces, these explicitly bring out a separation between women and the extended spaces occupied by men when they are seen to linger or stand as if in a lime. As indicated, women are not expected to linger on the inner roads. They will very rarely be on these inner roads, either during the day or at nightfall, for any length of time without a purpose. Exceptions relate to where a particular transformation occurs of an inner road into an explicit communal inner domestic space, such as at weddings. Houses and their extended physical spaces – the yards and, on some occasions, the roads in front – become literally known as wedding houses. In this particular village, there were no examples of women liming in front of houses (cf. Miller 1994: 48 on accounts in Trinidad). In a not-too-distant village on the same coastland, a few women would meet on the public road to lime, but never within the inner roads. In this instance, where this particular group felt 'easy' about meeting to hang out and talk as girl-friends in this public setting, they still maintained household boundaries by not liming on inner roads. Consider, again, the impersonal visibility of this public road that is not seen to be an extension of the house.

Those women and girls who are seen to transgress the boundary against liming on inner roads, where their presence is outside of any *accepted* extended transformed domestic space, attract 'talk-name' as a form of reputational loss. Their behaviour is discussed 'in secret' and considered wanting among one or more 'insider groups'[8] in the village. This is not idle or even *acknowledged gossip*: it has a differential presence in any mode of unifying a group or community. This is where it separates individuals whose behaviour, if known, would *affect* the group. It also serves to affirm individual self-worth (see Gluckman 1963; Paine 1967; Wilson 1974). Further, many find talk-name distasteful and would note the small number of individuals who haphazardly engage with one or more individuals – sometimes one person talking 'secretly' to another (but where others can overhear) at ceremonial events – who transgress respect by indulging in talk-name. Some efforts are made to limit this behaviour by others concerned with upholding respect as part of 'proper' group standards.

In the main village discussed here, a young girl would on occasion be seen to walk out on one of the two main inner roads with a young man. At times, the youth would have other male friends with him while he was walking out with the girl. Women, observing and discussing this behaviour, did not see it as a lime in the sense that the group were not really still (congregating for any period in one area) and they accompanied the others who had visibility as a couple; the very presence of this young girl 'walking out', being seen with a young man on the road outside of any known formal relationship, was a problem. This was a road of the houses as distinct from the public road. The 'talk-name' that ensued around her actions, where neighbours and others discussed her behaviour as something they would not do, rendered it in this problem category.

The young girl did not understand that she was transgressing a boundary. She had been allowed by her mother to travel singly to visit relatives in another country. She had travelled a number of times outside of the country on boats that plied the then unregulated border journeys between Guyana and Suriname. Later, she became a single mother. The young man failed to marry her. The women who had noted her behaviour felt that her actions, in being visible on the inner road, had led to this plight. By failing to observe the physical boundary on this inner road, she had also revealed herself as sexually available in a manner where it was not necessary to observe propriety or to consider the opinions of others in the village. It also became 'necessary' for the young man to take advantage of her and to leave her to become an unmarried single mother.

The capacity of these inner roads to disturb the equilibrium of how relationships are managed in intimate everyday settings further comes out in the way a mother notes, with some pride, that her daughters will never stand on these roads. They leave their homes to go to school in neighbouring districts and return promptly. Often, she would keep a watch to ensure they were at home and occupied with their 'school books'. The attentiveness to gendered boundary-making as a form of upholding respect further comes out in communal television-watching in the home. This also demonstrates the ascribed publicness of non-sexual capacities of persons as a *mode of intimacy* in domestic settings.

Communal spaces, respect and agency

Television in domestic spaces, more accessible after 1992, affords new opportunities for these boundaries to be displayed: mothers will note the proper behaviour of their girl-children in having the decency (shame) to move from communal spaces when romantic scenes appear in films or soap operas on the TV screen (see Halstead 2009 for extended discussions). One young girl noted how she would 'bend my head' when such scenes appeared on the screen if she was watching television in a communal space with men in the household, in particular, her father. Amid these forms of expressing shame are some – but not all – older woman, who expressly go against the boundary in a way that suggests a transformation of women's role. However, this might also be read as expressions of empowerment: this is where these women readily change their visibility to those who do not have to maintain their sexuality as invisible.

Examples include women who will curse in communal settings to at times 'shocked' laughter by visiting younger male relatives (at ceremonial events) and where they are often ignored by men and women in their behaviour. Note also other examples where an older woman would be accused of watching 'naked-skin' people on TV with too much comfort in such viewing and/or openly watching the 'immoral' soap opera, the *Young and Restless*, to the discomfort of men in the household (see Halstead 2009). This compares with a body of literature where women can move from the 'known' cultural upholder role and/ or have 'insider spaces' to express their agency and resistance. Lila Abu-Lughod

(1990) discusses these insider spaces in her work on the Bedouin and also shows changes in shared spaces where some women flout conventions. Relatedly, Jane Cowan (1991) discusses the Greek *kafenio* (coffee shops) to bring out new spaces for women 'acting out' in what were overtly dominant male settings. These women, *seen* to be behaving in a contra-traditional manner, represent a separate space as both sexual and non-sexual. This is where their lack of propriety is deemed to be secondary in favour of a new space to express their agency beyond particular kinds of gendered domestic boundary-making.

Boundary-making and the domestic

The older women could be similarly described in some contexts as flouting tradition in particular rituals where they have 'alternative' visibility alongside the greater emphasis on the appropriate behaviour of women. However, there are accepted spaces for women to overturn certain traditional settings and boundaries. This is particularly so at Hindu wedding ceremonies. Consider the Friday nightfall ceremony known as *dig-dutty* (*matakore* in Trinidad), which is held prior to the main Sunday wedding ceremony of these week-long celebrations. The latter part of this dig-dutty ceremony brings out the presence of women 'performing outside culture'. In this ceremony, the mother of the bride-to-be would go forth out of the house to lead a party of women to perform a ritual on the road as part of the wedding ceremonies; as the party of women led by the mother leaves the house, it would have a subdued and ultra-respectable appearance. Somewhere in the background and away from the group would be male *tassa* drummers, silent and waiting to be invited to beat their drums. The nightfall ceremony at a far part of the road (a more impersonal space or that leading to one) would involve literally digging the earth to make an offering with various items for the blessing of the couple.[9] Once the ritual has been performed, the subdued form of the celebration shifts dramatically. The first indication of this, to distant onlookers, is the sudden loud tassa drumming, as the drummers join the women-only party and walk alongside the mother, who leads the other women and dances with them as she makes her way back to the house. The mother does not have an option not to dance – it is a celebratory dance to show her joy at the completion of the ritual and her happiness for the overall wedding event. Other women also have to join in – the road itself is transformed through this dancing and the women's control of it for this celebratory event. This control can also be marked by laughter at specific dancing styles, not dissimilar to that which might be present at hen parties elsewhere and other women-only events such as bridal showers. The men keep away, historically, from this party of women in their triumphant dancing on the roads as they return to the wedding house, where personal and impersonal boundaries – roads and behaviour – are in an overturning of demarcated gendered visibility. As indicated, the house becomes converted into a wedding house, with tents in the yard and other physical arrangements for the weddings. Some of the spaces on the road in front of the wedding houses are also converted into areas where a few men would congregate. The dancing women, returning from the dig-dutty roadside ceremony, would go past the men, who would be gathered outside on the road or in the yard of the house; the women do so, leaving the periphery of the public road, to 'own' the inner road in their open, transgressive celebratory dance. The women would venture inside the house or a select area at the side or back of the house to continue a women-only celebration indoors – men are not expected to go into this area and those who do venture at their own peril and can expect to be the target of women's mockery and related behaviour. The event is known to continue into more suggestive sexual dancing between the women, where some take on roles of men in their dancing and performances on some occasions. The ritualistic dancing and event are an accepted part of wedding celebrations that unveil and hide the different roles of women in making boundaries. Note that, in more recent times, this dancing has spilled over into communal settings, marking particular transformations in terms of gendered roles and popular cultural expressions that also signal new spaces and negotiations for the gendered making of boundaries. This also relates to the shift in the idea of the unattractive, sexually unappealing older woman, implicitly presenced in everyday settings and overtly taking on 'community roles' at Hindu wedding ceremonies, for instance: examples can include the behaviour of a pandit helper, *Nowa*, who can exercise the 'older woman's space to use bad language without the need to consider respect issues (see Halstead 2001); an extreme visibility of this image of the sexually unappealing woman is that of the *Lucknee*, an older female who acts as a chaperone to the bride and groom. In *Kanyadaan* (gift of the maiden) wedding ceremonies, the Lucknee would usually accompany the bride and groom to the groom's home (usually his parents' home). This is also where the idea of Lucknee's non-sexuality is considered 'helpful'.

Lucknee

The Lucknee is expected to deter sexual relations for a particular 'post-wedding' ritual when the bride leaves with her husband to go to her marital home. The Lucknee travels and remains with the bride and groom for a week in these ceremonies and is a present-day figure in many Guyanese wedding ceremonies, in this village and elsewhere. The figure of the Lucknee is one much derided in popular culture[10] and resurfaces in comical attempts in Bollywood/Hindi films, for instance, by the groom to separate this chaperone from the bride. The Lucknee is there to keep watch over the bride so that there can be no consummation of the marriage before the bride returns to her parents' home for another ritual. Following this later ritual, she would then proceed again to her new home to commence her life as a married woman. The presence of the Lucknee adds to the merriment of celebrations, where there would be music and dancing amid the reception for the bride to meet invitees and receive gifts. The Lucknee is known as someone who 'sleeps between the couple'. However, she can be expected to keep the bride totally away from the groom so that the groom is not encouraged to be in the same room as the bride. The Lucknee sleeps at her side; there are many joking stories in circulation of brides and grooms circumventing Lucknees and this custom in order to be together. However, the presence of the Lucknee and the practice point to the envisaging of the larger collective setting: at the start of their lives together, the bride and groom are drawn into a collective setting where sexuality is publicly de-emphasized in one context.

The Lucknee enters into a performative space of unattractiveness – a person who must necessarily not be seen to encourage sex, where this ability can be supported by daunting appearance and attitudes. This restraint being imposed on the already married couple speaks to their relational appearance in communal settings where they first appear as married couples, through avoidance in favour of rituals performed with their relatives in their respective homes and where these ritualistic spaces will carry them forward into their new lives as part of being relational persons. The idea of a Lucknee as unattractive and unsexy also relates to the positioning of older women as prescribed upholders of respect and other relational practices in the domestic setting. This positioning, however, inadequately covers other behaviour where some women explicitly overturn their gendered visibility and claim other roles such as those that are also acceptable in remaking gendered forms of allowable boundaries. Thus, the idea of women as upholders of culture through particular types of public chaste behaviour, for instance, is also affected by other displays of changes in domestic communal settings.

Domestic boundary-making

The work of domestic boundary-making in ordering relations bears some limited comparison to how spaces and roles are conceived in gendered or other types of opposition to merit understandings of rules and sanctions in a given set of relations. Pierre Bourdieu (1977) points to such oppositions, variously bringing out the different treatment of the house and the space of intimacy that is conceived in relation to women as being of the house. Anjum Alvi (2013) notes how the domestic travels through *burqa* clothing: this is where, among Pakistani Punjab, women retain visibility as being within the house when present at the marketplace. They are fully covered by their clothing as a form of protection.

The notion of men having rights to outside spaces in their role as protectors marks some of these oppositions, but where some of the contemporary literature has engaged the oppressed–empowered divide of women seen to be without agency, this is also where women's positioning within the domestic attracts larger universal and geopolitical pressures in relation to universal understandings of human rights.[11] Counterarguments point to spaces for empowerment in such gendered divides. The positions of women as lacking voice and agency rest on essentialist constructs of religious–cultural practices: this position *becomes* evident in discourses about women needing protection against those who proclaim they are oppressed as simplistic notions in relation to universal rights versus cultural rights debates (see, for instance, Abu-Lughod 2002). This is also where it has contrasting visibility in bids by activists and others for rights against oppressive cultural practices. In this Guyanese context, these debates do not arise in the same way in the sense that women do not emerge as oppressed through 'popular' cultural rights issues.[12] Thus, change responds not simply to external rights 'pressures' as part of macro-dynamics, but also to how different experiences and aspects of a fluid identity are experienced. Public–private spaces, as extended spaces of the house, are configured and reconfigured to bring out these relations and to encompass change.

Concluding notes

Certain everyday practices and more formal ritualistic ceremonies have brought out varied negotiations of these forms of boundary-making as those that helped to produce and maintain extended domestic settings. These interactions, as part of the domestic, demonstrated relational modes of belonging where both men and women took on roles through the physical arrangement of space as extended domestic settings and their differing visibility in these spaces. The attentiveness to physical arrangements showed that, within fluid settings of public behaviour, forms of boundary-making still occurred that served to re-establish particular understandings of the domestic.

Being at home drew in the cultural modes of the boundary as everyday modes that were concerned with idealized understandings of behaviour and cultural practices to show that such ideals allowed for the management of close social relations in 'acceptable ways'. The capacities of men and women as sexual persons were both subsumed alongside rituals that also allowed expressions of sexuality. In an everyday guided by socio-cultural change and talk-name, household members were variously socialized into appropriate modes of behaviour that are expressed in physical boundaries and avoidance strategies and that rely on different configurations of the house – its extended spaces have differing explicit and implicit visibility in everyday relational arrangements.

Notes

1 A term used for small wooden 'crate-type' boxes that hold twenty-four bottles for soft drinks.

2 Eriksen (1990: 94) notes: 'The etymology of the word liming is obscure. It is a Trinidadian word, probably of recent origin since English has been a popular language in Trinidad for less than a century. It means, roughly, "hanging around" – but as I shall argue, there is no exact linguistic or cultural equivalent to liming in cultural contexts with which most of us are familiar.' See also Miller (1994: 33–5).

3 This classification of East Indian is in the Guyanese census and also used as a formal mode by East Indians. More generally, they describe themselves and are known as Indians. *East Indian* is also a term used in the Caribbean to describe persons who can trace their ancestry to India and to distinguish them from West Indians, seen to be largely those of African descent but also including others – these latter persons are also those who self-describe themselves as West Indians. Further, this term of *West Indian* is also used generally, particularly in diasporic locations such as New York, where it also has instrumentalist value to identify heterogeneous groups under one label. See Baumann (1998) for a related discussion of how different groups are homogenized in Southall, UK.

4 Literally, *hot music*. Women, latterly, are also chutney singers and dancers.

5 Also described and self-described as blacks.

6 The non-ethnic relates to Sydney Mintz's (1996) discussion of openness (see also Foner 1998), but is considered here to unveil the negotiations of an identity in and out of an essentialized category, where openness is part of this identity.

7 See Murphy (1964) for a different type of boundary-making where men don the veil for status. See also Busby's (1997) work for how men and women are fixed in gendered roles in South India and have negotiable and performative spaces for defining shifting forms of gender in Melanesia.

8 This notion of insidership excludes the person who is the subject of the talk-name and those who might disapprove of such talk-name, including other women and men. It does not exclude 'strangers' such as the anthropologist

who might be drawn into their confidences (Wilson 1974; see, however, Frankenberg 1957, as cited in Gluckman 1963: 312).

9 See also https://reshirish.wordpress.com/2009/10/21/indo-caribbean-hindu-wedding/.

10 See the description of choosing a Lucknee in Malcolm's Alves fictional work (2008) about an Indian wedding in Guyana, where he notes how the Lucknee had to be selected on the basis of being sexually unattractive.

11 See Abu-Lughod's critique of how this positions Muslim women as those needing to be saved (2002).

12 While cultural practices are part of people's everyday, and there has been some recent focus on domestic violence by nongovernmental organizations and external funding agencies alongside increased reporting of such violence, this is not seen as a culture-specific issue in the way, for instance, certain cultural issues in other countries are seen as detrimental to universal human rights (see Cowan et al. 2001).

References

Abu-Lughod, L. (1990). 'The romance of resistance. Tracing transformations of power through Bedouin women'. *American Ethnologist* 17, no. 1: 41–55.

Abu-Lughod, L. (2002). 'Do Muslim women really need saving? Anthropological reflections on cultural relativism and its others'. *American Ethnologist* 103, no. 3: 783–90.

Alves, M. (2008). *Once Upon a Time in Berbice*. Raleigh, NC: Lulu Publishers.

Alvi, A. (2013). 'Concealment and revealment: The Muslim veil in context'. *Current Anthropology* 54, no. 2: 177–99.

Baumann, G. (1998). *Contesting Culture. Discourse of Identity in Multi-Ethnic London*. Cambridge: Cambridge University of Press.

Bourdieu, P. (1977). *Outline of a Theory of Practice*. Translated by Richard Nice. Cambridge: Cambridge University Press.

Busby, C. (1997). 'Permeable and partible persons: A comparative analysis of gender and body in South India and Melanesia'. *The Journal of the Royal Anthropological Institute* 3, no. 2: 261–78.

Cowan, J. (1991). '"Going out for coffee?" Contesting the grounds of gendered pleasures in Everyday Sociability'. In *Contested Identities: Gender and Kinship in Modern Greece*, edited by P. Loizos and E. Papataxiachris, 180–201. Princeton, NJ: Princeton University Press.

Cowan, J., M.-B. Dembour and R. Wilson (eds) (2001). *Culture and Rights. Anthropological Perspectives*. Cambridge: Cambridge University Press.

Drummond, L. (1980). 'A cultural continuum: A theory of intersystems'. *Man* 15, no. 2: 352–74.

Eriksen, T. (1990). 'Liming in Trinidad: The art of doing nothing'. *Folk* 32: 23–43.

Foner, N. (1998). 'West Indian identity in the diaspora: Comparative and historical perspectives'. *Latin American Perspectives* 25, no. 3: 173–88.

Frankenberg, R. (1957). *Village on the Border*. London: Cohen and West.

Gluckman, M. (1963). 'Papers in honor of Melville J. Herskovits: Gossip and scandal'. *Current Anthropology* 4: 307–15.

Halstead, N. (2001). 'Ethnographic encounters: Positionings within and outside the insider frame'. *Social Anthropology* 9: 307–21.

Halstead, N. (2009). 'A landscape of respect relations. Television, status, houses'. *Home Cultures* 6, no. 1: 19–41.

Halstead, N. (2012). 'East Indians as familiars and partial others in New York'. *History and Anthropology* 21, no. 1: 149–69.

Hirsch, E. (1995). 'Introduction. Landscape between space and place'. In *The Anthropology of Landscape: Perspectives on Space and Place*, edited by E. Hirsch and M. O' Hanlon, 1–30. Amsterdam: Harwood Academic Publishers.

Jayawardena, C. (1980). 'Culture and ethnicity in Guyana and Fiji'. *Man* 15: 430–50.

Miller, D. (1994). *Modernity: An Ethnographic Approach. Dualism and Mass Consumption in Trinidad*. Oxford: Berg.

Mintz, S. W. (1996). 'Enduring substances, trying theories: The Caribbean region as Oikoumene'. *Journal of the Royal Anthropological Institute* 2, no. 2: 289–311.

Munasinghe, V. (2008). 'Theorizing world culture through the New World: East Indians and Creolization'. *American Ethnologist* 33, no. 4: 549–62.

Murphy, R. F. (1964). 'Social distance and the veil'. *American Anthropologist* 6: 1257–74.

Paine, R. (1967). 'What is gossip about: An alternative hypothesis'. *Man* (New Series) 2, no. 2: 278–85.

Premdas, R. (1996). 'Race and ethnic relations in Burn Hamite Guyana'. In *Across the Dark Waters: Ethnicity and Indian Indenture in the Caribbean*, edited by D. Dabydeen and B. Samaroo, 39–65. London: MacMillan.

Sidnell, J. (2003). 'An ethnographic consideration of rule-following'. *Journal of the Royal Anthropological Institute* 9, no. 3: 429–45.

Wilson, P. (1974). 'Filcher of good names: An enquiry into anthropology and gossip'. *Man* (New series) 9, no. 1: 93–102.

13

Recreational sex not-at-home: The atmospheres of sex work in Tel Aviv

Dana Kaplan

This chapter is about places where sex is bought and sold, theoretically far from the 'collective good, gift logic' of the pleasantness that supposedly characterizes the home (Douglas 1991; Pennartz 1999). My focus on commercial sex *not-at-home* is meant to help me address some key elements of sex and sexual relations under neoliberalism, specifically the spatial and atmospheric qualities or the material density of what sociologists term *recreational sexuality*. By atmospheres, I mean the complex ephemeral and affective amalgamation of spaces, objects and sociability (Anderson 2009; Löfgren 2014). I use the term *recreational sexuality* to address recent transformations in heterosexuality and the moral geographies associated with these transformations. Recreational sexuality is an entrepreneurial disposition that fuses together, in a distinctively neoliberal way, market and non-market logics (Attwood and Smith 2013; Hubbard and Whowell 2008; Kaplan 2011; Tyler 2011). It blurs the distinction between leisure and labour, home and work, between use and exchange values and between private and public spaces (Bernstein 2007b; Brents et al. 2010; Hubbard and Whowell 2008; Woltersdorff 2010). My interest in recreational sexuality follows Agustín's call to employ a cultural-studies approach to sex work. I shall emphasize the everydayness of commercial sex to reveal 'how our societies distinguish between activities considered normatively "social" and activities denounced as morally wrong.

This means examining a range of activities that take in both commerce and sex' (Agustín 2005: 619). Indeed, this chapter starts from the assumption that, under neoliberalism, some of these moral and spatial boundaries are shifting.

A key element in the current moral geography of recreational sexuality is the erosion of the home/market dichotomy that has animated much of the modern sexual hierarchy. Arguably, for most sexual-recreational practices, it is now hard to determine whether they fall within or without of 'respectable domesticity' and, concomitantly, to identify the spaces they inhabit as either home or non-home (Prior and Gorman-Murray 2015). E. L. James's bestseller, *Fifty Shades of Grey*, illustrates this new moral–spatial arrangement. It describes a 'designer' sex room in the home of Christian Grey, Ana's millionaire partner. The room is equipped with the latest, sleekest BDSM gear. The atmosphere is intoxicatingly rich. Ana is seduced by the clean, leathery scent of the furniture and the moneyed design. The room is designed as a glamorous space of consumption, resembling a sleek bachelor pad, a lounge at a cool, members-only club or a chic hotel (Osgerby 2005: 108–9; Williams 2013). It does not comply with the Goffmanian understanding of the middle-class home as a 'backstage' region, with its mundane, normal chaos, messiness and 'lived in' atmosphere (Birkebæk Olesen 2010: 33–4; Goffman 1959: 123; Ochs and Kremer-Sadlik 2013). Instead, this fictional sex room appears as a semi-private, third place of high living, set between work and home. It therefore suggests that, if sex is an adventure, it should look and feel as different as possible from the everyday aesthetics of the ordinary and from the enclosing feeling homes usually provide. Since the romantic–sexual relationship of the fictional couple relies on a plethora of sexual commodities (toys), the bestseller also proffers the idea that certain elements of commercial sex, packaged as consumer commodities, are glamorous and chic. In this regard, *Fifty Shades of Grey* exemplifies that the sex market – its atmospheres, commodities and scripts – is increasingly brought home to middle-class consumers, as the global success of the book itself attests (Martin 2013).

But the merging of private and commercial sex is not restricted to the home. Commercial sex *not-at-home* has become more socially and morally legitimate and, as will be discussed more broadly below, is increasingly also a part of middle-class spaces. In posing this, I take into account two major transformations in the spatial organization of sex work: first, the relocation of sex work indoors and second, the embedding of 'sexually oriented businesses' in cities' 'civil' and respectable quarters (Hubbard et al. 2009, see also Brents et al. 2010: 35; Martin 2015; Prior and Gorman-Murray 2015; Weitzer 2012). Commercial sex is no longer banished to the streets or the seamy parts of the city, but has entered indoors. This may mean not only that kinky elements are being absorbed into the cultural mainstream – an argument made extensively by sociologists of sexuality – but also that 'respectable domesticity' enters the sex industry, too. The chapter therefore asks whether home is brought to places of commercial sex too and, if so, how? Do sex businesses incorporate certain domestic aesthetic sensibilities? Do they induce, even faintly, a homey atmosphere, thereby conforming to what counts as 'good taste'? Clearly, 'good taste' – those cultural patterns that are regarded as the most legitimate, desired and morally respectable – is always associated with the middle class. While this chapter does not specifically discuss class relations and tastes, it is worth noting that moral geographies and affective atmospheres of both home and sexuality are fundamentally always classed (Birkebæk Olesen 2010; Hubbard 2002; Kaplan 2011; Ohad Smith 2013). Given the spread, legitimation and glamourization of sex work within middle-class purview, the question, then, is: Are the urban places of commercial sex filled with (middle-class) homeliness, the atmosphere of home?

My interest in the atmospheric qualities of sex businesses located in *home-like* spaces within Tel Aviv's residential and commercial centre relies on extensive scholarship that delves into the new formations of urban sex work under neoliberalism (Bernstein 2007a, b; Ferris 2015; Murphy and Venkatesh 2006; Weitzer 2012). However, this scholarship proffers a 'macro' perspective, usually dealing with governance, regulations and state policies. We lack research on individualization and emotionalization processes within commercial sex contexts. Compared with the abundant research on the marketization of the sexual home front, fewer studies address 'intimization' or 'careerism' in sex work, specifically by and for the middle classes (rare examples are Arvidsson 2007; Bernstein 2007a,b; Brents et al. 2010; Weitzer 2012: 31–3). Drawing on a burgeoning scholarship on affective atmospheres, I take a micro perspective, foregrounding cultural, experiential and affective *intersubjective* dimensions of recreational sex work (Anderson 2009; Bille et al. 2015; Edensor and Sumartojo 2015).

The first part of the chapter theorizes the concept of recreational sexuality. Next, I review recent transformations in the spatial organization of urban sex work and how these transformations are associated with the 'creative city' paradigm and the legal context of prostitution in Israel. The analysis relies on my own visits to brothels, located in improvised Tel Aviv apartments, as well as journalistic reportage and photographic documentation. While there is an array of sex businesses in Tel Aviv, I focus on brothels because they represent the most common practices and atmospheres of indoor commercial recreational sexuality and are 'the clearest evidence challenging popular images of degradation and oppression' (Weitzer 2012: 21). It should be noted that, for lack of space, the voices of sex workers, clients and city dwellers are missing from this chapter, as they deserve their own elaborate analysis.

Recreational sexuality

Recreational sexuality is a neoliberal disposition in which our sex life is supposed to raise our self-esteem (Kaplan 2011). The recreational 'pursuit of sex as sensation and adventure' no longer confines sex to the sphere of reproduction and intimate relationships (Attwood 2011: 87). Rather, sex and sexuality are normatively perceived as part of the economy. According to sociologist Elizabeth Bernstein, whereas the domestic sphere's *relational* sexuality 'derived its meaning precisely from its ideological opposition to the marketplace', the current 'recreational sexuality bears no antagonism to the sphere of public commerce. It is available for sale and purchase as readily as any other form of commercially packaged leisure activity' (Bernstein 2007b: 7, see also Attwood 2011; Attwood and Smith 2013; Brents et al. 2010).

In trying to make sense of the pervasiveness of sex in late modern economic life and public culture, most studies on recreational sexuality employ a 'sexualisation of culture' perspective. Studies on the sexualization of culture demonstrate the growing mediatization and marketization of sex, arguing that these processes blur the distinction between commercial and domestic sexualities to an unprecedented extent. To be sure, this historical generalization and periodization are too crude. Detailed historical case studies reveal more complex relationships, similarities and seepages between domestic and commercial sexualities than broad-brush analyses permit (see Brents et al. 2010: 48–51; Osgerby 2005; Preciado 2014). For example, Preciado's cultural account of the sexual-architectural imaginary of *Playboy* finds the 1960s as the starting point of our current sexual, gendered, consumerist and technological regime, characterized, inter alia, in the 'double process of the domestication of public sexuality and pornfication of the domestic' (Preciado 2014: 64). In the pages of *Playboy* and beyond, 'sex signified an intensity of experience, and intense experiences signified sex' (Jancovich 2006). In many respects, this socio-sexual regime has become the common sense of our time. This means that commercial sex becomes more normative and, furthermore, that sexual relations and practices are increasingly measured as individual lifestyles that should be sustained through the purchase of sexual commodities (Attwood 2011; Attwood and Smith 2013; Brents et al. 2010; Rutherford 2007). Thus, although most of us do not have a dedicated BDSM room at home, we *do* increasingly experiment with pornography, popular sexological advice or sexy lingerie, trying to enhance our sex life (Harvey and Gill 2011; Juffer 1998; Martin 2013; Tyler 2004).

The apparent lifestylization of sex means that the sex industry is losing its illicit edge upon entering mainstream culture. Not only are kinkier and queerer forms of sex normalized but commercial sex and various types of sex work also become part of the cultural repertoire and sex life of middle-class heterosexuals. However, most studies on the sex industry foreground gender inequality issues and sexual agency, or lack thereof. While sexism, sexual exploitation and sexual dis/empowerment are as pressing social problems as ever, we also need to consider the ways recreational sexuality may be transforming not just domestic sexualities but possibly also the sex industry (Bernstein 2007a,b; Brents et al. 2010; Murphy and Venkatesh 2006; Weitzer 2012). To the extent that the sex industry is simultaneously being normalized and glamourized, the question, then, is how normalcy and glamour are first, interlaced and second, made present. Does commercial sex lose some of its abject qualities, becoming more domesticated? These questions can be addressed by focusing on the atmospheric qualities of recreational sexuality set in brothels in Tel Aviv.

Moral geographies of sex: The spatiality of sex work

The abundant research on the spatial organization of prostitution 'has highlighted the dynamic nature of the moral and legal geographies of sex services in cities' (Prior and Gorman-Murray 2015: 101). According to Prior et al. (2012: 1838–9); 'within Western cities, the sex industry has long been figured as standing at the boundary between sexualities that are considered good, healthy and normal, and those that are not. Such distinctions are inherently spatialized in the sense that the state and law set limits on where commercial sex can be accommodated within the city' (see also Hubbard 2002).

Importantly, the penal code in Israel proffers a partial decriminalization approach (Scoular 2015: 9). Prostitution is not an offence, but it is prohibited to maintain or rent a place for prostitution.[1] For many years, this has directed commercial sex outdoors and towards the deprived areas of the city (Levenkron 2012; Zur 2016). For example, in 1976 there were around 500 street-walkers and fifty massage parlours in Tel Aviv (Zur 2016). However, things started to change in the mid-1980s, as 'an increasing preference for inner-city living triggered an influx of young people working in the new financial economy living, flourishing in the inner-city. ... As a result [the centre of] Tel Aviv became a fully middle-class area again, but with a much younger population' (Gonen 2015: 150). Municipal urban regeneration programmes followed, initiating various middle-class consumer zones that eventually helped raise the status of the city's centre and its current creative appeal.

Such processes are part of the creative city paradigm, according to which the new economy's creative class clusters in vibrant cities where its pluralistic and consumerist lifestyles can be realized (Florida 2003; Semi 2011). This clustering reinforces the city's economic success. Sex businesses are part and parcel of these class-based urban transformations, as Elizabeth Bernstein demonstrates in her study on the San Francisco Bay Area:

> The young, white professionals who flooded the city during the 1990s to work in high-tech, multimedia, and other industries – necessitating the 'renewal' of formerly impoverished areas – were at the forefront of a new economy in sexual services, both by creating a demand for them and by facilitating new conditions of production. ... Transformations in the forms and functions of urban space were accompanied by important changes in the prevailing practices and meanings of commercial sex. (2007b: 38–9)

The mainstreamization of commercial sex as a form of legitimate leisure characterizes many cities, even those that are not high-tech hubs. Spaces of 'adult entertainment' have recently come to increase the 'experience potential' and economic success of various cities (Brents et al. 2010; Hubbard and Whowell 2008; Löfgren 2014: 256). As Löfgren (2014) explains, there is now a marked tendency to brand cities through heightened multi-sensual atmospheres. In tandem with these developments, leisure-sex businesses have moved indoors and into the central, respectable and prime locations of many Western cities (Hubbard 2002; Hubbard and Whowell 2008; Martin 2015; Murphy and Venkatesh 2006; Prior and Gorman-Murray 2015: 102; Weitzer 2012). Whereas street prostitution is still denigrated and cast as an urban danger that needs cleaning up (Ferris 2015; Hubbard 2002), indoor sex work is constructed as more legitimate, safer, cleaner, discrete, business-like and even glamorous (Murphy and Venkatesh 2006; Weitzer 2012). According to Weitzer (2012), this is reflected in clients' demography as well. Indoor clients are 'typically more affluent, white collar, and well educated'. In practice, then, legal and municipal policies imply that 'not all sex-related businesses are anathema to the cultivation of a leisured and profitable "glamour zone" at the heart of the Western city ... and [they are] eminently marketable as part of a city economy designed to satisfy a multitude of consumer desires' (Hubbard et al. 2009: 198, see also Brents et al. 2010: 36–7).

An aspiring global city, Tel Aviv now brands itself as a connected, sexy and gay-friendly city, a 'site of seduction' (Hubbard 2011).[2] Accordingly, sex work has moved indoors. Selective arresting has cleaned up street-work areas. Court rulings and informal enforcement policies have tolerated sex businesses as long as they do not cause a tort (Levenkron 2012; Zur 2016). There are indications that the number of sex venues in Tel Aviv has risen in the last decade, that brothels and 'discrete' apartments are located in the city's centre and residential areas and that working hours have expanded to daytime as well (Lee 2012), all pointing to a changing moral geography of commercial sex and its growing mainstreamization.

The atmospheres of sex work in Tel- Aviv

My analysis of the atmospheric qualities of brothels in Tel Aviv is informed by a recent haptic move in geography, sociology and anthropology. Atmospheres are emotional – spatial phenomena surrounding 'people, things and environments' (Anderson 2009: 80). Assemblages of sensation, effect and touch, and atmospheres are the 'relation between environmental qualities and human states' (Böhme 1993: 114, 122). An atmosphere is a specific emotional charge that mediates between subject and object through interacting objects, lights, smells and people. In other words, it is the character of a particular space as we intersubjectively grasp it, and this perception is immediate, experiential, affective and embodied (Billie et al. 2015; Edensor and Sumartojo 2015). Such analyses ask how atmospheres shape everyday sociability, particularly in urban settings (Forss 2014; Green et al. 2010; Löfgren 2014; Thibauld 2015). Applications of this approach in sexuality studies have asked what atmospheric qualities *do* and not merely what they *represent* (Green et al. 2010; Hubbard 2002).

The fleeting, haptic nature of atmospheres calls for phenomenological methods of inquiry, and specifically auto-ethnographies and investigators' 'own and others' experiences of the sights, sounds, smells, temperatures and movements of other bodies that help comprise atmospheres' (Edensor and Sumartojo 2015: 261). The following analysis of brothels is based on three types of data: my own experience when I joined a vice-squad raid on brothels in Tel Aviv, photos taken by activist photographer Lihee Avidan in brothel rooms[3] and interviews I conducted with welfare professionals providing health care services to sex workers. I also use various journalistic articles, a memoir by a former sex worker (Anna 2009) and other media sources. I probe two of the main themes that arise from these data: *cleanliness* and *un-designed* quality.

Cleanliness

After a sleepless night, one hot morning in July (2010), I hop on a police minivan and join three detectives and two municipal inspectors.[4] Our first stop is located at the intersection of two of the most central streets in Tel Aviv. A street-level open door, above the sign 'Clinique for Natural Medicine' directs us to an apartment with a small, office-looking waiting room, with a 'secretary' named 'Maggie'. The apartment holds two or three other tiny rooms, all occupied. The detectives knock on the doors and interrupt the activity. The men and women gather in the waiting room. The women are not wearing extremely revealing clothes, or maybe they simply changed back into their non-work attire. The atmosphere is definitely unglamorous. Maggie handles the intrusion calmly and professionally. Everything seems strangely normal. ... Although the policemen check and record the women's and clients' IDs, only one of the clients, an ultra-religious young man, seems distressed. The two other clients know that nothing will happen to them and they quickly leave the premise.

Now that the rooms are empty, I can enter them. Cameras are everywhere. At the center of each of the three rooms stands a massage bed, a tiny shower and body cream or baby oil. Nude posters and canvases of poor artistic quality hang on the walls, in an attempt to liven up the rooms and induce an erotic atmosphere. The rooms are not nice-looking but they are not dirty, either. [field notes]

Beds are also the central focus of most of Leehee Avidan's photos. Her works focus mainly on massage beds in parlours where hand jobs are the main 'service' provided (Anna 2009). As much as could be inferred from the photos, the rooms look clean, floors are mopped and towels are always spread on beds and sofas to absorb bodily fluids. One of the health-care professionals I interviewed said much the same: 'In the treatment room there is always a bed and a tiny shower. The place is damp. The women change the bed linen after each client. ... They are obsessed with cleanliness.' This means taking many showers between clients, asking the men to wash up too and keeping the room as tidy and clean as possible (Anna 2009; Lee 2012). But the rooms are never pleasant. A good example is a short article published in the *Haaretz* newspaper (Elkayam 2013), in which a young American tourist who backpacked across Israel for three months shares his most bizarre moments. Short of money and having nowhere to stay the night, he rented a room in a hotel that turned out to be a brothel:

The bed was covered with a faux leopard, the ceiling was covered with mirrors and the TV had only porn on. I was afraid to lie under the filthy bed linen, so I slept on the bed with all my clothes on. I couldn't sleep because I kept hearing people having sex. At 2:00 I went out of my room to buy a can of coke and I saw fat, old men running naked in the corridor, switching rooms.

Thus, whether clean or not, the rooms are anything but cosy, designed and luxurious.

Staged but un-designed quality

Atmospheres are staged, as 'people actively try to shape experiences and moods of selves and others through organizing objects, bodies and spaces' (Bille et al. 2015: 33). Specifically, there is a growing scholarly interest in the professional design of urban ambiences and scenes (Löfgren 2014; Thibaud 2015). But urban atmospheres and places that create urban scenes are not always designed. Thus, there seems to be a crucial difference between the regular brothel studied here and 'big', designed brothels/strip clubs. The latter 'represent luxurious sites of conspicuous consumption' (Agustín 2005: 623), at least in the cultural imagination. Such places usually offer 'an array of activities – a bar, pool table, Jacuzzi, sauna, sitting room with sofas, pole dancing, and so on. At least some of the clients patronize these places for their party atmosphere' (Weitzer 2012: 31).[5] However, most brothels, even the bigger ones, are not that glamorous. They are also not professionally designed. Leehee Avidan's photographic documentation shows cluttered, disorganized rooms. The insides of the rooms look nothing like a luxurious hotel or spa. Thus, the welfare professionals I interviewed – one was previously a sex worker herself – who frequent the more regular brothels (even the bigger ones) to provide sex workers with healthcare services emphasized how sleazy the atmosphere is in such places. As one welfare professional interviewee sardonically said:

> There is this place in central Tel Aviv, on Hayarkon St., facing the luxurious hotel strip. It looks like [how I would imagine] a French brothel: there is a bar, [fancy] lighting fixtures, men smoking, [but] then the women emerge out of their crammed, suffocating rooms, parading in front of the men. These hideous rooms show what the women's true worth is.

This interviewee (and others as well) emphasizes the gap between the overdone glam of the club's front stage, and the horrible conditions workers must endure, symbolized by the backstage makeshift 'staff' room. As journalist Vered Lee (2012) puts it:

> There is a revealing contrast between the slight effort made to accord the rooms a 'sensuous' appearance, and the waiting room that the women who work in prostitution use in the breaks between clients. Here, the curtain is lifted and the face of the sex industry is exposed for what it is. In contrast to the rooms earmarked for clients, the working women's waiting room is cramped and unabashedly squalid. It's here that the women seemingly metamorphose from being in suspended animation to a state of 'heat' when a client arrives, the unfeeling body and mechanical

expression putting on the appearance of arousal, in a swift transition from unresponsiveness to fake pleasure.

This fakery was stressed by one of the professional aid worker interviewees, who said: 'Shabbiness is what encompasses the place. Cheap furniture purchased by the owners from the hardware store. Cheap curtains. Cheap lampshades. To create a certain respectability. There is a feeling of a staged luxuriousness, "as-if" classy atmosphere for pretend "VIPs"' Again, Vered Lee describes the sexy atmosphere brothel owners try to stage:

The corridors of the apartments used for prostitution are dimly lit to create a night-time effect; heavy curtains that block the outdoor light add to the effect. There is an obvious effort to create a feeling that time has come to a standstill, to cover up traces of the day, to make the client forget that outside the sun is shining. Doors open and close – creaking and slamming are constant sounds. Often, a feeble ray of sunlight that somehow manages to enter exposes the shabbiness inside: filthy, neglected apartments that sell cheap glamour and pretend crude artificial prestige. It's like a dusty, worn theatre setting.

Another interviewee similarly said: 'What is common to all of these places is the attempt to create a sexy atmosphere through the [dim] lighting, the curtains, or the scented candles. I can't stand this smell.'
My own fieldwork tells a similar story:

We drive to one of the largest places, also situated in the heart of Tel Aviv, next to a kindergarten. 'Police, open up!' No answer, so the police break down the metal doors using a battering ram. The place is two stories high, dimly lit. The first floor comprises the staff room and a waiting lobby, with ashtrays, a clutter of sofas and a bar. The place is clean and tries to look sexy with many nude pictures on the walls. The upstairs floor contains several small rooms, each with its own bed and shower. Un-matching bed linen. Next to each bed is a small dresser with towels, and body oil or cream and a small garbage bin. We then drive to a third place which was shut down by the police earlier this month. It looks closed, although one of the detectives opens the window from the outside, sniffs around, stating, 'it still smells like a brothel'. When I ask him to define this smell, he explains 'cheap perfume and scented candles'. [field notes]

But who creates these atmospheres? Who is in charge? The first pages of Anna's memoire, when she is still strong and optimistic, describe her daily routine at the brothel. 'Half-automatically I pull the sheet over the mattress, place the body lotion in an orderly manner, arrange my makeup kit and my vagina relief gel on the shelf. The folded towels get put inside the bathroom' (Anna 2009: 19). Half-automatically, but also half agentic, Anna carves out her own space. Some of Avidan's photos also show signs of personification: photos hanging from the walls, a pot or birthday balloons. Still, these rooms are not homely, unlike the Spanish private apartment described by Agustín (2005: 624). The Spanish rooms display 'few or no sexual signs; on the contrary, it may have floral-patterned covers and teddy bears on the beds, crucifixes and images of saints on the walls and the smell of home cooking wafting from the kitchen'. Thus, while the overall settings of brothels, massage parlours and other indoor sex venues are arranged by the business owners so as to stage a sexy atmosphere, in some rooms in Tel Aviv the women try to create or stage an even more personalized atmosphere, too. Indoor commercial sex then, is in un-designed spaces in which the atmospheric texture is doubly layered: first, by owners, who try to stage sexiness; and second, by the women, who try to stage homeliness.

Conclusion

In her research on Israeli culture of the early 1970s, Daniella Ohad Smith (2013, after Eco) terms various designing improvisations, such as those described above, 'anonymous designs'. Ohad Smith associates such 'making do' design practices with lower ethno-class aesthetics. The ethno-class hierarchies that still characterize Israel have been formed and started manifesting themselves as distinct cultural patterns and aesthetic tastes in the 1970s. Ohad Smith's description of lower-class 'anonymous designs' of homes from that period, 'furnished with used and salvaged furniture, a mix of colorful curtains, upholstery, and wallpaper with patterns that are not compatible with each other' (ibid: 31), is very similar to the look and feel of brothel rooms in contemporary Tel Aviv as well. This brings me back to my original question: Given the permeation of commercial sex into the fabric of middle-class everyday life in Tel Aviv, and considering the general public's acceptance of prostitution, do sex businesses incorporate atmospheric elements of home environments? And if so, does this homeliness fit with (Israeli) middle-class aesthetics that foreground nonchalant simplicity (Kaplan 2013)? While it would be reasonable to expect that brothels in residential areas would conform to middle-class tastes and, moreover, incorporate some home-like aesthetic in order to create a more respectable, ordinary and legitimate atmosphere, based on the analysis above, I would argue that this is not the case.

As I have demonstrated, the atmospheric qualities of indoor commercial sex are a function of both its outer emplacement within the city's centre and inner décor, objects and affective energies. We have also seen that the inside atmosphere has a staged texture that combines mass-produced sexiness on the part of business owners and hints of personalized homeliness on the part of sex workers. Surely, the analysis of the texture of sexual atmospheres is influenced by my – and most of my interviewees' – middle-class identity and bourgeois gaze. Still, I would argue that the commercial sex premises discussed here look and feel nothing like the 'zones of authentic pleasure' of cosmopolitan, urban middle-class consumers, such as cafes or cool boutiques (Semi 2011). Nor do brothels convey the simple taste of the Israeli (upper) middle class (Kaplan 2013) or the warm, personalized atmosphere of middle-class homes (Birkebæk Olesen 2010). The brothels' mismatched texture of poverty does not follow the unwritten aesthetic rules of the creative class (Edensor et al. 2009). Although clean, the rooms' un-designed, ragged quality does not convey a 'personal style', but rather, an abject atmosphere. This is almost as far as it gets from both the sleek, designer lifestyle sex depicted in *Fifty Shades of Grey* and the (supposedly) benevolent and empowering middle-class sex trade in San Francisco (Bernstein 2007b: 89–91). While the Tel Aviv brothels resemble the mess, clutter and shabbiness of everyday domesticity, and although they are sometimes personalized or look as if someone actually lives there, they lack respectability. This helps urban commercial sex to retain a taboo, exciting quality. This atmosphere, however, does not mean that the 'sexscapes' are transgressive, that they empower the disenfranchised or manifest a 'vernacular creativity' (ibid.). Rather, such abject atmospheres, places and practices are culturally valuable for middle-class consumers who, endowed with cosmopolitan cultural capital, may 'other' and 'salvage' them (Kaplan 2013).

As I noted above, the research on the urban spatiality of sex work tends to take a macro, institutional and regulatory perspective. These studies generally argue that, by turning indoors, sex work is being contained within the bounds of the neoliberal, creative city. Some studies even propose that this changing moral geography of sex work plays a part in the branding of cities, which makes sense considering the recent emphasis on the experiential, sensory and atmospheric qualities of 'brandscapes' (as described by Löfgren 2014). Following this emerging line of research, but focusing not on macro processes and regulatory policies but on micro and everyday practices, I propose that the 'bad' taste and unrespectable quasi-domesticity the rooms display is one way in which a touch of kink may stain the realm of neat, designed and normal urbanscape. Arguably, this touch of abjection may actually add value to the city by giving it a certain sense of 'authenticity' and vibrancy (Kaplan forthcoming). Thus, the less-than-respectable brothels do not so much demarcate the dividing moral lines between 'good' and 'bad' recreational sexualities so much as they contribute to the city's branding as a creative city.

Notes

1 See the pivotal *Criminal High Court of Appeals 94/65 Turjeman v. Attorney General 19 (3) 57.* The court rendered that it is illegal for a prostitute to work in her own home (Levenkron 2012: 175–177).

2 This is official policy. See: https://www.tel-aviv.gov.il/en/abouttheCity/Pages/TelAvivBrand.aspx, and https://www.tel-aviv.gov.il/en/Pages/EventPage.aspx?WebID=9336473c-1537-4ab6-8a69-d299b5db8bcc&ListID=0ac6b290-896c-4fcb-bb36-0c5252101eff&ItemId=8.

3 See http://www.haaretz.co.il/magazine/the-edge/1.1894484 and also http://liheeavidan.com/photography/rooms/.

4 The 'municipal business licensing' enforcement policy has been in use from 2006 onwards (Levenkron 2012: 190–1). Until 2013, licensing regulations were highly specified in terms of hygiene and public safety of massage parlours.

5 The 'Baby Dolls' strip club is the best example; see http://www.babydolls.co.il (adult content).

References

Agustín, L. M. (2005). 'New research directions: The cultural study of commercial sex'. *Sexualities* 8, no. 5: 618–31.

Anderson, B. (2009). 'Affective atmospheres'. *Emotion, Space and Society* 2, no. 2: 77–81.

Anna. (pseud). (2009). *The Bright Side of the Moon: The World of a Young Woman in the Israeli Sex Industry.* Tel Aviv: Resling [Hebrew].

Arvidsson, A. (2007). 'Netporn: The work of fantasy in the information society'. In *C'lickme: A Netporn Studies Reader*, edited by K. Jacobs, M. Janssen and M. Pasquinelli, 69–76. Amsterdam: Institute of Network Cultures.

Attwood, F. (2011). 'Sex and the citizens: Erotic play and the new leisure culture'. In *The New Politics of Leisure and Pleasure*, edited by P. Bramham and S. Wagg, 82–96. Basingstoke: Palgrave Macmillan.

Attwood, F. and C. Smith. (2013). 'Leisure sex: More sex! Better sex! Sex is fucking brilliant! Sex, sex, sex, SEX'. In *Routledge Handbook of Leisure Studies*, edited by T. Blackshaw, 325–36. London: Routeldge.

Bernstein, E. (2007a). 'Sex work for the middle classes'. *Sexualities* 10, no. 4: 473–88.

Bernstein, E. (2007b). *Temporarily Yours: Intimacy, Authenticity, and the Commerce of Sex.* London: University of Chicago Press.

Bille, M., P. Bjerregaard and F. T. Sørensen. (2015). 'Staging atmospheres: Materiality, culture, and the texture of the in-between'. *Emotion, Space and Society* 15, no. 31–8.

Birkebæk Olesen, B. (2010). 'Ethnic objects in domestic interiors: Space, atmosphere and the making of home'. *Home Cultures* 7, no. 1: 25–41.

Böhme, G. (1993). 'Atmosphere as the fundamental concept of a new aesthetics'. *Thesis Eleven* 36: 113–26.

Brents, B. G., C. A. Jackson and K. Hausbeck (2010). *The State of Sex: Tourism, Sex and Sin in the New American Heartland*. New York: Routledge.

Douglas, M. (1991). 'The idea of a home: A kind of space'. *Social Research* 58, no. 1: 287–307.

Edensor, T., D. Leslie, S. Millington and N. Rantisi (eds) (2009). 'Introduction: Rethinking creativity: Critique of the creative class thesis'. In *Spaces of Vernacular Creativity: Rethinking the Cultural Economy*, edited by T. Edensor, D. Leslie, S. Millington and N. Rantisi, 1–16. London: Routledge.

Edensor, T. and S. Sumartojo (2015). 'Designing atmospheres: Introduction to special issue'. *Visual Communication* 14, no. 3: 251–65.

Elkayam, L. (2013). 'Departures Arrivals: Tahar and Mirit Find in Rhodes the Vacation Eilat Could Never Give Them.' *Haaretz* (November 13). Available online: www.haaretz.com/israel-news/.premium-1.529612

Ferris, S. (2015). *Street Sex Work and Canadian Cities: Resisting a Dangerous Order*. Edmonton: University of Alberta Press.

Florida, R. (2003). 'Cities and the creative class'. *City & Community* 2, no. 1: 3–19.

Forss, A.-M. (2014). 'The aesthetics of dwelling'. *Journal of Aesthetics and Phenomenology* 1, no. 2: 169–90.

Goffman, E. (1959). *The Presentation of Self in Everyday Life*. New York: Anchor Books.

Gonen, A. (2015). 'Widespread and diverse forms of gentrification in Israel'. In *Global Gentrifications: Uneven Development and Displacement*, edited by L. Lees, H. Bang Shin and E. Lopez-Morales, 143–64. Bristol: Policy Press.

Green, A. I., M. Follert, K. Osterlund and J. Paquin (2010). 'Space, place and sexual sociality: Towards an "atmospheric analysis".' *Gender, Work & Organization* 17, no. 1: 7–27.

Harvey, L. and R. Gill (2011). 'Spicing it up: Sexual entrepreneurs and the sex inspectors'. In *New Femininities: Postfeminism, Neoliberalism, and Subjectivity*, edited by R. Gill and C. Scharff, 52–67. London: Palgrave.

Hubbard, P. (2002). 'Sexing the self: Geographies of engagement and encounter'. *Social and Cultural Geography* 3, no. 4: 365–81.

Hubbard, P. (2011). 'Gender, power and sex in the world city network'. *L'espace Politique* 13, no 1: 2–38.

Hubbard, P., R. Matthews and J. Scoular (2009). 'Legal geographies – controlling sexually oriented businesses: Law, licensing, and the geographies of a controversial land use'. *Urban Geography* 30, no. 2: 185–205.

Hubbard, P. and M. Whowell (2008). 'Revisiting the red light district: Still neglected, immoral and marginal?' *Geoforum* 39, no. 5: 1743–55.

James, E. L. (2011). *Fifty Shades of Grey*. New York: Vintage Books.

Jancovich, M. (2006). 'The politics of *Playboy*: Lifestyle, sexuality and non-conformity in American Cold War culture'. In *Historicizing Lifestyle: Mediating Taste, Consumption and Identity from the 1900s to 1970s*, edited by D. Bell and J. Hollows, 70–87. London: Routledge.

Juffer, J. (1998). *At Home with Pornography: Women, Sex, and Everyday Life*. New York: New York University Press.

Kaplan, D. (2011). 'Sexual liberation and the creative class in Israel'. In *Introducing the New Sexuality Studies*, edited by S. Seidman, N. Fisher and C. Meeks, 357–63. London: Routledge.

Kaplan, D. (2011). 'Sex cards in Tel Aviv: Mood work, recreational sexuality and urban atmospheres'. In *Shopping for Emotions or How Commodities Became Authentic*, edited by E. Illouz. London: Routledge.

Kaplan, D. (2013). 'Food and class distinction at Israeli weddings: New middle class omnivores and the "simple taste"'. *Food, Culture & Society* 16, no. 2: 245–64.

Lee, V. (2012). 'Hell du Jour: Meet Israel's daylight prostitutes'. *Haaretz* (November 11). Available online: www.haaretz.com/israel-news/hell-du-jour-meet-israel-s-daylight-prostitutes-1.469461.

Levenkron, N. (2012). 'On legal clinics, policemen and women in prostitution'. *Hamishpat* 17, no. 1: 161–208 [Hebrew].

Löfgren, O. (2014). 'Urban atmospheres as brandscapes and lived experiences'. *Place Branding and Public Diplomacy* 10, no. 4: 255–66.

Martin, A. (2013). 'Fifty shades of sex shop: Sexual fantasy for sale'. *Sexualities* 16, no. 8: 980–4.

Martin, A. (2015). 'Sex shops in England's cities: From the backstreets to the high streets'. In *(Sub)urban Sexscapes: Geographies and Regulation of the Sex Industry*, edited by P. J. Maginn and C. Steinmetz, 44–59. London: Routledge.

Murphy, A. K. and A. S. Venkatesh (2006). 'Vice careers: The changing contours of sex work in New York City'. *Qualitative Sociology* 29, no. 2: 129–54.

Ochs, E. and T. Kremer-Sadlik (2013). *Fast-Forward Family: Home, Work, and Relationships in Middle-Class America*. Berkeley: University of California Press.

Ohad Smith, D. (2013). 'The "designed" Israeli interior, 1960–1977: Shaping identity'. *Journal of Interior Design* 38, no. 3: 21–36.

Osgerby, B. (2005). 'The bachelor pad as cultural icon'. *Journal of Design History* 18, no. 1: 99–113.

Pennartz, P. J. J. (1999). 'Home: The experience of atmosphere'. In *At Home: An Anthropology of Domestic Space*, edited by I. Cieraad, 95–106. New York: Syracuse University Press.

Preciado, P. B. (2014). *Pornotopia: An Essay on Playboy's Architecture and Biopolitics*. New York: Zone Books.

Prior, J., S. Boydell and P. Hubbard (2012). 'Nocturnal rights to the city: Property, propriety and sex premises in inner Sydney'. *Urban Studies* 49, no. 8: 1837–52.

Prior, J. and A. Gorman-Murray (2015). 'Housing sex within the city: The placement of sex services beyond respectable domesticity?' In *(Sub)urban Sexscapes: Geographies and Regulation of the Sex Industry*, edited by P. J. Maginn and C. Steinmetz, 101–16. London: Routledge.

Rutherford, P. (2007). *A World Made Sexy: Freud to Madonna*. Toronto: University of Toronto Press.

Scoular, J. (2015). *The Subject of Prostitution: Sex Work, Law and Social Theory*. London: Routledge.

Semi, G. (2011). 'Zones of authentic pleasure: Gentrification, middle class taste and place making in Milan'. *M/C* 14, no. 5: 8.

Thibauld, J. P. (2015). 'The backstage of urban ambiences: When atmospheres pervade everyday experience'. *Emotion, Space and Society* 15: 39–46.

Tyler, M. (2004). 'Managing between the sheets: Lifestyle magazines and the management of sexuality in everyday life'. *Sexualities* 7, no. 1: 81–106.

Tyler, M. (2011). 'Tainted love: From dirty work to abject labour in Soho's sex shops'. *Human Relations* 64, no. 11: 1477–1500.

Weitzer, R. (2012). *Legalizing Prostitution: From Illicit Vice to Lawful Business*. New York: New York University Press.

Williams, R. J. (2013). *Sex and Buildings: Modern Architecture and the Sexual Revolution*. London: Reaktion Books.

Woltersdorff, V. (2010). 'Sexual politics in neoliberalism. Managing precarious selves'. In *Care or Control of the Self? Norbert Elias, Michel Foucault, and the Subject in the 21st Century*, edited by A. D. Buhrmann and S. Ernst, 210–22. Newcastle upon Tyne: Cambridge Scholars Publishing.

Zur, H. (2016). *The Geography of Prostitution in the City of Tel Aviv During the Years 1975–1995*. Unpublished MA thesis. Tel Aviv: Tel Aviv University.

14

Letters home

Ben Campkin and R. Justin Hunt

In 2012, artist Benjamin Sebastian performed 'Home' as part of the 'Sundown Schoolhouse of Queer Home Economics' (2012) – an exploration of queer domesticity led by the architect and artist Fritz Haeg, held in a geodesic dome erected on a terrace at London's Hayward Gallery. Haeg had invited a mix of individuals and organizations to the Schoolhouse, and had advertised for what he termed the 'queer community' to partake in a dialogue about 'making ourselves at home' and 'LGBTQ home-making (inspired by the program of "home economics" developed in the nineteenth century to educate young women in domestic duties)' (Haeg 2012). As a result of previous collaborations, we had been in conversation with him to help facilitate the participation of local audiences and artists, including Sebastian.

The Sundown Schoolhouse's programme included talks, discussions, film screenings, performances and domestic activities: exercise, cooking, meals, craft, gardening and study. Through this constellation, 'queer domesticity' was conceived in multiple ways and used as a lens through which to view historical and contemporary communities and individuals. For example, conversations focused on safe spaces for LGBTQ minorities in contemporary London; how sexual orientation and queer identities are expressed in the material culture of homes; the domestic designs and buildings of LGBTQ architects and interior designers; queer kinship and family trees; the queering of domestic spaces by historical figures such as Edward Carpenter, The Bloomsbury Group, Claude Cahun and Marcel Moore; the heritage of queer domestic space, from stately homes to squats, illegal occupations and models of collective living; and queering as a methodological tactic in research on homes, domesticity and housing.

For Sebastian's contribution, on one of the Hayward's iconic Brutalist concrete terraces, aside the geodesic dome, he erected, occupied and burned a soft pitched-roofed tent-like home, sewn together from paper (Fig. 14.1). This chapter comprises abridged versions of two letters we wrote individually to him in response, shortly after the event, and later read at an academic workshop with him present (Campkin and Hunt 2012), and which are elaborated here through two commentaries.

Prompted by 'Home', as performed at the Hayward and in subsequent iterations, we approach sexuality, home and their relations from the distinct perspectives of scholars working in performance studies (Hunt) and urban studies (Campkin). Rather than attempting to produce a seamless argument, we use the letters to the artist and commentaries on the letters to work beside each other. In this, we draw on Eve Kosofsky Sedgwick's spatialized notion of 'beside' (Sedgwick and Frank 2003) as an alternative to dualistic thinking, permitting a number of elements to run in productive parallel through varied kinds of relation. We adopt an epistolary method as one suited to traversing multiple arenas of queer domesticity, at once intimate and public. And we purposefully fold in the commentaries to draw attention to modes of knowledge production afforded by the events of writing and reading.

Hunt extends from his letter with a reflection on the queering of methods and epistemologies. He draw a relation – via the notion of the fold – between the letter, a document of Sebastian's performance that conflates two separate moments of writing (that of the workshop, in 2012, and the preparation of this chapter, in 2016), and the artist's own body. The performance of the fold in this writing makes a home for sexuality through the act of recounting Sebastian's intervention: an archive that accepts and plays on the impossibility of capturing the original event. Also returning to the folds of Sebastian's performance, Campkin's letter connects home to the urban scale. His commentary develops this link by exploring three processes and categories at the core of contemporary urbanization in London, and which featured in the Sundown Schoolhouse discussions of LGBTQ homes: failure, heritage and dispossession. This draws a relation between the politics of sexuality, gender and home in queer theory, and debates about housing and regeneration in urban studies, and suggests future potential in this move.

At home, then, with queer theory and in the theoretical debates of performance studies and urban studies, respectively, both authors address Sebastian's evocative work directly (epistle) and tangentially (disciplinary specific discourse). A purposeful construction of this chapter is the way in which subjects within each author's work fold onto and into one another, never supporting a clear inside or outside to an argument. Never locating an argumentative home, this chapter asks, queerly, for the reader to engage in a process of homing – a relational engagement with uncertain territory made familiar in its traversal.

***

Dear Benjamin,

I've thought a lot about your piece at the Hayward. It, and the subsequent iterations that I've witnessed, hinges, for me, on the space of home as transitory: not static, not stayed, not placed.

You carry out a parcel; a mass of paper folded and kept in plastic and tape. You rip the parcel open and unfold the papers. Sewn together they fly up, there in the wind on the Hayward's balcony, into the shape of a house. You rip a door into the side of the house and step inside. The house crumbles and re-forms, shaped by your body and the whipping wind. Your arm emerges from a tear in the house. Following is your half naked body. The house becomes a giant dress. You are at once the man of the house and child born of its womb. What happens to gender here? What happens to you? There amongst the folds of paper, once home, now costume (some sort of technological interface), something changes about you, for us, witnessing the action. You pull out a needle and thread. You sew the figure of a house on your arm. It bleeds a bit. The passage from house to home, marked by the unfolding of various sheets of paper and various threads, reminds us of the journey we might take towards home, ever wandering, ever (un-en)folding.

I wanted to write to you because I think that letters have a lot of power. Whenever I write one I think of PJ Harvey's song 'The Letter' – in her song the pen becomes (of course) the phallus, and the envelope a cavity, of sorts. It's not exactly a vagina or an anus. It's a space folded somehow between those, a vessel to transmit the desire of what the phallus attempts to communicate. The interesting thing about the envelope, of course, is that it is a fold that unfolds to carry something different; it is, perhaps, heterotopic.

Foucault writes about heterotopias, spaces that are un-placed. Not dis-placed necessarily. Heterotopias exist in normative space and time but function differently. You and I have discussed utopia before. How artistic collectivity may be utopic. Following Foucault and especially Ernst Bloch, José Muñoz says that utopias are always futural and figural – they do not exist outside of the space of our imagining of what will be. I am coming around to the hope of what someone like Muñoz instills in utopic projections, but I like to consider heterotopias a lot more. There in the fold of that envelope exists a space, in transit between bodies while remaining somewhat em-bodied by the act of its being written on, and in; its folding and sealing, the techniques of its departure and arrival.

The envelope becomes a home, of sorts: a queer little home. You've heard me blather on about homes before. How homes are a production, performatively announced through a set of iterative factors. Home, in this way, becomes an epistemological question – a set of known relations that shift and move. Home, perhaps, in this way, registers as heterotopia. The envelope acts as a home for the letter (this letter perhaps), acting as a transitory boundary between bodies so that a new set of relations can be found there in the new, next, home of the letter (in your hands, in your mind, kept or thrown away).

I want to write to you about a couple things (now has moved too, this is 2016); and I'm jumbling them. They're all connected in my mind, within the figure of the fold: the fold of these sheets in a folded envelope, the folded paper that begins your performance, the queer fold that has enveloped us here in London, the fold of your lover's arms there in the home you share with another queer couple (now, a then of folding). Folds keep folding in on themselves and out again. Where is the outside to our queer little group? Where is the inside?

I'm not much of a Deleuzian, as you know. But in Deleuze's book on Foucault he takes up the figure of the fold quite elegantly. It makes me think about your piece, and about our positions in our queer life-worlds. Deleuze uses the fold to think creatively about the production of subjectivity. The fold helps Deleuze do away with interiority and exteriority for a subject, as opposition. The fold announces that the inside is nothing more than a fold of the outside. Deleuze's folding of Foucauldian thought centers around the madman put to sea on a ship. Foucault and Deleuze consider the state of that man as passenger on a vessel between homes who is also housed as prisoner. The fold of the sea becomes his interior to the social exterior – landed, stable homes. This figure is also one of the primary examples Foucault uses to describe heterotopias – the floating ship is heterotopic because of its non-place placeness.

I see you as passenger/prisoner. Not that I think you're a madman, honey. At least not in the terms of the Renaissance madmen that Foucault is thinking about (just like us, he loved a bit of rough trade). But because you are there, representing the fold, within folds, you remind me of the revelation and conscription made possible by our attempts to creatively produce our subjectivity – you perform for us this folding as unfolding. And within the limitless folds I feel a relation to you that is entirely sexual.

But this sexual relation isn't about fucking, per se. It is a desire to know something through your work, through your body, that is more like what Odysseus found, tethered to his ship (passenger/prisoner), arriving at the Sirens. There, sutured to his not house/not home, he encountered the songs, temporally folding past present and future, and began to understand things differently. What you communicate is a potential to refashion, to remold and of course, to keep with the theme here – refold. We are wrapped with attention, or at least I was, on that journey with you – through a house into a home and on again.

When I wrote you then (2012), I asked you:

'What will the inside of this confusion regarding the space of home look like when it has unfolded, presenting itself as an exterior to this time – when our journey has taken us elsewhere?'

I can still only hope it will be as gorgeous as you there, atop the Hayward, in a billowing paper skirt.

Justin

✱✱✱

Folds: Queer address, time and the performance of knowing

R. Justin Hunt

Two questions mark this writing:

1 To whom is this addressed?

2 When is this writing?

One might remark that the spatiality of each question requires a further inquiry of 'where'? But 'where' is certain and, perhaps, supports the answers to these questions. 'Where' is folded among the words on this page. Where is a negotiation of a you, reader, and this, four texts: there. There among the words folding in on you and him (implicating an 'us': a transaction of the text); there in some future of reading wherein the questions are marked, again.

The writing that precedes was originally addressed to the artist Benjamin Sebastian, though the intention of the writing was not solely for him. 'Ben', as he is addressed in my letter, was present at the conference where my co-author (another Ben) and I presented two letters. Writing letters for an academic workshop was, for me then, a test of academic protocols: the mode of address purposefully athwart of normative academic papers. The second-person narrative voice offers two things, then: a way of addressing academia and of addressing queerness.

Performance studies scholar José Muñoz has offered that queerness might 'interrupt the regime of rigor to make ... dominant institutional ideology visible'

(1996: 7). Rigour, a mode of writing ensuring plausibility to one's argument through normative structures of citation and evidence, is not to be done away with, but queer acts require a different mode of address. For, as he says, 'queerness is often transmitted covertly' (Muñoz 1996: 6). As a student of Muñoz, it was impressed upon me that

> performance studies, as a modality of inquiry, can surpass the play of interpretation and the limits of epistemology and open new ground by focusing on what acts and objects *do* in a social matrix rather than what they might possibly mean (Muñoz 1996: 12, emphasis in original).

The home for sexuality that this letter attempts to recount to its subject (a queer biographical sketch, surely) cannot say what it means but it might open up methods of approaching what it did.

In this response to a letter to my friend, I take up William Haver's position, methodologically. He argues that a queer scholarship 'can never amount to an epistemological capture of an object by an understanding on behalf of knowledge' (Haver 1997: 283). While I have edited down the letter from its original format, I have not included citations or buoyed various external references (scholarly or friendly, though these needn't be in opposition). This commentary on the letter follows the protocols of the edition you are reading, mostly. It cites its literature, providing examples that affix various meanings to the methodology of its output. It provides reference, then, but it does not affix meaning, fully.

Meaning is mobile. Despite the security I have afforded these words (having them printed for you, for example), what they do for you cannot be fully my job. And this commentary on the actual text, a letter, results in a useful strategy: the fold. I have to fold in the *then* of the writing of the letter into this *now* of crafting remarks for a *then* of your reading. So, I affix the marks on this page, remarking on their crafting to undo any tidy security of 'epistemological capture'. But such a remarking provides another aspect of the queer method of scholarship that I have taken up: one that seeks to address identification.

If, for instance, I identify that I was using philosopher Michel Foucault's notion of heterotopia (1984) to underpin a mobile relation to 'home' as a means to unpack the queer body's performance, there on top of the Hayward Gallery, then I have required of you, the reader, to fold back your thinking. I have made a fold in this text that meets the moment when Foucault is introduced above (not cited) and provided scholarly identification outside of normative protocols. Such a fold invaginates, as scholar Jacques Derrida would have it, my text. It 'traverses, yet also bounds the corpus' (Derrida and Ronell 1980: 71) of this text and of Benjamin's body.

In thinking about how to comment on a letter whose purpose was to respond, in a scholarly mode of address, to an action, I began to think of

FIGURE 14.1 *Benjamin Sebastian, 'Home', curated by I'm With You, 2012, London. This piece formed part of Fritz Haeg's 'Schoolhouse of Queer Home Economics', held in a geodesic dome at the Hayward Gallery, in its Wide Open School programme. Photographs by Christa Holka.*

Derrida and Avital Ronell. Derrida and Ronell's article 'The Law of Genres' (1980) considers the body, both textual and somatic, in terms of a series of identifications that will be useless because their limits are ever in question. They too try to remark on an event, recounted in literature, but find that 'it is thus impossible to decide whether an event, account, account of event or event of accounting took place' (Derrida and Ronell 1980: 71).

This is precisely where I find myself and am attempting to write myself. So, as I mentioned at the outset of this writing, I know exactly where but not to whom or when. Derrida and Ronnell, in their essay on the limits or edges of classification – and thus, identification – find, like Bachelard (1994 [1958]), that opening the 'inside' to the 'other' denies both inside and outside a stable identity. They write:

> There is only content without edge – without boundary or frame – there is only edge without content. The inclusion (or occlusion, inocclusive, invagination) is interminable: it is analysis of the account that can only turn in circles in an unarrestable, inerrable, and insatiably recurring manner – but is terrible for those who, in the name of the law, require that order

reign in the account, for those who want to know, with all the required competence, 'exactly' how this happens (Derrida and Ronell 1980: 70).

An endless folding occurs between the inside of one classificatory boundary and another. We cannot know what happened but can attempt to perform the account, a queerer mode of knowing. And such a mode of knowing cannot be forged in teleological time, or what queer scholar J. Jack Halberstam has called 'repo time' (2005: 5). Then and now are folded onto each other. I am not seeking to reproduce knowledge but to interrogate our (mine and your) coming to know. The letter above blurs the boundaries between scholarly and personal address. You are present within us in this, but delayed, a then-ness that could be called queer. This commentary has sought to set out, performatively, a case for the use value of an inocclusive scholarship: it cannot tell you what you want to know but it can show you how it might be knowable.

* * *

Dear Benjamin,

'Can I bleed? What about fire? Graphic nudity?' This was your response to the invitation to be part of the Schoolhouse of Queer Home Economics last summer. There is a notion and privileged experience of home as a stable and comforting space. The architectural theorist Jonathan Hill writes that, conventionally, the point of the home is to keep the 'inside inside, and the outside outside'. I hadn't seen your work before, but your question suggested that you wanted to trouble that relation, and to create a primal home where blood, fire and the sexualized – graphically naked, not nude – body would have a place. These elements feature in any mythical home, even if it is against the latent threat of them and other enemies that the myth is founded.

Fritz Haeg's Schoolhouse of Queer Home Economics had been inspired by the Victorian programmes through which young women were taught how to 'keep home', invoking not only domestic labour but the most claustrophobic of bourgeois interiors: stuffy home-making in which bodies were oppressed and repressed within normative limits. Using a utopian architectural form – the geodesic dome – Fritz had occupied a terrace of the Hayward Gallery. Like the mushrooming dome tents outside London's St Paul's Cathedral of the Occupy Movement at that time, this temporary home claimed a territory within a semi-public space: on the edge of an institution, questioning given structures but also beholden to them: menacing from the inside.

Occupying this already occupied institutional edge, the queer domesticity you seemed to be imagining was the antithesis of the bourgeois home: an uncanny and unpredictable home, a home in or of a crisis, even if productively so. The intricately sewn white paper house you eventually unpacked and moulded, fought your way into, and out of, brought home a tension at the heart of the Schoolhouse: a tension between the desire to domesticate queerness, or make the queer acceptable, and a politics of actively queering domesticity.

At times you seemed in control; and at others you struggled: this home had a life of its own. You possessed and then dispossessed it (or it, you). The form it took was partly your own, and partly shaped by the elements as it blew in the wind. (I remembered the stress of putting up my tent as a boy scout.) We cheered when the house you'd made stood up, with you inside. But against the Hayward's timber-impressed concrete it still seemed fragile, and you quickly transformed it into something else.

Was this an allegory of a struggle to make meaning from inherited ideas of home? You appeared both child-like and adult (not necessarily in that order). The house itself was the shape kids are taught to draw as if it were the natural shape of home – the kind of Wendy house that little boys and girls play home in.

At first we could not see what you were doing inside your home, but then you defecated/birthed an egg – the ultimate symbol of home – but an egg that went nowhere; a symbol that messed up and came to nothing. You held it in your mouth and cracked it open, so that yoke mixed with white spewed over the paper walls. The comfort of home, reproduction, inheritance disrupted in one fell swoop.

In architectural history I'm always pulled towards unstable homes: slums, ghettos, sink estates: you get the picture. This graveyard of degraded domestic ideals, returning to the ground, are often associated with sexual and gender 'deviance'. The inhabitants of these unstable homes are misrepresented and the histories of these places misrecognized, benchmarked – from a privileged perspective against a fictional ideal – as failed. I often look at these homes through other representations – plans and sections, photos and models. But yours is hard to place: a hybrid between drawing, model, dress and skin that came to life. As with those degenerate homes I study, bound to powerful narratives of decline and degraded materialities that move us and them, in the home you built, the physical, symbolic and imaginary dimensions of domesticity intertwined: inside outside, outside inside. Flat-packed, tattooed into your arm and sewn into your skin, the house arrived and travelled on in and with you.

As we took refuge in the geodesic tent to discuss all kinds of radical homes and home lives – of faeries, squatters, artists, aesthetes – we kept coming back to the home as a site for collective politics: where radical ideas and actions could be formed or nurtured. One of the questions we kept coming up against had to do with the possibilities for such configurations to emerge in a city like London today, with its high rents and rapacious regenerations, its right to buy, but not to stay. All the elements of your occupation – abjection and crisis, placement and displacement, possession and dispossession, carrying and being sheltered by home – move us in this direction, making a transition from a queer domestic politics of identity to a wider politics of collectivity.

As the London housing crisis intensifies, what I'm left wondering is: how might a queer take help to think it, feel it, act it out?

Ben

***

From queer homemaking to queer place-making: Failure, heritage and dispossession

Ben Campkin

I signed off my letter to Benjamin with a question, prompted by his 'Home' at the Hayward Gallery. I now reorient this as: What do queer domestic tactics and imaginaries offer in the context of an intensely unequal city characterized, for many, by increasing insecurity about being 'at home', and pressure to move elsewhere? Benjamin's intervention was a tactical queering of the Hayward Gallery terrace, working at the interstices of bodily, imaginary and institutional homespace. It evoked the way that ideal homes can act violently in enforcing or reproducing normative constructs of sexuality and gender, repressing difference. Enacted in public, it also encapsulated some of the liberating ways that, as we had been learning in the Schoolhouse, refusals and reconfigurations of domestic social and spatial relations could be conceived and realized.

Sebastian does not conceive of queerness as an identity but as 'a current or imperative moving through and between our bodies ... relations in time and space' (Sebastian 2013). Since the summer of 2012, the elimination of queer space – as safe venues for LGBT and queer-identifying people – in London has galvanized debate and collective action through performance, research and activism, and has emerged as an issue of wider media and public discourse. This has focused in particular on commercial nightlife space, which in these communities enwraps civic and welfare space (see, for example, Campkin and Marshall 2016; *The Gay UK* 2015; Margolis 2015; Walters 2015; Webber 2016).[1] In this context, and following discussions of canonical and everyday architectural and urban sites of queer domesticities in the Schoolhouse, I am interested in how we might traverse discussions of queer homemaking and place-making. Prompted by Sebastian's intervention, and led by my initial letter of response, here I will address three processes at the core of debates about London's urbanization and consider them specifically in relation to queer space: failure, heritage and dispossession. These categories link the domestic to the urban scale and connect contemporary discussions of queer sexuality, subjectivity and relationality to debates about housing and regeneration in urban studies.

Given that queer space and heritage have risen to the surface of public debate lately, reflection on the housing crisis involves not just housing per se – unaffordability, homelessness, tenure insecurity, poor quality of accommodation – but also wider processes such as gentrification (Glass 1964). Minorities, the spaces they occupy, and the heritage they value, are a core concern in this debate. In reference to LGBT and queer-identifying people, this concern translates to a question of where they can be collectively at home when many cultural and nightlife venues and safe spaces have been closed, sold and/or converted to other uses, even when apparently vital. The closures have taken place rapidly, in the shadows, serving to maximize developers' profits at the expense of established communities, and frequently underpinned – typically for property-led regeneration – by opaque and offshore financial transactions (Campkin 2013; Campkin, Ross and Roberts 2013; Minton 2012).

Higher-profile spaces, such as the iconic cabaret and performance venue the Royal Vauxhall Tavern, London, billed as one of the UK's oldest LGBTQ pubs and predating the legalization of homosexuality, have become symbolic battlegrounds and have drawn attention to the wider and longer-term elimination of queer space (Alwakeel 2015; Brown 2015). Media attention has emphasized the closure of commercial LGBTQ entertainment venues, but civil society organizations and charities are closing at an alarming rate as a result of the combined pressures of government and local government cuts and the costs of space.[2] Such organizations have often formed part of clusters with commercial and nightlife venues and so are equally if not more vulnerable to waves of gentrification. LGBTQ night-time spaces also form important roles within their neighbourhoods, providing specific welfare services to their clients, but also boosting business for local shops, integrating with other elements of localized cultural and creative industries.[3]

Queer and feminist theorist Judith Halberstam has called for critical attention to a logic of success or failure in culture, arguing for a conceptual reorientation of failure as a positive practice that acknowledges that 'success in a heteronormative, capitalist society equates too easily to specific forms of reproductive maturity combined with wealth accumulation' (2011: 2). As cities change, 'failure' is frequently used to legitimize the need for certain modes of development. For example, degradation and failure are dominant tropes in the imagination of London's post-war social housing stock (Campkin 2013). These narratives inhibit creativity about how to change in order to move forward, causing division or confusion about who or what to blame.

In contemporary urbanization in London, there is a need to deploy a queer sensibility to this logic, given that success (equated to economic growth based on wealth accumulation through property) has unevenly distributed benefits and enforces failure on others, because failure is attributed in ways that reflect status and taste and privilege certain ways of knowing, and because risk is needed to imagine alternative urbanisms and ways of making home.

One angle on the history of queer space in London, as in other Western metropolitan centres, suggests that it has flourished most readily in failed, closed, ruined, marginal and stigmatized space (Binnie 1997; Andersson and Campkin 2009, and Campkin 2014). This is as true of radical utopian queer art as it is of middle-class gay pioneer gentrifiers or everyday cruisers. As such, it is notable that a contemporary moment of apparent failure – when multiple venues have closed or been forced to close – has witnessed, rather than the vanishing of queer space, a rejuvenated queering of London through the actions of campaigners.[4] In this context, artists, activists, venue owners and customers, entrepreneurs, academics and others have been propelled to debate and assess the histories, qualities of, and present and future need for queer home – and to act individually and in networks to protect it.[5]

In response, there has been an urgent direction of energy – first reactive, but now more proactive and strategic – towards the protection of certain spaces. This has coincided with, and has begun to capitalize on, a new prioritization of minority heritage by institutions. This has included attention to built heritage associated with LGBTQ-identified people (Historic England 2016; Smith, this collection), as well as a wider inclusion of LGBTQ heritage narratives in museum discourse and the public sphere (Mills 2006). There are also parallel discussions in other cities about the effects of gentrification on queer space, the assimilation of former LGBTQ neighbourhoods, and/or the desexualization of spaces formerly associated with sex (Doan 2011; Bell and Binnie 2004).

Mainstream discussions of built environment cultural heritage, such as the 'The Farrell Review' (2014), point out that heritage now has to be seen as integral, rather than anathema, to modernity and development. In this context, the conception of cultural heritage is both retro- and prospective. Questions of 'future heritage' – potential values – are as important to collective memory and the tourism sector as past heritage. Yet rapid development and regeneration, which privileges those heritage values that can be easily commodified and turned into cultural capital, poses specific challenges for the protection of LGBTQ heritage.

The recent pressure on and closures of queer venues prompt reflection on how LGBTQ identities, cultures or histories are shaped by, present in, passed on, or inherited through the built environment, specific buildings, places, landscapes. Central to the intellectual challenge of this project are questions of what should be included under the auspices of LGBTQ heritage, how sites should be identified and presented, and how to use built heritage productively both to communicate changes in the presentation of non-normative gender and sexual identities over time and to positively impact contemporary publics by informing them about the histories of LGBTQ people.

In reference to museums, popular history and LGBTQ History Month, the art historian Bob Mills has contested the ways that recent expressions of queer history often resort to a limited range of tropes that emphasize sexual orientation, above gender nonconformity, and a narrative of repression and coming out. He challenges us to bring out these contradictions and rethink the norms of presentation and consumption of queer heritage. Of particular relevance is Mills' argument that LGBTQ heritage projects need to recognize 'multiple temporalities of sex and gender within a single moment' (Mills 2006: 256). How, then, could a critical approach to queer urban heritage be developed?

Heritage, etymologically linked to inheritance, is at heart a heteronormative conceptualization of transference, associated with the devolution of land and property by birth or succession. In contemporary property-led regeneration in London, the collective heritage of minorities often succumbs to 'spatial cleansing', driven by conservative and consumerist heritage values, or features falsely linear, static, simplistic or passively nostalgic evocations of history and culture (Herzfeld 2006). Heritage has actively contributed to the elimination of queer space – especially sexualized queer space – in contemporary urbanization (Andersson 2012, 2014; Campkin, Ross and Roberts 2013). London's King's Cross in the 1980s was home to a cluster of LGBTQ venues and organizations and was associated with the production of radical queer art and politics (Campkin 2014). Yet there are no signs of this in the redeveloped King's Cross, which has been praised for its sensitivity to the area's industrial heritage and which benefitted from massive public subsidy.

In the context of built heritage, there is often a need for rapid action and there is growing momentum, propelled by community groups, towards the protection of buildings, spaces and their social values through, in the UK, the use of planning mechanisms such as 'community asset value' and the architectural listing process (Brown 2015; *Hackney Citizen* 2015; Webber 2016). Thinking through the tensions between heritage and queerness, or heritage-led urbanization and the queering of space, is a longer-term project. Yet, even in this context of rapid action, as in past moments of synergy between queer and urban activism, there is a need for affinities across minority groups whose rights to heritage are being infringed and a critical awareness of inequalities wrought by contemporary neoliberal urbanization and gentrification (Schulman 2012). If queering domesticity involves turning instability into a productive critical orientation, as in Sebastian's piece, how does this work at the scale of urban heritage in practices of queer place making? What clues are there in recent queer theory?

In his polemic *No Future* (2004), Lee Edelman examines the way that heteronormative reproductivity is upheld through cultural figurations of the child. Drawing on the work of Jacques Lacan, Edelman critiques the way that the modern social and symbolic order relies upon embodiments of the child as the representation of a future secure in its own reproduction. Even while lesbians, gay men and others with queer sexualities might strive to be part of this system, it necessarily excludes homosexuality, with its detachment of sex and reproduction and its association with the death drive, as a symptom – what Edelman refers to as *sinthom*osexuality, referencing Lacan's use of an earlier formulation of sinthom for symptom. The child, Edelman argues through reference to canonical literary, philosophical and cinematic works, is a fetish and fantasy, ostensibly comforting in the face of death terror, the death drive and the reality of death itself, yet inevitably 'an erotically charged investment in the rigid sameness of identity that is central to the compulsory narrative of reproductive futurism' (Edelman 2004: 21). In this view, queerness is not an identity but an unnameable threat to undo 'the identities through which we experience ourselves as subjects' (ibid), identities which are made falsely coherent by the fantasy of self-realization through reproduction. Edelman argues for an ethics that embraces queer association with the negativity of the death drive, with *jouissance*, and 'disidentification from the promise of futurity' (27).

Edelman's thesis exposes how homosexuality is deemed other or inferior in respect of heteronormative notions of reproduction, underpinned by unconscious narcissistic intentions:

> Futurism … generates generational succession, temporality and narrative sequence, not toward the end of enabling change, but, instead of perpetuating sameness, of turning back time to assure repetition – or to assure a logic of resemblance (more precisely: a logic of metaphoricity) in the service of representation and, by extension, of desire. (60)

However, there is also an acknowledgement of reproductivity and the child as a symbol of care. The question of how to embrace the logic of 'no future' in a way that promotes care and self-care is not clearly answered in this text. It also leaves us wondering about the potential importance of queerly imagining forms of reproductivity which do not straightforwardly reinforce sameness or fulfil a narcissistic desire for repetition. In relation to the project of queer history, it raises tensions with tactics of mourning, holding on, not letting go, and indeed with any future-focused project of queer heritage, if 'what is queerest about us, queerest within us, and queerest despite of us is this willingness to insist intransitively – to insist that the future stop here' (Edelman 2004: 31). Yet perhaps Edelman still leaves room for the possibility of attempting approaches to urban heritage if they can take a critical stance towards reproductivity, refusing sameness and acknowledging or embracing the death drive's 'disarticulation of forms' – the death drive being, according to Freud, a 'nostalgia for a state before the appearance of individuality and sexual differentiation' (quoting Lacan, Edelman 2004: 61).

Muñoz, as a queer scholar who has suggested a politics of mourning, has offered a critique of the romanticization of the negative and the 'anti-relationality' in Edelman's and related theses that, he argues, prioritize sexual difference in ways that inhibit a sense of queer collectivity (2009). As his intervention within this debate, and in response to the pragmatism of popular gay politics, Muñoz proposes a blueprint of queer futurity that embraces utopianism and sees queerness as potentiality. Through this lens, we might more clearly see the project of queer heritage as connected to the struggles of others, subject to the same pressures of displacement; as primarily concerned with the past for its possibility to imagine the future differently. 'Concrete utopias', in Muñoz's terms, outlined through Ernst Bloch's Marxian discourse on hope, are grounded in historically situated struggles, even if at times they can still be whimsical. Like Sebastian's 'Home', Muñoz's associative methods of researching and writing history – interweaving theory, autobiography, artwork, official archives and the traces of performance – are suggestive, projecting us into a space where we might 'do' domesticity and heritage queerly.

The responses of London's queer communities to recent threats to close iconic performance venues, such as the Royal Vauxhall Tavern – where queer utopias have been staged and imagined – has involved systematic use of legal and policy frameworks for protecting architectural and community heritage and media interventions, in conjunction with performative activism, and performance as activism, in which queer history has been mobilized towards the future. In this, there is a refusal of conservation, per se, as well as a refusal to let go. In this context, working in utopian ways against the structures of neoliberal urbanization, there is bound to be difficulty and disappointment, but that is why a grounded politics of hope is important.[6]

The present dispossession of queer space emphasizes the importance of the queering of space as an enactment of dispossessions. Perhaps economic dispossession is the fundamental operation within London's housing crisis, in London's queer space crisis, and in the philosophical, psychic and sexualized crises that comprise the search for a place to be queerly 'at home'. Queer theorists have investigated dispossession as, on the one hand, a psychoanalytic process of becoming, whereby subjectivity is constructed through a series of losses of, attachments to, and relations with others; and as a series of ideologically driven processes whereby normativity is imposed as a form of control, disowning and abjecting to preserve power for an elite while actively enforcing precarity on others (Butler and Athanasiou 2013). Negotiating dispossession therefore involves us in a psychic and social process of collective becoming with others – akin to Sebastian's queer action – whereby loss has to be, and can creatively be, continually confronted. Yet it also involves actively protecting one's place, faced with the constant political, economic, cultural and social realities of eviction.

Notes

1 Queer space is produced in diverse forms but might include, for example, safe social and/or work environments for those with minority gender or sexual identities; and/or spaces deemed important because a significant proportion of the clientele identify as LGBTQ; or spaces associated with LGBTQ people through the ways that they are designated or marketed.

2 For example, Broken Rainbow, a national service for LGBT victims of domestic violence based in Manchester, currently faces closure, and PACE, which provided mental health support services and promoted well-being among LGBT+ communities from 1985 to 2016, has already closed. There is a notable lack of non-commercial LGBT-designated social spaces in London at present in comparison with the 1980 and 1990s, because of a range of interacting factors. See Campkin and Marshall 2016.

3 Ibid.

4 See, for example, http://www.weareblackcap.com and http://www.rvt.community/ for active campaigns at the time of writing.

5 See, for example, Raze Collective, http://razecollective.com/, a charitable body supporting queer performance and Campkin and Marshall 2016.

6 Here, queer reclamations of utopianism may intersect with Marxist and feminist re-evaluations of the modernist utopian project in social housing (Campkin 2013; Hatherley 2009; Rendell 2012).

References

Alwakeel, R. (2015). 'Royal Vauxhall Tavern: Another London gay venue threatened by developers'. *Evening Standard* 16 April. Available online: http://www.standard.co.uk/news/london/royal-vauxhall-tavern-another-london-gay-venue-threatened-by-developers-10181665.html.

Andersson, J. (2012). 'Heritage discourse and the desexualisation of public space: The "historical restorations" of Bloomsbury's Squares'. *Antipode: A Radical Journal of Geography* 44, no. 4: 1081–98.

Andersson, J. (2014). 'Desexualising public space through "restoration"'. *Urban Pamphleteer* 3, 9–10. London: UCL Urban Laboratory.

Andersson, J. and B. Campkin (2009). '"White tiles. Trickling water. A man!": Literary representations of cottaging in London'. In *Ladies and Gents: Public Toilets and Gender*, edited by O. Gershenson and B. Penner, 208–17. Philadelphia: Temple University Press.

Bachelard, G. (1994 [1958]). 'The dialectics of outside and inside'. In *The Poetics of Space*, G. Bachelard, trans. M. Jolas. Boston: Beacon Press.

Bell, D. and J. Binnie (2004). 'Authenticating queer space: Citizenship, urbanism and governance'. *Urban Studies* 41, no. 9 (1 August): 1807–20.

Binnie, J. (1997). *A Geography of Urban Desires: Sexual Culture in the City*. Unpublished PhD dissertation, University of London.

Brown, M. (2015). 'London gay pub the Royal Vauxhall Tavern is given grade II listing'. *The Guardian* 9 September. Available online: http://www.theguardian.com/uk-news/2015/sep/09/london-gay-pub-royal-vauxhall-tavern-given-grade-ii-listing.

Butler, J. and A. Athanasiou (2013). *Dispossession: The Performative in the Political*. Malden, MA: Polity Press.

Campkin, B. (2013). *Remaking London: Decline and Regeneration in Urban Culture*. London: I. B. Tauris.

Campkin, B. (2014). 'Derek Jarman's King's Cross'. *3:AM Magazine*. Available online: http://www.3ammagazine.com/3am/derek-jarmans-kings-cross.

Campkin, B. and R. J. Hunt (2012). 'Letters home', *Sexuality at Home*, University College London, 11 December.

Campkin, B. and L. Marshall (2016). *LGBTQI nightlife in London, from 1986 to the present*. London: UCL Urban Laboratory.

Campkin, B., R. Ross and D. Roberts (eds) (2013). 'Regeneration realities'. *Urban Pamphleteer* 2. London: UCL Urban Laboratory.

Deleuze, G. (1988). *Foucault*, translated by S. Hand. Minneapolis: University of Minnesota Press.

Deleuze, G. (1993). *The Fold: Leibniz and the Baroque*, translated by T. Conley. Minneapolis: University of Minnesota Press.

Derrida, J. and A. Ronnel (1980). 'The law of genre'. *Critical Inquiry* 7, no. 1: 55–81.

Doan, P. L. and H. Higgins (2011). 'The demise of queer space? Resurgent gentrification and the assimilation of LGBT neighborhoods'. *Journal of Planning Education and Research*, 6 January.

Edelman, L. (2004). *No Future: Queer Theory and the Death Drive*. Durham: Duke University Press, 2004.

Farrell, T. (2014). *The Farrell Review of Architecture and the Built Environment*. Available online: http://www.farrellreview.co.uk.

Foucualt, M. (1984 [1967]). 'Of other spaces, heterotopias'. Architecture/mouvement/continuité, trans J. Miskoweic. October. Available online: http://foucault.info/documents/heteroTOpia/foucautl.heteroTopia.en.html.

The Gay UK (2015). 'Gay bars that have closed in London since the turn of the century'. *The Gay UK* (5 November).

Glass, R. (1964). *London: Aspects of Change*. Centre for Urban Studies ed. London: Macgibbon & Kee.

Hackney citizen (2015). 'Hope for The Joiners Arms as campaigners win protective status'. 16 January. Available online: http://hackneycitizen. co.uk/2015/01/16/the-joiners-arms-wins-asset-of-community-value-status/.

Haeg, F. (2012). 'Sundown schoolhouse of queer home economics'. 11 June to 11 July 2012, Hayward Gallery, London. Information available online: http://www. fritzhaeg.com/schoolhouse/projects/queer-home-ec.html.

Halberstam, J. (2005). *In a Queer Time and Place: Transgender Bodies, Subcultural Lives*. New York: New York University Press.

Halberstam, J. (2011). *The Queer Art of Failure*. Durham, NC: Duke University Press.

Hatherley, O. (2009). *Militant Modernism*. Winchester, UK: Zero Books.

Haver, W. (1997). 'Queer research; Or, how to practice invention to the brink of intelligibility'. In *The Eight Technologies of Otherness*, edited by S. Golding, 277–92. London: Routledge.

Herzfeld, M. (2006). 'Spatial cleansing: Monumental vacuity and the idea of the West', *Journal of Material Culture* 11, nos. 1–2:127–49.

Hill, J. (2006). *Immaterial Architecture*. London: Routledge.

Historic England (2016). 'Put LGBTQ heritage on the map'. Available online: https:// historicengland.org.uk/research/inclusive-heritage/lgbtq-heritage-project/.

Margolis, E. (2015). 'Closing time: The loss of iconic gay venues is a nasty side-effect of London's sanitization'. *The New Statesman* (11 March).

Mills, R. (2006). 'Queer is here? Lesbian, gay, bisexual and transgender histories and public culture'. *History Workshop Journal* 62: 253–63.

Minton, A. (2012). *Ground Control: Fear and Happiness in the Twenty-First-Century City*. London: Penguin.

Muñoz, J. (1996). 'Ephemera as evidence: Introductory notes to queer acts'. *Women and Performance* 8: 5–16.

Muñoz, J. E. (2009). *Cruising Utopia: The then and there of Queer Futurity*. New York: New York University Press.

Rendell, J. (2012). 'May Mo(u)rn: A site writing'. In *The Political Unconscious of Architecture: Re-opening Jameson's Narrative*, edited by N. Lahiji, 109–42. Farnham: Ashgate.

Schulman, S. (2012). *The Gentrification of the Mind: Witness to a Lost Imagination*. Reprint edition. Berkeley: University of California Press.

Sebastian, B. (2013) http://www.benjamin-sebastian.com/

Sedgwick, E. K. and A. Frank (2003). *Touching Feeling: Affect, Pedagogy, Performativity*. Durham, NC: Duke University Press.

Walters, B. (2015). 'Closing time for gay pubs – a new victim of London's soaring property prices'. *The Guardian* (4 February).

Webber, E. (2016). 'Why are London's gay bars disappearing?' *BBC News*, 29 August. Available online: http://www.bbc.co.uk/news/uk-england-london-33608000.

Index

Lightning Source UK Ltd.
Milton Keynes UK
UKHW02n0637150218
317860UK00009B/336/P